REWRITING MAGIC

THE MAGIC IN HISTORY SERIES

FORBIDDEN RITES
A Necromancer's Manual of the Fifteenth Century
Richard Kieckhefer

CONJURING SPIRITS
Texts and Traditions of Medieval Ritual Magic
Edited by Claire Fanger

RITUAL MAGIC
Elizabeth M. Butler

THE FORTUNES OF FAUST
Elizabeth M. Butler

THE BATHHOUSE AT MIDNIGHT
An Historical Survey of Magic and
Divination in Russia
W. F. Ryan

SPIRITUAL AND DEMONIC MAGIC
From Ficino to Campanella
D. P. Walker

ICONS OF POWER
Ritual Practices in Late Antiquity
Naomi Janowitz

BATTLING DEMONS
Witchcraft, Heresy, and Reform in the
Late Middle Ages
Michael D. Bailey

PRAYER, MAGIC, AND THE STARS IN THE
ANCIENT AND LATE ANTIQUE WORLD
*Edited by Scott Noegel, Joel Walker,
and Brannon Wheeler*

BINDING WORDS
Textual Amulets in the Middle Ages
Don C. Skemer

STRANGE REVELATIONS
Magic, Poison, and Sacrilege in
Louis XIV's France
Lynn Wood Mollenauer

UNLOCKED BOOKS
Manuscripts of Learned Magic in the Medieval
Libraries of Central Europe
Benedek Láng

ALCHEMICAL BELIEF
Occultism in the Religious Culture of
Early Modern England
Bruce Janacek

INVOKING ANGELS
Theurgic Ideas and Practices, Thirteenth to
Sixteenth Centuries
Edited by Claire Fanger

THE TRANSFORMATIONS OF MAGIC
Illicit Learned Magic in the Later Middle Ages
and Renaissance
Frank Klaassen

MAGIC IN THE CLOISTER
Pious Motives, Illicit Interests, and Occult
Approaches to the Medieval Universe
Sophie Page

The Magic in History series explores the role magic and the occult have played in European culture, religion, science, and politics. Titles in the series bring the resources of cultural, literary, and social history to bear on the history of the magic arts, and they contribute to an understanding of why the theory and practice of magic have elicited fascination at every level of European society. Volumes include both editions of important texts and significant new research in the field.

MAGIC in HISTORY

REWRITING MAGIC

AN EXEGESIS OF THE VISIONARY AUTOBIOGRAPHY *of a* FOURTEENTH-CENTURY FRENCH MONK

CLAIRE FANGER

THE PENNSYLVANIA STATE UNIVERSITY PRESS
UNIVERSITY PARK, PENNSYLVANIA

Chapter 5 of *Rewriting Magic* appeared in a preliminary form as "Libri Nigromantici: The Good, the Bad, and the Ambiguous in John of Morigny's *Flowers of Heavenly Teaching.*" *Magic, Ritual, and Witchcraft* 7, no. 2 (2012): 164–89. © 2012 University of Pennsylvania Press.

The following extracts are reprinted with permission from:
Polity Press, excerpt from Pierre Bourdieu, *Pascalian Meditations.* This translation © 2000, Polity Press.
Springer Science + Business Media, excerpt from Ludwig Wittgenstein, "Philosophy: Sections 86–93 (pp. 405–35) of the so-called 'Big Typescript' (Catalog number 213)," trans. C. G. Luckhardt and M. A. E. Auel, *Synthese* 87 (1991): 3–22. This translation © 1991 Kluwer Academic Publishers.
The C. S. Lewis Company Ltd., excerpt from *The Silver Chair* copyright © C. S. Lewis Pte. Ltd. 1953.
Wiley Books, excerpt from Ludwig Wittgenstein, *Philosophical Investigations,* trans. G. E. M. Anscombe, P. M. S. Hacker, and Joachim Schulte, 4th ed., rev. Hacker and Schulte (Malden, Mass.: Wiley Blackwell, 2009). Copyright © 1953,1958, 2001 by Blackwell Publishing Ltd.
Random House, excerpt from *Possession: A Romance* by A. S. Byatt, copyright © 1991 by A. S. Byatt. Used by permission of Random House, an imprint and division of Penguin Random House LLC. All rights reserved. Any third party use of this material, outside of this publication, is prohibited. interested parties must apply directly to Penguin Random House LLC for permission.

Library of Congress Cataloging-in-Publication Data

Fanger, Claire, author.
    Rewriting magic : an exegesis of the visionary autobiography
    of a fourteenth-century French monk / Claire Fanger.
        pages   cm — (Magic in history)
Summary: "Examines the text and background of The Flowers of Heavenly Teaching, an autobiography by the fourteenth-century Benedictine monk John of Morigny. Explores how the author negotiated the categories of magic and heresy in relation to Christianity"—
Provided by publisher.
Includes bibliographical references and index.
ISBN 978-0-271-06650-9 (cloth : alk. paper)
ISBN 978-0-271-06651-6 (pbk : alk. paper)
1. John, of Morigny, active 13th century–14th century. Liber florum celestis doctrine.
2. Magic—Religious aspects—Christianity.
3. Christian heresies.
I. Title. II. Series: Magic in history.

BR115.M25F36   2015
271'.102—dc23
2014046791

Copyright © 2015 The Pennsylvania State University
All rights reserved
Printed in the United States of America
Published by The Pennsylvania State University Press,
University Park, PA 16802-1003

The Pennsylvania State University Press is a member of the Association of American University Presses.

It is the policy of The Pennsylvania State University Press to use acid-free paper. Publications on uncoated stock satisfy the minimum requirements of American National Standard for Information Sciences—Permanence of Paper for Printed Library Material, ANSI Z39.48–1992.

CONTENTS

List of Figures / vii
Preface / ix
Structure and Referencing System for the
   Liber florum New Compilation / xiii

Introduction: Lost and Found Knowledge / 1

PART 1 FOUNDATION

Chapter 1 Like Stones of Fire: I Encounter the Book of Visions / 15
Chapter 2 A Mysticism of Signs and Things: The *Ars Notoria* and the Sacraments / 35
Chapter 3 Penance: The Sacrament of the Middle of Life / 58

PART 2 RESTORATION

Chapter 4 Errors of Intellect, Errors of Will: I Encounter the Book of Figures / 83
Chapter 5 Magical Objects of Knowledge: Categorizing the Exceptive Arts / 109
Chapter 6 Visionary Exegesis and Prophecy: Milk and Meat / 132

Conclusion: Future History / 154

Notes / 169
Selected Bibliography / 203
Index / 209

FIGURES

1 Bodleian Library, University of Oxford, fol. 1r / 92
2 Bodleian Library, University of Oxford, fol. 66r / 96
3 Letter braid / 100
4 Arts and gifts / 119
5 Reg. lat. 1300, fol. 137r. © 2015 Biblioteca Apostolica Vaticana / 129
6 Universitätsbibliothek Salzburg, M I 24, fol. 79r / 152

PREFACE: *MISE EN SCÈNE*, CORRIGENDA, AND THANKS

As I write this, the Latin edition of John of Morigny's *Liber florum*, which I have edited with Nicholas Watson, is in press at the Pontifical Institute of Mediaeval Studies and scheduled for release in the summer of 2015. This edition will be an important resource for all serious readers of *Rewriting Magic*, since it makes available not only John's original Latin text in both its versions, but also more of the background data on which my readings and interpretations here are based. We have a collaborative English translation in progress that we hope will shortly make this remarkable work still more accessible to a broad audience.

Over the two decades involved in the making of our edition, manuscript discoveries have continued to yield new information that has gradually reconfigured our picture of John and his world. Inevitably in this process some of what we described or conjectured in our earlier publications has become outdated. In order to ease readers who are familiar with our old work into the purview of the more recent hypotheses and better readings represented by the new edition, I take this opportunity to correct a few points where names, locations, facts, or probabilities have shifted from our earlier projections.

- In this book, as in our edition, following our sense of the most authoritative manuscripts of John's text, I adopt Burgeta (Bridget) as the name of John's sister, not Gurgeta (Georgette) as she appeared in our 2001 edition of the *Liber visionum*.
- "*Liber visionum*" itself is now obsolete as a title for the whole text; we retain its more limited use as a title for the first of the text's three books, the visionary autobiography (which we edited as the "Prologue" in 2001). In the Old Compilation, John lists twelve titles for the work, one of which was in fact *Liber visionum*; however, by the end of the New Compilation, he explicitly wants *Liber florum celestis doctrine* to be received as the title for the whole book. We take him at his word.
- Also, contrary to earlier suggestions that John's visionary experiments with the *ars notoria* took place at Chartres (based on the fact that several

visions are situated there), we now believe the location of these experiments is far more likely to have been Orléans, where John was sent to take a degree in canon law—and presumably to learn civil law, the subject in which Orléans specialized. Canon law was one of the only two university studies open to professed monks, the other being theology, a specialization allowed at Paris but not Orléans. (For more background on this topic, see *Liber florum,* Introduction A by Nicholas Watson, §8 and notes.) John does mention studying at Orléans, and his location at the university there makes better sense both of the chronological data we have and the fact that he is evidently rubbing shoulders with friars and Cistercians (as well as visiting his sister) in the course of his work with the *ars notoria,* and later too, during the composition of his own Book of Prayers.

- The scope of John's ambit is further clarified by our identification of Otrouiacum (mentioned several times in the Book of Visions as the location of John's mother's house, and not translated in our earlier edition) as Autruy, now Autruy-sur-Juine, a village on the Roman road that runs between Morigny and Orléans, forty-five kilometers north of Orléans and twenty-two kilometers south of Morigny. (For details of our identification of this location, see *Liber florum,* Sources at I.i.4.)

- The provenance of the "Barking Dogs" who condemned John's work in 1315 is no longer securely located at Sens, where I placed it in publications after 2001. Our original manuscript reading for this place name turned out to be in error. While other noteworthy condemnations originated in Sens in this time period, this is only one possible point of origin, and cannot now be nailed to textual evidence.

- The manuscript count has changed almost yearly since the initial discovery, so it is now the case that all published lists of manuscripts prior to 2015 are outdated. At present I am aware of twenty-three manuscripts containing John's work in whole or in part. One manuscript contains the original draft or Old Compilation. Eighteen manuscripts contain all or substantial portions of the New Compilation *Liber florum.* The remaining four manuscripts are prayer collections containing unattributed sequences of prayers drawn from John's work. I do not publish a complete manuscript list here; I do, however, maintain a list online of the main manuscripts at societasmagica.org/userfiles/files/manuscripts.pdf. I have written more fully about the manuscript situation in *Liber florum,* Introduction B.

Readers curious about further facts of John's biography, and the background, composition, and reception history of the text, are invited to consult the extensive materials in the introduction and commentary of our edition of the *Liber florum celestis doctrine*.

All histories, however new the data they rest on, peek at corners of knowledge that are colonized to a large or small degree by other scholars, and they depend on institutional support. This one is no exception. For institutional support, I am grateful to the Social Sciences and Humanities Research Council of Canada and the American Philosophical Society for travel grants that enabled me to consult manuscripts in situ, and to Harvard University and Rice University for ongoing research and publication assistance.

Though the *Liber florum* is a virtually unstudied work, there is a small but growing body of writings on John of Morigny, and several scholars who have pursued research projects that importantly engaged *Liber florum*. I remain grateful to Sylvie Barnay, the pioneer in this territory, for her initial kindness and conversation in Paris in the summer of 2000. I owe intellectual debts also to Frank Klaassen, Benedek Láng, Sophie Page, and Julien Véronèse, friends and colleagues whose writings remain an ongoing point of reference for my own work. I am glad when younger scholars engage with John of Morigny, too; Luis de las Cuevas, Nell Champoux, and Denva Jackson have all written interestingly about John of Morigny in graduate and undergraduate research projects and have inspired and delighted me with their ideas.

More specific and particular debts are owed to several people. For reading and responding to the initial manuscript draft of *Rewriting Magic*, as well as for his sustained interest in my work over the years, and for much else besides, I owe very special thanks to Richard Kieckhefer. Substantial thanks are also owed to Rachel Fulton Brown, who identified herself as one of the readers for the press, and to the second still anonymous reader, for a set of exceptionally detailed, generous, and knowledgeable responses. Both have helped enormously in developing my understanding of what readers might expect to see in (and get out of) this book, and thus in honing its presentation. To my colleagues at Rice, Donna Beth Ellard and James D. Faubion, I owe additional thanks for their insightful comments coming from outside the field; their readings also have informed the book's shape. Finally, my research assistants Minji Lee and Anya Parker assisted with many tasks necessary to this book's final state, including proofreading, formatting, Latin checking, and bibliography. Without them this book would be much the poorer. Errors remaining are of course my own.

To John of Morigny himself I owe a very considerable debt. For twenty years I have worked with him, reading and rereading his words, seeking answers to puzzling questions, imagining his responses. As I learned to listen more closely to what he said, and to cooperate with him in representing the flow of his thought (a project in which he has a been a strong and hardly disinterested collaborator), he has taught me a great deal, challenging or changing nearly everything I thought I knew about the Middle Ages.

It is not too difficult to take advice from the dead, once one learns the trick of their speech. Living friends are a different story, and their advice does not always immediately feel welcome, perhaps especially when it happens to be correct; but despite this (or because of it), I want to express my deep gratitude to my collaborator on the Latin edition of the *Liber florum,* Nicholas Watson, longtime friend, reader, listener, and sparring partner, who in many ways—some more annoying than others—always pushed me to read more deeply, see more clearly, learn more thoroughly, and write more accurately. This book would not have been possible without him.

STRUCTURE AND REFERENCING SYSTEM FOR THE *LIBER FLORUM* NEW COMPILATION

REFERENCE	DESCRIPTION
	I. BOOK OF VISIONS
I.Gen Prol	General Prologue to entire work
I.Prol	Prologue to the Book of Visions
I.i	Visions induced by the *ars notoria*
I.ii	Good visions after John laid aside the *ars notoria*
I.iii	Testimony of two other witnesses against the *ars notoria*, Bridget and John of Fontainejean
I.iv	Preparations for the Book of Prayers. This brief section includes an exhortation on the right intention of the operator and some notes on distinguishing true from false visions of Mary.
	(The Old Compilation version, OC I.iv in *Liber florum*, was more extensive, additionally including a rite of profession, information about drawing the figures, a longer section on distinguishing true and false visions of Mary, and further preliminary rituals.)
	II. BOOK OF PRAYERS
II.Rit Prol	The Ritual Prologue is a page of prayers and visualizations meant to precede the entire book. In some manuscripts (including the base manuscript used for the edition), it comes at the beginning of the Book of Prayers; in others, it appears at the front of the book.
II.Prol	Epistolary prologue to Book of Prayers; tale of John's redemption briefly sketched

II.I *1–*7 SEVEN PRAYERS

II.i Prayers *1–*7 Opus 1: Acquisitional. Seven Prayers, to God, Mary, St. John, Mary Magdalene.
> Composed by John during the *ars notoria* period, these prayers enable operators to request permission to continue to the work of the Thirty Prayers.

II.II 1–30 THIRTY PRAYERS

II.ii.1–12 Opus 2: Auxiliative. Prayers 1–12 of the Thirty Prayers, to God, the angelic and blessed orders, and Mary
> These prayers seek divine assistance for the work in the form of nine spiritual gifts. Since angelic invocations are somewhat similar within the three major hierarchies, these prayers have many repeated parts.

II.ii.13–16 Opus 3: Preparative. Prayers 13–16 of the Thirty Prayers, to God in Trinity and the whole heavenly court
> These transitional prayers invoke God, Mary, the angels, and the divine dispensation to purify the senses, preparing the operator for the spiritual gift of knowledge.

II.ii.17–20 Opus 4: General Executive. Prayers 17–20 of the Thirty Prayers, to Christ
> Prayers for primary faculties: intellect, memory, eloquence, and stability.

II.ii.21–27 Opus 5: Special Executive for the liberal arts. Prayers 21–27 of the Thirty Prayers to Christ, the angels, and the blessed
> Each prayer addresses one angelic order from Angels to Principalities to request one art.

II.ii.28 Opus 6: Special Executive for philosophy. Prayer 28 of the Thirty Prayers, to Christ, the cherubim, and the blessed

II.ii.28B.1–2 This two-part prayer is located in different places in different textual traditions. Called the "first prayer of the book," it is said to be good for having visions. It is used with the prayers of the Ritual Prologue.

II.ii.29 Opus 7: Special Executive for theology. Prayer 29 of the Thirty Prayers, to Christ, the seraphim, and the blessed

II.ii.30.1–2 Opus 8 and 9: General Executive for all sciences, Thanksgiving. Prayer 30 of the Thirty Prayers, to God, all angelic and blessed orders, and Mary

II.III FIRST PROCEDURE

II.iii.prol	Prologue to the First Procedure, a manual compiling ritual instructions for using the prayers for the first time
II.iii.cap 1	First chapter concerns preliminaries, attitude of the operator, time, place
II.iii.cap 2	Second chapter lays out the opera, grouping the prayers into weeks
II.iii.cap 3	Third chapter has a Service of the Angels and an additional prayer, "Prepotentissima"
II.iii.cap 4	Fourth chapter on certain additional precepts; includes ritual for consecration of the book

III. BOOK OF FIGURES

NC III.i	In this first part of the New Compilation of Figures, John rewrites part of the Old Compilation of Figures in response to challenges from "barking dogs." He describes the attack on the figures, makes specific corrections to the Old Book of Figures, and outlines a new, simplified Second Procedure (a way of using the figures with the prayers), and some new versions of other rituals.
	(The Old Compilation Book of Figures, OC III in *Liber florum*, originally contained many figures, mostly no longer extant. The surviving book preserves the lettering of most of the figures and some petitions accompanying them, surrounded by two sequences of visions; various rituals associated with some of the figures; an exegesis of these rituals; and a set of instructions on petitioning for a vision.)
NC.III.ii	The Book of Particular Experiments included here is a brief essay describing what "particular experiments" are, and including just one experiment. It refers to, and updates, a much larger "old" book of experiments, perhaps no longer extant.
NC III.iii	This part narrates visions of revelation of the seven figures, before describing these to enable execution by operators, completing the new Second Procedure ritual. It also describes the revelation of the ring, containing instructions on how to make a ring, to be worn by the operator on special occasions, in what it occasionally calls a Third Procedure.

INTRODUCTION:
LOST AND FOUND KNOWLEDGE

[A]sk yourself whether our language is complete;—whether it was so before the symbolism of chemistry and the notation of the infinitesimal calculus were incorporated in it; for these are, so to speak, suburbs of our language. (And how many houses or streets does it take before a town begins to be a town?) Our language can be seen as an ancient city: a maze of little streets and squares, of old and new houses, and of houses with additions from various periods.

—Wittgenstein, *Philosophical Investigations*

"We've got to start by finding a ruined city of giants," said Jill. "Aslan said so."
  "Got to start by *finding* it, have we?" answered Puddleglum. "Not allowed to start by *looking for it*, I suppose?"

—C. S. Lewis, *The Silver Chair*

John of Morigny, the man whose work is the principal target of my investigation here, was a fourteenth-century Benedictine attached to the Abbey of Morigny near Étampes. He was highly educated, a monk and priest with an advanced degree in canon law from the University of Orléans, whose writing reflects deep acquaintance with the most important literature, poetry, art, and theology of the later Middle Ages. The extant book through which we principally have access to him, the *Liber florum celestis doctrine* or *Flowers of Heavenly Teaching*, is a complicated and polyvalent work that John wrote in installments and circulated to an expanding audience of ritual operators over many years. Until very recently there have been no printed editions of this text,[1] which is one reason it has remained unknown and inaccessible since the early sixteenth century. Over the past two decades, I have been one of the primary vectors for transmission of information about John's *Liber florum*, so when I write that "we" have access to John through this work, the pronoun includes a much smaller range of readers and knowers than is usual even for the authorial "we" in scholarly writing.

John's book deserves to be better read and more widely understood; it is a serious, impassioned, and original work that was important to a readership across Europe for over two hundred years. While its most interesting features resist easy analysis, the overarching structure is clear: the *Liber florum* in its finished form breaks down into three principal parts. Part I is a visionary autobiography and apologia for the work, explaining its personal background and divine delivery (the Book of Visions); part II is a lengthy liturgy addressed to God and the angels for infusion of divine and curricular knowledge (the Book of Prayers, culminating in a set of ritual instructions called the First Procedure); and part III contains more visions and a set of figures designed to work with and enhance the ritual process (the Book of Figures, whose operations are sometimes called the "second procedure").[2]

In the Book of Visions, John confesses to experimentation with both necromancy (*nigromancia*, or black magic[3]) and a widely used and broadly condemned angel magic text called the *ars notoria*, a ritual aiming to gain heavenly knowledge of the liberal arts, philosophy, and theology, which John's own Book of Prayers is clearly structured to imitate. But John's work is no lay or partially learned dabbling in magic; it flaunts its erudition unabashedly. Using a biblical trope well known from the writing of Saint Augustine, John explicitly plunders the *ars notoria*, pulling its "sacred and divine words" into his own book "as the Hebrews plundered the Egyptian treasure." And even as it reflects John's knowledge of late medieval magic texts, the whole work also records the process of its own composition under the guidance of the virgin Mary; its prayers, visualizations, and figures are geared to enable the same sort of visionary communication with the Virgin, Christ, and the angels that John himself experienced.

John's literate intertextual references, layered composition, and interweaving of visions, rituals, and autobiography all add to the complexity of his book. However, a further complication was introduced when the book was, in effect, broken in the middle by a condemnation in 1315 from certain "Barking Dogs," who are not named but must have had professional knowledge of canon law.[4] The Book of Figures, which had already been circulating for some years, contained figures which, to the Barking Dogs, too much resembled "necromantic" figures. The scandal ensuing from this condemnation effectively blocked further use of the original Book of Figures. John could not very well recall the condemned part of the text from his community of operators (after all, it had been approved and confirmed by the Virgin to begin with, and in all probability consecrated by individual operators when they copied it, too). Rather, he elected to add a new installment that offered an alternative model for the ritual and spiritual processes described in the first version. In great haste he rewrote the last part of his book, leaning even more heavily than before on the divine guidance and prophetic dreams that he describes to us as he goes along. The process of composition that resulted in the *Flowers of Heavenly Teaching* is thus partly represented as a rewriting of magic, but it is equally represented as a "delivered" text, a divinely inspired record of sacred communication that is mapped onto the work of the sacraments.

Introducing this work to a modern audience, even an audience of medievalists, is something of a challenge. This is not only because of its internal reflexivity and its erudite frame, but also because of how recently it was discovered in extant manuscripts. Until 1987, when the French scholar Jean Dupèbe briefly noticed one of the Munich copies of *Liber florum* in an article on the *ars notoria*,[5] the work had been referenced in modern times only through the record of its condemnation. The first extended notice of this condemnation occurs in an entry for the year 1323 in the *Grandes Chroniques de France*, where it is written that a certain monk of Morigny had wanted to "inspire and renew a condemned heresy and sorcery called in Latin *ars notoria*." The *ars notoria* is described, in a way conventional for the time, as a science that bestowed different branches of knowledge when its figures were contemplated with fasting and prayers, but which involved the invocation of "little known names which were firmly believed to be the names of demons." According to the writer of this account, the monk, who himself condemned the *ars notoria*, nevertheless had compiled a book filled with images in honor of the Virgin, the use of which procured for the operator not only all branches of knowledge but also "any riches, honours or pleasures one wanted to have." In the end, the book was declared "false and evil, against the Christian faith, and condemned to be burned and put on the fire."[6]

To any interested and serious reader of the text, aspects of this description will appear in some respects inaccurate, if not unfair (*Liber florum* is explicitly not concerned with earthly honors or pleasures, for example), but at least it makes clear that John's book is a work distinct from the *ars notoria*. Later paraphrases of this entry, however, blurred the distinction, eliding John's *Liber florum* ever more closely with the *ars notoria* itself. A much-compressed version occurs already in the fourteenth-century chronicle of Guillaume de Nangis, in which the invocation of names "firmly believed to be the names of demons" are cited as part of the description not of the *ars notoria*, but of the anonymous monk's own book.[7] Later, in a notice in the sixteenth-century *Antiquitez, croniques et singularitez de Paris*, the still anonymous monk of Morigny is falsely credited with inventing the *ars notoria* itself.[8] And later still, in a single, hastily compressed sentence in the compendious history of the inquisition by Henry Charles Lea, published in 1887, John is not credited with writing anything at all: "A monk was seized at Paris in 1323 for possessing a book on the subject; the book was burned, and he probably escaped with abjuration and penance."[9]

Thus a loose chain of quick paraphrases over six hundred years gradually effaced any mention of the long, complicated, and difficult text constructed and reshaped over more than a decade by John himself. The trail that might have led back to John's work was sufficiently cold that even Lynn Thorndike did not catch its scent, though he may have held a copy of John's work in his hands (the same Munich manuscript later identified by Dupèbe). Thorndike alluded to condemnations or to manuscripts of John's book several times in his *History of Magic and Experimental Science* (noting in passing a reference to the work in the Augustinian Jacques le Grand's 1405 encyclopedia *Sophologium*, which also represents the text as a version of the *ars notoria*) without connecting these references to the *Grandes Chroniques* account, or to one another.[10]

It was not until the early 1990s that independent discoveries of manuscripts containing full and complete texts of John's New Compilation *Liber florum* by Sylvie Barnay in France, and Nicholas Watson and myself in Canada, made it clear that this work survived the burning.[11] Indeed, by now it has become clear from ongoing discoveries of manuscripts across Europe that it had a vigorous life and was not nearly so successfully repressed as the Chronicle suggests.[12] The spread of the *Liber florum*—at least in part via Benedictine monks traveling from monastery to monastery—may have begun before 1323, but it certainly did not end there. Predictably (in terms of normal manuscript distribution rates, which tend to increase with time as manuscripts proliferate), all known copies postdate the burning. Manuscripts have been located in England, Germany, Austria, Italy, and Spain. Several of the copies still reside in Benedictine monasteries in Austria, and others were known to have been in the possession of religious houses at one time.[13] It is clear, too, that most of the existing copies were made for use. John instructs that the book should be personalized and consecrated, and the majority of known copies are so personalized, with individual names in the prayers, and, where figures still exist, in the figures as well.[14] All of these are men's names, so far: Albert, Andreas, Bernard, Erasmus, Geoffrey, Jacob, Peter, Rupert, Ulric. Copies that do not contain personal names are exemplars, at least in two cases held in monastic libraries for monks to copy and personalize for themselves.[15]

We must thus be very cautious in accepting the "final" feel of the Chronicle account, with its suggestion that whatever illicit practices the monk of Morigny may have been dabbling in, they were nipped in the bud. The evidence of widespread transmission and ritual use of the *Liber florum* in the milieu of literate monks after 1323 challenges the widespread belief that book condemnation constitutes effective censorship.[16] As far as John himself is concerned, we must remember, too, that the Paris burning was not the first condemnation his work suffered. Evidence of John's continued work on the *Liber florum* after the initial condemnation in 1315, eight years before the sensational account in the *Grandes Chroniques*, challenges the static conception of categories like heterodoxy and orthodoxy by showing how, even in the face of condemnation, magic texts may continue to be consciously drawn into and engage with learned Christian discourse and practice.[17] John's own work offers us a detailed account of how he negotiated the categories of magic and heresy, and how, in collaboration with Christ and the Virgin, he evolved, from the basic principles supplied by the *ars notoria*, a lived theology of liturgical and paraliturgical practice. The continued popularity of his book through the fifteenth century suggests that this was seen as a successful negotiation by its readers, many of them religious men sufficiently well educated to read and grasp the ritual force and theological claims of John's work, and thus in a reasonably good position to make judgments about its orthodoxy.

The story told about the *Liber florum* in the Chronicle account of its condemnation is a simple and recognizable story about a monk punished for the use of illicit magic. The *Liber florum* itself tells a story about a monk punished for the use of illicit magic, but it is about much more than that, too; as I will argue here, it is in a larger and more important way a story about knowledge acquisition—in particular about the personal process of John's own intellectual formation, but in a larger way about learning in general. It has theological and ethical ramifications that make it considerably more complicated than the story found in the condemnation account.

How to present the knowledge-arc of John's story to twenty-first-century readers remains a puzzle, however. Prima facie it might seem as though John's own extensive knowledge—his embeddedness in the intellectual contexts of twelfth-century Chartrain literature, liturgy, exegesis, and canon law (all relatively familiar turf to medievalists, at least in theory)—ought to give an advantage to modern readers in finding access to his work. Yet in fact, while his literate background provides important starting points for study, John integrates devotional, exegetical, and natural knowledge in ways that are somewhat unusual. His use of the angel magic of the *ars notoria* to gain knowledge of the liberal arts—indeed, the remarkable witness he offers to its popularity in his milieu—is both striking and so alien to modern intellectual practices as to make the grounds for condemnation of his text perhaps a little too easy to accept. The fact that his knowledge derives from a store of other magic texts, too, many no longer available to us in any form at all, makes certain aspects of his experience quite hard to get at. In the end, the *Liber florum* has been lost on several levels at once. It was lost in one way because the allegation of magic that is the inevitable reference point for history even now creates in readers a predisposition of disbelief in John's own claims for the text's sacred delivery; lost in another because the knowledge practices John engages are so much further from the practice of history than they used to be; and lost in a third way because history (by which I mean the interpretation of the record of events, not the stream of events as such) actually does have a tendency to repeat itself when the record of an original local memory disappears.

Rewriting Magic is part of a project shared with the handful of other scholars now engaged with John's work to restore more of the local memory of the book under condemnation. The Latin edition of the *Liber florum* is an important piece of that work, the product of almost two decades of interpretive labor, but the access it provides to the *Flowers of Heavenly Teaching* is necessarily somewhat specialized. *Rewriting Magic* aims to tell a story that will open the work up further, embedding the knowledge-arc that governs John's narrative in an account of its medieval sacramental and magical background, so that readers—especially readers completely new to John's work—will have a stronger base for understanding the quest for knowledge that drove him to the study of magic and beyond it.

An inevitable part of that story is my own quest for knowledge about John, my search for manuscripts of his text, and my personal involvement in the labor of piecing together evidence for the layered composition and transmission of his work. The way in which John's *Liber florum* comes into being as knowledge in the twenty-first century cannot, at least for me in this book, be divided from the way I came to know it. For even as John was aware of being a medium that transmitted, to the best of his ability, the words of Mary, first-century mother of Jesus, to a fourteenth-century audience, I am aware of being a medium transmitting, to the best of my ability, the words of John of Morigny, fourteenth-century Benedictine, to an audience of twenty-first-century readers.

While I am far from resolving all the problems or answering all my own questions about his book (questions naturally proliferate at a greater rate than answers), I do have a great deal more to connect it to than I did when I started—an array of memories, ideas, other manuscripts, other texts, and other historical and theological writings that are connected, or might be connected, to the way John thinks and writes. The sheer volume of detail, the very intimacy of my view of John's work, has, to use the modular image of my epigraph from Wittgenstein, gone from being something like a model home to something more like a model city. And not a finished model, either; it is not that kind of thing. Wittgenstein's metaphor allows knowledge to be viewed simultaneously as a genuine whole system and an unfinished aggregate of historically striated regions. Like memory, it is also, and simultaneously, crumbling and being rebuilt, reinventing itself not as a whole, but in pieces. Yet the sense of identity—of being one thing (as a city is one thing through successive rebuildings)—remains. Thus, mutatis mutandis, my grasp of John's work has built itself into a construct that has its newish parks and subdivisions, its historic districts, its condemned and burned-out husks of buildings, its neighborhoods where cabbies would refuse to drive you if this city were real—a model so extensive, with so many bits trailing here and there off the edge of the cultivated land, paths winding up in great rutted heaps and piles of uncultivated data edging the virgin forest where the precise topography under the arboreal canopy is still only dreamt of, that this knowledge becomes increasingly difficult to hand on to new readers.

The problem is genuinely acute. It cannot now, if indeed it ever could, be unloaded all at once. In our collaborative edition of *Liber florum*, Nicholas Watson and I offer John's text with an apparatus that is something like a map of the central area, with various keys, tables, indices, and other *legenda* that guide readers to interactions between different parts of John's system, and between John's system and other systems. The edition, of course, is designed for a fairly advanced user, a reader of Latin, a knower and consumer of information about medieval manuscripts. In this volume, I am attempting something different. I am writing here something more like a memoir of a journey, which is not just about my knowledge of John of Morigny but also my learning of him; it is about the way he has taken shape in my mind (acquired a personality, behaviors, tricks of speech, traits I recognize when he performs them), but also the way he has shaped me, made me who I am, which cannot be entirely disentangled from the way I know him. My book is thus part ethnography, with John as a primary informant. It is part exegesis, as I try to glean from his book, with the aid of my own slowly accrued knowledge of medieval exegesis and liturgy (a knowledge that was truly not there at all at the point of encounter), a picture that might suggest a shape for what is missing. It is part intellectual history, and it is also a meditation on magic and religion. The object of this book is to map my own journey in a way that others might be able to follow it.

The exercise of thinking of the book as a journey-memoir suggests itself because John of Morigny's *Liber florum* is a journey-memoir of the kind I am trying to describe. His book is about knowledge acquisition: it represents both a ritual means of acquiring knowledge and a narrative of that acquisition, and these two things influence each other. At the same time, he is engaged in representing his own knowledge process in such a way that the reader/operator may follow in his footsteps. His book resembles Wittgenstein's language-city, in being composed of some old and some new regions, some being built and some decomposing; it also resembles a great many poems, in the way that it records and actualizes its own process. It attempts not to tell about an experience in language other than that experience, but rather to create an experience in language for us—one that must transform us if we engage it, for it is also a work of conversion.

Underlying my exposition of John's *Liber florum*, and part of the purpose of the memoiristic parts of this book, is an argument that the sacral knowledge process that John lays bare is a fundamentally familiar one, for it is still possible to perceive knowledge acquisition experientially as a transformation of self that is integrated with the transformation of knowledge in a larger communal sense. In the *Liber florum*, this transformation is conceived on a cosmic scale, as part of a divine transformation of the order of the universe in the work of human creation and redemption. The experience of internal transformation that is involved in this process is actually part of an external transformation that is tied to the entire community of the Christian faithful, and thereby also to the dispensation that maps a divine *telos* for this process. These inner and outer things are not merely parallel or analogous, but one single process in which John is always consciously and dynamically engaged.

In scholarly discourse now there are philosophical and social-scientific models for the way knowledge works that may be useful to certain readers for translating John's theological process, because they also cast knowledge as processual, dynamic, simultaneously local and general, inner and outer, individual and communal. The theoretical approaches nurtured by Wittgenstein's work on language games and by Bourdieu, with his terminology of "field" and "habitus," offer related models of knowing as a constituent part of learned selfhood that is communally shared, produced and reproduced in the experiencing subject who is fluent in the rules of a specific knowledge practice, habitus, or language game. The term "language game" identifies a sphere of knowledge in practice that overlaps with (but is not identical to) the idea of habitus. Both terms rest on an assumption that when we seek to understand knowledge in its local manifestations, the target of our attention cannot be static abstract referents for knowledge bodies, nor specific rules of play, but rather must be knowledge as dissolved in the medium of practice (the "game"). Obviously a "game" is not the rule card, nor the game board, nor the playing pieces, nor even the players, but the processual engagement with the rules in the forward motion of "play." Knowledge occurs in the state of play at the interface between the interior self or subject and the outer (communal and social, but also elemental) world.[18] The body of theory underlying these knowledge models lacks the directionality governed by divine *telos* that exists in John's model, but as soon as you begin seeking to locate ethical action in the matrix, a certain directionality, a kind of shadow of an eschatology, begins to appear.[19]

But we do not really need social theory to grasp the dynamic, inner and outer, forward motion of knowledge; it is experientially available in other ways. When we write books, we settle into a habitus that may rest at the nexus of a plurality of fields (in the common sense), and we engage a game that, if well played, may show fluency (or expertise) in several areas. The book, once published, is a material object that comes into being as knowledge when it is engaged by others, becoming communal in the forward motion of play. In discussions of habitus and practice theory generally, for the most part simpler examples are used than writing books, for the same reason that Wittgenstein provided simpler examples of language games to establish what he meant by them. (The "builder's game" is the critical topos,[20] and comes up in most discussions of language games, but it is not the only example, and perhaps not even the best one, of what a language game can be.) Knowledge practices need not be engaged through books, but I point out that they can be, and that the writing of a scholarly book is a valid example of how, embedded in a complex intersection of habitus, we pursue historical language games.

I place this example strategically here, because, though it is not simple, the writing of books is something that I expect many of my readers will understand fluently, expertly, and viscerally as experts in its practice, though many readers may not have as expert a familiarity with the other knowledge practices that John engaged (whether the lettered practices, like canon law, liturgical composition, or exegesis, or the contemplative practices like praying the hours, using the *ars notoria* figures, or conversing with the virgin Mary). A few may know what it is like to pray the hours, but more of us will know what it is like to write a book. Composing a book, like praying the hours, is something that rests on daily habits. Any seriously written book changes the writer. Any given moment in the writing of a book is also engagement with a dynamic communal knowledge that we are trying to *push* on, to *manipulate*, to *authorize* changes in. At the same time, depending upon our initial position, we may be trying to change our status in a given field (in both the common sense and Bourdieu's). In writing, we seek not merely to produce a material object—that least of all, perhaps, especially in this digital age—but really to adjust the knowledge system in which the written object is about to take its place.[21] All writers are familiar with the extent to which, in doing this, we live in the book's imagined future even as we lick it into shape.

My investigation of John's theology, and the entwined role of magic and the sacraments in his book, is at its basis an attempt to describe his engagement with certain language games. After this introduction I will limit my direct engagement with the vocabulary of Bourdieu and Wittgenstein because this is not a book about the ways they construct knowledge, but about the ways John of Morigny constructed it, the apparatus of meaning-making constituted in the Latin theological tradition that was the substrate of habitual daily knowledge for him. For we do have the potential to engage any language games we choose, including medieval ones, where a sufficient record is left of how they were played in the first instance. Learning the rules of these older and more recondite games—learning how to play them, and even to play them well—is really what all historians do, and I am not doing anything very different here, except that in certain places I try to lay my own writing a little more open to expose its process.

I want to make clear here at the outset that my interest in the narrative of discovery is not the story for its own sake. The object of the game is actually to locate and articulate the functioning of the hinge between personal and institutional knowledge processes. The location of this hinge is necessarily internal. I am not the only actor in the story of John's discovery, not the sole or first reader of his work. The knowing of John of Morigny is a communal project, and all the people who have also been holders of, and contributed to, the infant body of knowledge about John of Morigny (most especially my collaborator in the editorial process, Nicholas Watson) are all the more important just now because they are still so few.

At the same time, it is really only my own story that I can tell. And because John's work was almost entirely untouched by history, so nearly pristinely institutionally unknown at the point of my engagement with it, the story of my learning of John's book offers a unique opportunity to demonstrate how new knowledge must begin interior to a self even as it engages what may sometimes appear as an institutional overdetermination, the preexisting, necessarily oversimplified grid of historical knowledge as it begins to be known in curricula and in textbooks. I am, finally, interested in how the creative play of meaning-in-use both uses and gains leverage from, and exerts force on, the institution whose rules it follows.

In uncovering this process, I am aware of myself as in some instances performing more or less Wittgensteinian operations, but I am also aware of doing what John of Morigny did in his Book of Visions and Book of Figures, showing how knowledge initially exterior to the self (whether first encountered in books or visions) becomes interiorized through reading and rereading, and through practice, and then transforms the systems it exists to uphold. Thus, I engage to preach about John's practices by practicing his manner of preaching. If I have a single overriding goal, it is to make John's work accessible, as much as possible *experientially* available to my audience, to create an experience in language that is homologous with my own experience of coming to know John, condensed into a smaller and more efficient format, a record of engagement with his text.

Because my readers are about to be plunged into this record of engagement at the deep end (because I began, as we all must, with a knowledge of John's habitus that was partly missing, partly wrong, and generally inchoate, and I must set the reader *in medias res*), I here offer a brief overview of the book's shape as a reassurance that there is in fact a path to knowing embedded in it. The book is divided into two parts of three chapters each, with similar patterns in both. The titles of the two parts, "Foundation" and "Restoration," imitate the terminology of the two-part division used by Hugh of St. Victor to structure his work *De sacramentis* (*On the Sacraments*). John's own book also reflects this structure, in the sense that his New Compilation Book of Figures offers a restoration of the world described in the Old Compilation Book of Figures, mapping John's redemption onto an idea of sacramental supersession within his book.[22]

Part 1, "Foundation," primarily draws its evidence from John's Book of Visions, although it touches base with things further on in the work. Its main external referent is the *ars notoria*. This part seeks to answer the question of why, even while he sought to destroy the *ars notoria*, John would re-create some of its most characteristic features in his own book. In pursuing my investigation, I am mainly engaged with John's visionary autobiography, but I do, particularly in chapter 3, touch on some of John's prayers as well. This is necessary because of the way parts of John's autobiography are fed into the prayers, where we see his life experiences refracted in different ways. The Seven Prayers in particular are so linked to the visions that it is all but impossible to limit the autobiographical discussion exclusively to the prose narrative.

Part 2, "Restoration," primarily draws its evidence from John's Book of Figures (in both the Old and New versions), although it engages with episodes earlier in the work. Its main external referent is necromancy. This part of the book aims to answer the question of how John succeeds in continuing to understand his work as divinely delivered even after it gets broken by the accusation of the Barking Dogs—a question that cannot be entirely disentangled from other, harder questions about what necromancy actually meant to John, and how it, too, might partake in the sacramental and dispensational understanding that he begins with.

Both parts have a similar interior structure. The first chapter of each section is narrative and descriptive, the second chapters are broadly contextualizing, and the third chapters involve close reading. Chapters 1 and 4 open with personal narratives of my first encounters with John's Book of Visions and his original Book of Figures, respectively. Chapters 2 and 5 zoom out to elaborate broader contexts that are meant to domesticate the contingencies of the language games in which the *ars notoria* and necromancy acquire their significance and manifest their rules of play. Chapters 3 and 6 offer close readings of crucial moments in John's narrative, showing how John's expertise in theology is crucially compounded of vision and prayer. These chapters highlight both the game and the game-changing qualities of John's work, where the reader is invited to observe whole clouds of philosophy condensed into a few drops of grammar.

Part 1 | FOUNDATION

1

LIKE STONES OF FIRE:
I ENCOUNTER THE BOOK OF VISIONS

Now and then there are readings that make the hairs on the neck, the non-existent pelt, stand on end and tremble, when every word burns and shines hard and clear and infinite and exact, like stones of fire, like points of stars in the dark—readings when the knowledge that we *shall know* the writing differently or better or satisfactorily, runs ahead of any capacity to say what we know, or how. In these readings, a sense that the text has appeared to be wholly new, never before seen, is followed, almost immediately, by the sense that it was *always there*, that we the readers, knew it was always there, and have *always known* it was as it was, though we have now for the first time recognised, become fully cognizant of, our knowledge.

—A. S. Byatt, *Possession*

Knowledge is a journey. It is for this reason difficult to map as a schema. There are no partitions between the elements. One's knowledge of a person, or any complex thing, a language, or a topic or area does not accumulate in a straightforward way. With a person, one attends to countless behaviors and learns to see new patterns. The image of the person is adjusted as we move forward. With a language, one acquires an alphabet and a grammar, and later, a sense of how the words make sense when they cluster. One learns to relate to, to translate, the recurrent clusters; one fits in new learning around the clusters already recognized. This is a process. There may be a spot that one recognizes as the "beginning," or the "end," but that point is sometimes hard to locate.

Yet always, as A. S. Byatt describes it, one retrofits new discoveries to some sense of the already known. The beginning of knowledge is in the shock of recognition, a moment in which "here is the sought-for thing" jockeys with "here is a new thing, an unsought thing, a thing I have never before seen." The unseen, unexpected nature of the thing clears its own space. The whole event encloses a prayer that the object that so holds one's attention—person or thing—one day may be known more and better. Whatever one learns, there is always in the back of one's mind a whole picture that one represents to one's self as the "whole thing"—the "Latin language," for example, or otherwise, "Richard Kieckhefer," or in another register "Mary Douglas," or again "Augustine of Hippo." Unless one is engaged in a deliberate exercise of averted vision, the "whole" tends to appear less sketchy than it really is, more real at any given moment than we have any right to think.

Because inevitably most of it is *missing*. It cannot really be looked at. Our sense of the "whole" always governs the way that our knowledge must be partitioned, developed, and represented, yet at the same time the "whole picture" is the most mutable thing of all. It can crumple at the learning of one new fact. The whole picture must be raised again and again from its ruined self, represented in the mind's eye as pristine, an image where all the lines connect, a figure that always appears whole even after being wholly destroyed. That is the work of memory. Scholarship too is a work of memory.

The most difficult part of this work of memory is that the picture of what one knows is always simultaneously, in some part or other, a picture of one's self. To identify it too closely with the self would be a misapprehension, even a pathology, but so would be a representation that constructed it as entirely other, entirely an object. As long as the self continues, the picture must always be there; it is part of consciousness. But how do you take this ever-changing, elusive, miragelike, mutable, and dynamic thing that is your own view at a distance of the knowledge of a subject that is simultaneously an object (for this thing is also your memory, it is also you yourself) and turn it into a guide, a book to inform others? How in fact do you share it? This is not a problem that is in any way specific to introducing a new historical discovery to an audience that does not know it yet, for there is always some aporia, some philosophical bemusement engaged in undertaking any complex communication. The aporia between knowing and speaking is especially assumed to plague "mystical" knowledge, but it is hardly exclusive to the experience of divine transmutation of the soul. Yet it is fair to say that the greater the gap (of whatever sort) between your knowledge and that of your projected audience, the more acute the problem becomes.

Here is a more concrete instance, an exemplum about the gap between discovering and knowing. Once, after I had delivered a presentation on John of Morigny, very early in the process of learning about him, someone asked me why no one had looked for this text before: "Was it presumed lost?" It was difficult to know how to answer this. The text was not "presumed lost" in the sense that nothing about it was presumed at all: it was simply lost. There appeared to be no epistemic quiddity to presume a loss *from*—it was so lost that there was no other knowledge to which to attach it, no map with a blank spot on it crying out to be filled in. When you lose an object—a wedding ring, a favorite pair of glasses, a document—you know what it looks like, you can describe it to someone else, and you may remember where you were standing when you realized it was missing. But in the case of John of Morigny, there appeared to be no contiguous contingency, nothing it sat by the side of, by means of which it could be located as knowledge on the map of medieval Europe. Of course John's work draws on many known genres, and many works that preceded his are in some aspect or another similar: confessions, meditations, exempla, mystical autobiographies, visionary accounts of the virgin Mary, works of liturgical exegesis, the *ars notoria*, and so on. But all the most striking aspects of the way these things are *combined* in John's work are unrepresented elsewhere. Simply put, there is no other visionary autobiography by a self-confessed magic user seeking to produce a prayer book in the way John produces it. There was so little context for this that there might as well have been none at all. This work was lost in a way that was wholly new to me: there was no memory of a previous possession, nowhere we were standing when it disappeared, no way to describe it, and no hypothesis about where it might be.

It does seem odd in retrospect that a profound lack of information about some historical topic is not recognizable as a discontinuity at the moment of encounter. It seems as though it *ought* to be, as though the historical record prior to the discovery of the various manuscript versions of the work of John of Morigny should have appeared as a break in the story, a clear gap, a blank space crying out to be filled in, but evidently it did not. The process of knowledge has to begin with an awareness, however dim, that a discontinuity exists, that there is some sort of gap in the memory, some difficulty, some irritating problem with the record that needs to be opened up and examined. One of the difficulties, perhaps especially for the junior scholar, with locating such a gap in the first place is that it feels personal. It feels like ignorance. The worse the institutional lack, the harder the problem, the less the scholar may feel that she wants to admit it to anyone else. Yet its admission is crucial. Recognizing the difference between personal and institutional ignorance, or personal and institutional knowing, is not easy or immediate because of all the ways in which they are not actually different. Ultimately the institutional foundations are inside of us. That is why the primary practice of the scholar's discipline is agnosticism: learning to stay mindful of how much is always unknown, learning to be aware of discontinuities in knowledge (one's own and that of others), of uncertainties and doubts, without rushing to fill the gap with things that only sort of fit, "without any irritable reaching after fact & reason," as John Keats put it.[1] The poet's discipline is not that much different from the scholar's.

This awareness of a discontinuity, experienced at first as a vexing state of ignorance, first stirred in me twenty years ago after a telephone call from Nicholas Watson, an old friend then already teaching at the University of Western Ontario, though we were graduate students together, entering the University of Toronto in the same year, and both medievalists—he in the Department of English, I at the Centre for Medieval Studies. Nicholas, who later became my collaborator on the edition of John's *Liber florum*, is the most important of the contemporary dramatis personae to appear in these pages, and I indulge in a brief characterization here. His temperament is in most ways opposed to mine: he is jovial, sanguine, easily gregarious, ebullient (to a fault?), energetic, ambitious, with speech and manner indexing Oxbridge, trained in English literature but as time wore on moving more toward the institutional history of Christianity, interested in vernacular theology and middle English writers, especially those often thought of as "mystics." Nicholas writes from the outside in, always quite a lot, always in long full sentences, hewing down and inwards as he feels for the shape of a work coming into being through his own words. He cannot think without a great spill of words first, nor do his dark corners—he does have some—ever seem to curb the flow of his optimism.

I am saturnine, choleric, and melancholic, somewhat socially phobic, which makes me seem aloof and "difficult" at times (unless I am comfortable with you, in which case I may talk too much), energetic too, but cynical, with speech and manner for fellow initiates indexing Reed College (a place that prized a traditional education, where in fact my grandfather taught physics in 1923–24, but is perhaps better known for the quirky brilliance of its famous dropouts, including Steve Jobs and James Beard), trained in English literature but as time wore on moving more toward the sociology of knowledge, interested in medieval Latin writers, but especially those concerned with liminal knowledge areas (which for some reason does not boil down to what is usually called "mysticism" in my case, though that too). I write from the inside out (have practiced poetry), and am a chary spiller of words, building up slowly as I feel for the shape of a work, so to speak, "in the air." I have bright corners that rarely attain their full incandescence in public circumstances. Nicholas and I are so nearly temperamentally opposite that I sometimes wondered how on earth we would be able to engage in a successful collaboration. (Nicholas—the ebullient one—often assured me that it *was* successful, though less often lately, perhaps because this became more obvious as the work drew to a close.)

At the time of his phone call to me, shortly after the first manuscript of the work we later came to know as the *Liber florum* was handed to him by a librarian at McMaster University, I was just finishing up a dissertation at the University of Toronto on the intellectual history of magic. He had been commissioned to deliver a five-minute talk on a manuscript for an educational video being made about the rare books collection in the McMaster University Library. He suspected (rightly) that this manuscript might be of interest to me, and also (wrongly) that I might know something about the text it contained.

He explained that the book in question, uncatalogued and unnumbered at that time (now MS 107), was in Latin and had a modern binding that labeled it simply a "prayer book." Nothing at all was known about it by the library, but the idea of a prayer book suggested to the librarian that it might be his sort of thing. It was missing the first fifteen folios, and began *in medias res* with a long rambling prayer that described itself as being for *feria secunda*, the second day of the week, Monday. The Sunday ritual was missing; there was no introduction and no rubric announcing author or title, though the copy was dated to 1461 in the colophon at the end. The seller had been Italian. The book contained a few devotional images of Mary and Christ, not of any great artistic merit, and perhaps later than the text they illuminated, though in color, which may have been why the book was singled out for attention.

Beyond the images, there was nothing to suggest that this was a work of particular interest. (Though of course the word "interest" itself flags no more than the place where one feels the beginning of knowledge branch off, differentiate itself, from the homogenous landscape of one's ignorance;[2] I knew nothing about prayer books then either.) I must emphasize the fact that this, the first discovery, contained nothing but a ritual text, prayers with instructions; it did not have any of the autobiographical passages found in later copies, which would have made everything different. John's name and byname were not mentioned in it.

The first half of the book was occupied with rhapsodic prayers addressed to the virgin Mary, which, if not all immediately recognizable, did not appear unusual. The second half, however, was definitely eccentric. It contained a sequence of prayers addressed to the nine orders of angels. More unusual still, the first seven angelic orders were aligned with the liberal arts, and each of the prayers was in search of knowledge of one art: grammar, rhetoric, dialectic, arithmetic, geometry, music, and astronomy; the remaining two orders, the cherubim and seraphim, were petitioned for the disciplines of philosophy and theology. There was a sequence of folios at the end that described how to make a ring, consecrated to the Virgin, that enabled further divinatory work—a magic ring, as we then too quickly thought of it. (This manuscript did not contain John's original qualification, "that signifies perfection and love ... and in all other ways signifies like the rings of prelates."[3])

Nicholas sailed through the early prayers, mentally preparing a five-minute talk, but when he came to the angelic prayers he began to suspect that the manuscript was more unusual than it had seemed at first. When he came to read about the embossed ring (which could be made of gold or silver, or amber, or artificial amber, each signifying different attributes of the Virgin) that would help the wearer answer questions, his suspicions became more pressing. He was most startled of all by the practice involving an experiment to induce a vision before continuing. Nothing he had encountered in his field had prepared him to read about a devotional practice in which having visions was actually a *necessity*. In search of more information, he made three telephone calls. (I do not know what order he made them in, only that I was the third, but will impose an order for the sake of the narrative.) The first call was to Frank Klaassen, then a graduate student at the University of Toronto, like me, writing a dissertation on intellectual magic in the Middle Ages, already culling data from manuscript catalogues and trying to put them in some sort of order. Frank told Nicholas that the angelic prayers sounded like an *ars notoria*, a work of illicit magic—condemned by theologians but rather common in manuscript, actually—that used angelic prayers to access knowledge of the liberal arts. The second call was to Richard Kieckhefer, a well-known scholar whose works bridged magic and what usually gets called "spirituality," and the author of many books, of which perhaps the best known at that time was *Magic in the Middle Ages*. Richard remembered the entry in the *Grandes Chroniques* describing the 1323 burning of a work by a French monk, like an *ars notoria*, but with Marian images in it.

I was the last person Nicholas called. I was energized to hear of this interesting set of prayers and vexed to be able to add nothing to the information already in play. It was not just my own lack of knowledge that bothered me; it was my complete lack of resources. What had I *failed to read* that might have connected me to the sort of thing this appeared to be? I had read about the *ars notoria* in Lynn Thorndike, of course, but it was described in a way that made it sound less than relevant to my engagement with intellectual history; Thorndike mentions several works of notory art in manuscript, in a paragraph ending "but all alike are apt to impress the present reader as unmeaning jumbles of diagrams and magic words."[4] I was not interested in unmeaning jumbles. In fact I did not really think of prayer as all that pertinent to intellectual history, either, though these prayers were a little different because of the way they embedded the liberal arts, whose importance for intellectual history one could hardly deny (though at the same time one could easily imagine many ways of dismissing their role here as unimportant just the same, *because they were prayers*). I wanted to learn more and had no idea where to go. I thought perhaps at least I could try to find more manuscripts, naively assuming that I needed to know only where to go to look them up.

Some days after this conversation with Nicholas, I asked my dissertation supervisor, George Rigg (world-class expert on Anglo-Latin literature, deep well of information on Latin philology, steeped in manuscript culture and the practices of medieval editing), how I might go about finding more copies of an obscure Latin prayer text that Nicholas had found in an acephalous fifteenth-century, perhaps Italian, copy. We were walking across Queen's Park together for some reason I cannot now remember. His answer, given in a cheerful and not uninterested tone, was definite: "I have absolutely no idea!" This was characteristic insouciance on George's part, but it was also a critical observation for me. Since George was an expert, it let me know that the ignorance I harbored uneasily was not just mine; there was an institutional component to it. One was allowed to be at a loss.

I soon came to realize more intimately that there were layers upon layers to the institutional difficulty—or otherwise put, as all medievalists work out sooner or later, a great deal of stuff in manuscript holdings that no one knows very much about. What gets written down in a catalogue or handlist for a given collection depends largely on what is available to know outside the text, that is, in the knowledge that has already been institutionalized. Cataloguers can rarely afford to put time into reading the entire contents of a manuscript. Sometimes they do, and catalogues may offer detailed information about the contents of a book, but more often the cataloguer skims through, looking for dates and rubrics, making notes. It is obviously easier to classify a text with a famous author than one with an unknown author, and if there is no available secondary literature, the record will be skimpy. Much medieval Latin material is only crudely categorized, if at all. This includes Latin of all sorts and genres, not just works of a putatively magical nature; anonymous treatises, commentaries, miscellanies, computus texts, prayers and liturgies, and the work of many lesser-known authors all may be relatively hard to track. In a manuscript holding or archive, one is at the very periphery of institutional knowledge: at the edge, so to speak, of the knowledge-world. This can be exciting but may also induce vertigo.

There were two additional difficulties with the McMaster manuscript that made the catalogue indices even less useful than usual. First, although the book was personalized throughout the prayers with an owner's name (Bernardus), it had no author's name associated with it; second, it was missing the first fifteen folios, which meant there was no introduction describing the work, and more importantly no opening phrase, no *incipit*. It is not possible to hunt for any text in any standard indices without at least one of these terms. Existing databases and manuscript catalogues were thus of almost no use to us at the outset. Looking for the text would involve random leafing through catalogues and indices for individual prayer incipits and hoping to get lucky. It could take years.

Beyond the intrinsic (and continuing) problems of finding manuscripts, much that has been uncovered since the 1990s about medieval magic texts and manuscripts still waited in the wings. This was prior to the publication of any of Sylvie Barnay's work, which we were not to find for another few years. Richard Kieckhefer's *Forbidden Rites* (1997) had not yet crystallized into an edition. Only after this came the steady trickle of new writings trying to piece together the topography of this area: the preliminary reflections on magic in manuscript collected in my volume *Conjuring Spirits* (1998), Hedegård's edition of the *Liber iuratus* (2002), the work of Julien Véronèse on the *ars notoria* (2004), Boudet's *Entre science et nigromance* (2008), and many other works that have emerged only in this millennium. Much else that has advanced the area was still nascent then, including the Internet itself. There was no Google.[5] There were no digitized manuscripts, nor was there high-speed data transfer to facilitate downloading pages from them. Not even the Twilit Grotto, Joseph Peterson's collection of online esoterica, yet awaited the intrepid browser of the newly accessible World Wide Web.

Thus it was that when Nicholas described the McMaster prayer book for me, with those odd prayers for the seven liberal arts, there was almost nothing to attach it to, nowhere to look it up, and no systematic way of searching for more copies. Richard Kieckhefer had tipped us off to the entry in the *Grandes Chroniques*, but at that point we could not know for sure whether the text in this manuscript could firmly be identified with that work, or whether it was, as I then thought vaguely, "just another *ars notoria*." Thorndike indicated, and Frank confirmed, that there were many variants and versions of these. There was nothing in this manuscript copy to identify it with any "monk of Morigny" or otherwise with the book described in the account of the 1323 burning. The manuscript itself was quite a bit later than the burning, and the indications of its Italian origin did not suggest a strong link. Overall, the likelihood that it was "just another *ars notoria*" seemed relatively greater to me, but the whole was really a bog of probabilities that contained scarcely a single stepping-stone of hard fact. This was partly because I did not have enough data to correlate it with any known copy or version of the *ars notoria* either.

This also was a problem with the institutional knowledge of the *ars notoria*, not just mine, for it, too, was in some sense a lost text, one of many works traveling under the pseudepigraphic authority of Solomon that have only recently begun to attract the sustained attention of scholars.[6] Though the *ars notoria* had seen early printed editions, and manuscript copies persisted well into the modern period, until quite recently it was treated by historians as hardly more than a medieval curiosity. Historical works tended to repeat the same phrases about it, mostly drawn (as with accounts of John of Morigny's work) from condemnations, or, post-Thorndike, from *The History of Magic and Experimental Science*. The text's history was obscure, its origin unknown, the number of versions uncounted, and their relation to each other unguessed. How the *ars notoria* was used, or how it might have "worked," was not even a matter for speculation. Perhaps there was too little to go on, or perhaps it so obviously did not work that questions of what results anyone might have obtained from its use were never raised. Importantly, the absence of real knowledge about the *ars notoria* did not initially appear to me as a big blank space on the map of knowledge, either. One must be quite close to spot the shimmer, the boundary where knowing shades into not-knowing.

Experientially, knowledge always has to start with the sense that one has been handed a really resistant puzzle, an enigma that induces one to waste an extra hour or two trying to find an answer. In this case I wasted rather more than an hour in random searches of manuscript catalogues in the Pontifical Institute Library without result. I pondered the prayers in the McMaster manuscript and looked up the early printed editions of the *ars notoria*, which really did not seem all that similar. I returned to Thorndike's account of *ars notoria* variants more than once. It is a jumble of data, which I quote here to show both its breathtaking quality (remember that he stands on a cliff at the very edge of institutional knowledge) and how little it actually says. He wrote,

> There seems to be little difference between the notory art of Solomon, that of Solomon, Machineus, and Euclid, and the *Golden Flowers* of Apollonius, in which Solomon is mentioned almost every other sentence. Cecco d'Ascoli may have had it in mind when he cited the *Book of Magic Art* of Apollonius and the *Angelic Faction* of the same author. In one manuscript at the close of the *Golden Flowers* of Apollonius are prayers which one "brother John Monk" confesses he himself has composed in the years 1304–1307.[7]

The book with the *Golden Flowers* and the prayers of "brother John Monk" was in the Bayerische Staatsbibliothek in Munich, Clm 276. It felt significant that Thorndike indicated two works of interest in this book, one slightly less anonymous than the other. In fact Dupèbe had already connected this manuscript to the burned book in the Chronicle account in 1987, but I did not know this at the time. Remember that the McMaster manuscript had lost its opening pages; there was no author named; it thus contained no irrefragable link to the Chronicle entry in any event. For all I knew there were multiple versions of the *ars notoria* with Marian prayers in them. (This is in fact the case.) The Chronicle itself does not specify the monk's name, only the location of his abbey, so I had no reason to connect Thorndike's reference to "brother John" to the Chronicle account. With so much missing data, it could have been no more than a hunch, more like a shot in the dark, that led me to order a microfilm.

It was a low-risk shot, of course (the microfilm was inexpensive, and no matter what happened with the prayers, I was getting two potential *ars notoria* versions for the price of one), but it turned out to be a golden ticket. Scrolling through the pages, it did *make hairs on the back of my neck stand up* to look at the prayer texts of Clm 276, and to realize, even before comparing the texts closely, that these prayers were already familiar, the same as the ones we had in the McMaster manuscript. There was more, too. Though it was incomplete, the Munich copy did contain the first clear author identification, with the words "I, John, a monk of Morigny" on the opening folio. It also offered an incipit, "Here begins the book of Visions of the blessed and undefiled virgin Mary, mother of God,"[8] so the tools for searching manuscript indices and bibliographies were now in our hands. Beyond this, though it was very brief and allusive, the Munich copy included a sketch of John's engagement with the magical or "exceptive" arts, from which he was redeemed by God and the Virgin, from whom he sought and received license to compose a new book to attain to the pinnacle of all arts and sciences. All this, taken together with the dates of composition, was quite sufficient evidence to link the work contained in these two manuscripts to the Chronicle account of the burning.

Dabblers before, Nicholas and I now began a more earnest quest, undertaking more systematic catalogue searches, sending queries to librarians and others we thought might be positioned to turn up medieval Latin manuscripts of this sort. Frank Klaassen added John of Morigny's name and "Incipit Liber visionum" to his list of search terms, hoping to find more work by John among the texts he was hunting for his dissertation. We learned of the next three manuscripts at around the same time, in early 1997, when Nicholas and I had completed a draft transcription of the Munich text and written what we believed to be final drafts of our chapters for *Conjuring Spirits*. This book had gone enough past the submission deadline in my contract that I was receiving annoyed notes from the publisher and I was anxious to finish, but the representation of knowledge it contained was fated to be slowed down by a virtual landslide of new information. One manuscript of John's work in London, British Library Additional 18,027, had just been located by Frank Klaassen; Nicholas had found out about two additional copies in Austrian libraries—Vienna, Schottenkloster 140, and Graz University Library 680—via a query to the Hill Monastic Manuscript Library in Minnesota.[9]

I got an altogether more breathless call from Nicholas shortly after his receipt of the microfilm of the manuscript from the Graz University Library. He had browsed through it. He told me that it contained a longer version of the text than any we had yet seen, including a much longer visionary autobiography, confirming a number of things we had only been able to guess at before: a use of the *ars notoria* fully documented, a blow-by-blow account with many detailed visions; mention of John's friends and family members—evidently John had a sister who had used the *ars notoria* too; and he was putting it the mail immediately. ("The kind of story in it," he joked, "is one I could imagine you writing for yourself, if it had not turned out to exist!") Of course I could never have written anything like it, though I also knew what he meant: what he was sending me was filled with *stones of fire*.

When the mail came that brought me the Graz microfilm, I was digging through my closets trying to find a box suitable for mailing two rather bulky copies of the *Conjuring Spirits* manuscript to the press. After I dropped the microfilm into the reader, however, all thought of immediate delivery of the book was dismissed. I spent the rest of my day browsing the visions in the Graz text, electrified by this voice from the past speaking so clearly to me of curious visionary dreams (*sompnia*). The tale offered far more than one expected from such a confession, too. Details of the visions were closely noted and did not allow any quick or easy mapping of the text onto a known medieval genre. Perhaps the closest sort of thing would be the exemplary tales of magicians who overreach and repent their ways (like the sorcerer's apprentice, like Theophilus). Yet from the very first ars notorial vision, John's account struck me as coming closer to the way one tells real dreams than anything else:

> One day, at a late hour after I had fasted, I uttered some of the prayers from it which are called *ars nova*. And lo, in the night, as though put into an excess of mind, I saw the following vision. It seemed to me that I was in a field next to my mother's house in the village of Autruy, and it was night, and the moon was shining, and there was moonlight on the western wall of the aforesaid field. I was facing that direction, and there on the wall appeared the shadow of five fingers of someone's hand. And the shadow of those fingers was very horrible, because each of them was so big and fat that one could hardly fight it with five human hands. But I turned towards the moon and looked into the firmament so that I could see where the shadow of the fingers was coming from. And there in the firmament I saw the figure of a malign spirit (that is, the devil), so terrible, so formless, so foul, that no ear has heard of it, nor has it arisen in the human heart. And it was holding its hand open

in front of the moon, so that the shadow of its fingers appeared on the wall of the field.[10]

The account positions John carefully in the landscape of his vision, which is a place both strange and familiar, beside his mother's house, facing the wall, looking at it as the diabolic vision begins to be "screened" against it as in a kind of shadow play. At first he sees only the fingers of a monstrous hand (why "fingers"?), and only when he turns around does he get a fuller view of the sky-devil, from the hips (at the horizon) to its head (at the zenith). Its nether regions are not visible.[11] The top half takes up most of the sky, appearing with a strong light behind it, so it is still blacked out—merely a larger shadow.

Demonic apparitions in general may have been cultural archetypes. Certainly demons of monstrous forms, outsize shapes, inhabit the demonic stories (e.g., in the life of Saint Anthony and others later modeled on it), but this account differs by its close attention to the subject's positioning, the height and bulk externally measured with respect to the zenith and horizon, but lacking attention to any particular aspects of the demon's face or figure. Blazons of demonic forms would have been commonplace in the literature John read, animals or animal hybrids with claws, horns, muzzle, and tail appearing frequently in stories and images from the period, yet John does not evidently draw on them. Neither was this the way of medieval dream visions as a literary genre, which tend to pan the visionary landscape with more attention to the external visual field than the positioning of the subject in relation to it.

More strikingly, this apparition of monstrosity is attenuated by the account as it goes on, in a way that is surprising, but still dreamlike:

> And when I saw this figure, I could not look at it long because of its great foulness, but fell flat on the ground so that I could not see it, saying, "Truly, truly, inexplicable is the figure of demons!" After saying this I roused myself and went into my house, which was beside the field, and said to those who were inside, "Come and look at some amazing things in the sky!" And I went up into a kind of solar, and some others came with me, so that I could show what I have described to them. When we were looking out through the solar window, I pointed out to them the aforesaid figure, terrible as before, although I had seen it only a little. But then suddenly the figure descended into the field I had come from in the likeness of a holy man, and now he was very simply dressed in a black garment and was wearing a black diadem around his head. When I saw him I repented somewhat that I had called him a malign spirit, and then I immediately woke up.[12]

While it would not be unusual in a hagiographic narrative to have a demon appear in the guise of a holy man, the saintly protagonist would typically recognize the demonic apparition and drive it away. John's narrative takes the opposite trajectory: the monstrous form has already appeared and been recognized as the devil. Alone in the dark, John is so frightened that he falls face down on the ground. When he collects himself and enters the house (with lights, with other people), the fear diminishes; when he invites others to observe the apparition, the demon also diminishes in stature, descending from the sky and entering the field now looking more like a holy man than a demon, simply dressed in black (like John, like any Benedictine), but distinguished by a diadem. More true to life than to any sermon exemplum or hagiographic narrative, John tells us that he repented (a little) that he had said it was a malign spirit—a detail that is plausible as an internal response to a social situation where he fears he will be perceived as having misrepresented the "wonders," the *mirabilia*, but is hardly explicable save as a real dream fragment. There is no mystical or hagiographic narrative model for such an ambiguous and inconclusive vision.

This oddity and ambiguity is characteristic of other dreams in the course of his narrative. The other dream that caught my attention in this first reading was vision 4 (by John's numbering), where the entire Trinity appears, or seems to. Yet the apparition is not entirely visual:

> After I had begun the work of this book, when I had already laboured in it all the way to the twenty-ninth lunation, the day the moon completes her course, in the night after twilight, after uttering a certain prayer from this book which is called the "Sign of Grace," I immediately extinguished the candle and got into my bed, and when I had laid myself down, I fell into an ecstasy. And lo, suddenly the room in which I lay was filled with a great light, and there appeared to me two men whom I saw but I could not quite catch what they looked like. And between them there came a third, but I could neither see nor hear him, I only sensed him. One of the ones I saw stood at the head of my bed and the other at the foot, and the one at the head spoke to me, saying proudly, cruelly, and arrogantly, "If you had been praying to me for eighty days and more, you might have been able to attain what you seek by now." And the other, standing at the foot, responded "John, hear what father says." At once believing that he who spoke first was the Father, he who spoke second the Son, and the Holy Spirit was the one I did not see but sensed, rising and weeping with my hands joined, I said to the Son, "Remember, Lord, that you were God and man at the same time, and are, and will be." Right away he answered,

"And I say unto you that in eight days you will have a vision." And as soon as he had said that I immediately woke up.[13]

Here also, the details recall experiences of real dreams: the way the two dream figures appear, and yet seem only partly visible; their ambiguous behavior, and their speeches which command definite things, but elude a satisfying reading as clearly divine or diabolic; the sense of invisible presence felt as the Holy Spirit.

Other details from this vision stand out in relation to the *ars notoria* itself. John tells us how long he had been working with the text (all the way to the twenty-ninth lunation, the day of the full moon) and names a specific prayer from the *ars notoria*, one called "Sign of Grace," *Signum gracie*,[14] that he used to induce the dream. The experiences he records in this part of the text completely shatter anything that might have been expected about usage of the *ars notoria* from the knowledge available outside of it at that time. Indeed, neither the prayers themselves, which Thorndike (pardonably) described as "unmeaning jumbles," nor the rather abstract (and by nature improbable) notion of "instantaneous learning" of the liberal arts, nor the grandiose mythic histories the *ars notoria* provides for itself really suggest that a person might usefully put its prayers into operation. Certainly they do not suggest the process that we see John using here, in which they are being put to work as a technique for dream incubation.[15]

John's process is the same before each vision: he waits for twilight, says a prayer from the *ars notoria* (the fact that he names or mentions the prayer in at least some cases suggests that the prayer may be selected for the kind of information he wants to receive), puts out his light, and gets into bed. The content of the dreams that follow this procedure seems quite free ranging and not at all self-explicating; his visions do not appear to be led by sequences of visualizations in the *ars notoria* itself (though prescribed visions in the glossed B version do suggest that the vision will be angelic). Rather, the dream information often comes in response to specific questions or desires and needs to be decoded after the fact. The operating assumption is that dreams will generally have a communicative purpose, so the decoding process may be put to use in natural dreams as well as solicited ones. This expectation of finding meaning in the dream content can most easily be seen from the fact that John's dream solicitation is sometimes explicitly intended to help him decode information from previous dreams; for example, in his account of the induction of vision 9 (to be discussed further in chapter 3), he writes, "A certain great tribulation happened to me, and persisting in this tribulation, I saw many horrible visions each day. And one day I wanted to know what they meant, and in order to find this out,

I offered a certain prayer which was said to be for memory from the aforesaid book of the *ars notoria*."[16]

But divination of the signification of specific dream messages, while prominently figured in John's narrative, is not the only kind of use to which John puts the *ars notoria*. At the end of the Book of Visions, after John finishes with his own story, he goes on to narrate the visions of two others, to both of whom he taught the *ars notoria*, and who later, following his lead, forswore the practice. The first of these was his younger sister Bridget, who had been asking him for a long time to be taught to read. Although initially he had suggested that, at fifteen, she was too old to become very good at it,[17] in the end he yielded to her requests:

> I again considered that she might be able to succeed by means of the *ars notoria* in knowing how to read in a brief space of time, with her age not hindering her, and without hardship. So at that point first I set her to the *ars notoria*, as boys learn who have learned nothing, and I showed the letters to her. And she learned so much—she who had never seen letters—that within the reckoning of half a year she was reading and writing everywhere; and what's more, in the church before all the people she sang an alleluia perfectly all by herself, without help, as graciously as an angel.[18]

The *ars notoria* may have seemed a natural and obvious choice for John, in part, of course, because the goal of these particular prayers was learning quickly, but also because when children were taught to read, the text would normally have been a book of prayers—sometimes a missal or antiphonal or sometimes the hours of the Virgin.[19] Prayers had a number of advantages for the teaching of literacy. The language would have been familiar (even for quite young children, some prayers would have been known by heart), and prayers have a repetitive structure readily recognizable to the ear of a child brought up listening to Latin in church. The Latin prayers of the *ars notoria*, like those of any missal, repeat familiar references from the Vulgate, especially the Psalms; the unknown words may also have helped train her memory for letter and sound associations.[20] It should not be surprising that Bridget learned quickly.

But her rapid learning had a cost, and soon after her miraculous acquisition of literacy, the nightmares began. Like John, she had many horrible visions, among them one that was more frequent than the rest: "In ecstasy while sleeping, she saw, or rather sensed, that a malign spirit came and stood near her in her bed, and the malign spirit pressed so hard upon the girl's sides and back that she could neither speak nor cry out. He was always talking to her, threatening that he would kill her and torment her and not leave her in peace. . . . [S]he was so greatly terrified by him . . . that she dared no longer lie down alone at night."[21] On one particular occasion, John describes her lying in bed with a female companion.[22] John himself is sleeping somewhere nearby, perhaps in the same room, when the demon comes in to trouble her:

> Stricken with fear, she cried out to me and said, "My brother, the spirit is here, I feel him, for God's sake chase him away if you can!" I answered her, "My sister, what's wrong? Commend yourself to God, cross yourself and say an Our Father and the Creed and Hail Mary, and he will do you no harm." But although she said these prayers, lo! the spirit came nearer to her, and began to torment her and whip her so that she cried out loud as though demented, and she said to me, weeping tearfully, "Oh my brother, look, he's got me now!" When she had spoken I silently incurred great pain and fear, thinking that she endured these things on account of the work of the *ars notoria*. Then I said to her, "Dear sister, renounce the *ars notoria* and its pomps and works, and tomorrow promise God and the blessed Mary before her image in church that you won't operate through this art any more if the blessed virgin Mary will lift the fear of this spirit from you." This she promised she would do, and immediately the spirit moved some distance away from her. Rising from my bed, I got some light burning in the chamber, and when I looked in her bed I saw nothing. And she said to me, "Look: up to now I sensed that I was in his power, but he has withdrawn from me somewhat." And still I saw nothing, but I comforted her as best I could, speaking to her about God's trustworthiness and his love, and as I comforted her the spirit withdrew completely. And on the next day she did as I had told her.[23]

John's perspective as external to the vision, a listener and observer, heightens the contrast between Bridget's mad outcries in the dark and the apparent peace of the candlelit room once John has put the light on. He shares his sister's fears to the extent of actually expecting an apparition, yet he does not see one. Bridget's terror and the gradual recovery of her proper senses in her brother's comforting presence were easy to believe in; I've recovered from nightmares of this kind myself. And yet for all its experiential realness, Bridget's story follows a standard medieval model of virtuous thought ultimately triumphing over demonic attack. (John later describes his sister trampling the demon underfoot in the mode of many women in hagiographic narratives.)

The last vision in this part of the book returns to the divinatory structure and function already remarked in the majority of John's own dreams, though it concerns someone else. John of Morigny had a friend, a Cistercian monk, also named John, from the Abbey of Fontainejean, to whom—again, after repeated requests—John of Morigny taught the practice of the notory art. When John of Fontainejean had been working with the art for some time, he solicited a dream asking after an interpretation of the names or words of the art.[24] John of Morigny describes the important details of his friend's vision, following it with an exegesis:

> As he recounted it, it seemed to him that he was in the cloister of his abbey, namely Fontainejean, and he entered a place in which his books of this art, and others, were lying around. And he found a monk there holding a psalter. He was reading this psalm in it: "Grant to the king, O God, your judgement." And then this monk began to look on in the psalter with the person who was reading, and the one who was reading, seeing this, said to him, regarding him rather indignantly: "What are you looking for? What are you after? The thing you're looking for is not here." . . . Since that which he sought concerned the operation of the *Ars notoria*, it was said to him that what he was looking for was not in the Psalter. And since the Psalter concerns divine law and is pleasing to God, it plainly appears that the *Ars notoria* does not concern the divine law and is not pleasing to God.[25]

Once again, the details are realistic. The dream has a familiar setting, the monastery of Fontainejean, but the actual room ("a place where books were lying around") was not. Here, John of Fontainejean learns through a rapid but pointed allegory that God will not be answering divinatory questions put to him through the *ars notoria*. The vision cuts two ways, because of course God actually *is* answering a question, albeit not with the answer that was expected. (Or was it?) This is not a diabolic vision in the style of Bridget's. It is read as offering a clear divine message: the *ars notoria* is not the Psalter, neither a good basis for monastic practice nor a good tool for scrying. If God does not appear in the dream, he speaks nevertheless.

It struck me as odd at the time that even though the *ars notoria* was painted in diabolic colors, God appeared through it. Theologically, of course, there can be no prohibition against God's speaking when and as he chooses, but the whole account was confusing to me because I felt I could never be certain whether God was actually behind the visions; the visions in which God's voice makes itself heard seem neither less scary nor less odd than the demonic ones, and in fact, sometimes both demons and good angels often appear quite close together in the same dream. My initial view of this part of the text was no doubt further confused because of the extent to which it was still colored by the Chronicle account of the condemnation, which suggested that John was "feigning" to be inspired by the Virgin but "in reality" reviving the *ars notoria*. The Chronicle account could not but lend the whole business in the prayers the air of a hole-and-corner operation: John "feigned" that the Virgin had delivered these things to him, as though he had been trying to conceal what he was really doing. Though it added a few autobiographical details, the last manuscript I'd encountered, Munich Bayerische Staatsbibliothek 276, said little to discourage this idea.

Finding this visionary autobiography at the front of the prayers in the Graz manuscript was a revelation, but also a puzzle, because of the intimate details it offered about John's performance of the *ars notoria*. It was clear that John meant this to *introduce* his prayer text, but how could a thorough account of what must surely constitute the very worst of his misdeeds, his magical operations, be the *introduction* to this devotional cover-up operation? The more one tried to figure out how it worked as a cover-up, the more puzzling it became. For what was being covered up? The thing was a *confession*. No detail, however incriminating, of his own willfulness is allowed to escape the net of his prose; he admits to taking the *ars notoria* for a holy book, to using it against express divine warnings. Later, he admits to using even the most blatantly transgressive forms of magic. There seemed no reason for John to tell us all this.

Unless of course he actually *meant* to write a confession, in the full medieval Christian and literary sense of that term: a document considering the interventions of divine grace into his personal life as a sinner. In some ways the very vividness of John's autobiography belies its true nature, as its reports seemed so real and immediate. For all that, it stands to reason that John's account of how he came to write the book could not have been written until *after* the book was done. It was hard not to take his visionary descriptions as a blow-by-blow telling, effectively a *diary*, rather than an after-the-fact representation, a *memoir*. But it is a memoir, and the difference matters. The story told in the Book of Visions is the one that John intended to represent him, a crafted product, a picture of his own state of understanding about his spiritual development as it probably stood circa 1311, when, as he thought, he had finished his book.[26]

Ultimately, as seems clear to me now, the only way to make sense of the *Liber florum* at all is by accepting the ways in which all of its autobiographical parts constitute genuine confession, in this sense, and taking all the things he says about his own motivation and understanding to be more or less true, at least as true as any literary confession, or any autobiography. I do not mean that one should fail to implement the usual hermeneutic suspicions necessary around all personal accounts of memory. But I have come to appreciate its cod-ing more than I could have at first. John's prose, though quirky and sometimes baffling in its quick swerves of direction, is limpid enough at the most crucial narrative junctures in the Book of Visions, and it is ultimately unambiguous about representing his conversion as God's triumph. It is God who brings his work round, filling out and completing his knowledge despite John's own willfulness. To summarize an understanding I came to only later, if the whole visionary autobiography is intended as a confession, if John therefore reveals himself in error or in confusion, or tormented by demons, this is because, just as with Augustine's *Confessions*, the document is constructed to reveal the active and particular interventions of divine grace in the life of one particular sinner. The sins must be particular to demonstrate the particularity of the interventions. The book itself may be seen in this manner as an imprint of the action of divine grace on John's person; he understood it throughout the long composition process, which took many years, as God's working through him, informing him, and building his knowledge—in part through nurturing, and in part through chastisement, that he might be converted and live. At the same time, it is clear that John saw himself as working to blaze a trail, in intertwined prayer and narrative, so that others, similarly entangled in the *ars notoria*, could follow the path that God had opened in him.

This way of seeing the text was still somewhat alien to me, or at least barely nascent, in 1998. We had no idea how much information the Graz manuscript would turn out to contain (far more than we had from either of the previous manuscripts). We could not know, either, of the revelations still to come in the Old Compilation text in the Bodleian Library, nor of the unique text we were going to find in Bologna that helped us make better sense of the text's transmission.[27] Within the few days following my first encounter with the Book of Visions, I digested it to a summary to include as an appendix to my *Conjuring Spirits* article, which went to press long before I had time to put together all the visions with the prayers they inspired, to work out a proper chronology, to reconstruct the order in which these things must have been written, all information that came to me and to Nicholas over a longer period of time with much labor. I felt then, and still do feel, that the information we had about the work, scrappy as I knew it to be, was too important not to share. Waiting is sometimes prudent, but it would have been a vanity to wait for the perfection of this particular knowledge.

The Book of Visions was obviously significant on its own terms, and three years later we published a preliminary edition of this part of the text based on the Graz manuscript.[28] However, it must be remembered that the Book of Visions is only the antechamber of a considerably larger structure; it was written to introduce a work that preexisted it and already had many moving parts.

The Visions show John's conversion away from the *ars notoria*, and in order to understand the whole, it is necessary to take seriously his strong initial engagement with the *ars*, the form his conversion took, and also the form of the follow-up actions that constitute his emendation of life. It is important to see what error he was confessing to, and why, but we also need to see why the error of magic needed to be amended in this particular way: by *rewriting* it. Throughout his book, John asserts that his goal is to destroy the *ars notoria*, but he does this not by burning it but rather by plundering it: restoring its intended good, reconsecrating its purpose, and renovating its prayers. The whole work cannot be properly understood without the Book of Visions, but the Book of Visions needs the rest of the work to contextualize it.

In the next two chapters, I will elaborate some of the metaphysical surround. The first part brings out key aspects of what John sees as the "error" of the *ars notoria*—sacrilege and disobedience—and the second examines the way the sacrament of penance is enacted in John's visions.

2

A MYSTICISM OF SIGNS AND THINGS:
THE *ARS NOTORIA* AND THE SACRAMENTS

In this chapter, I will be concerned with the *ars notoria* and the process of John's reaction to it (the path, that is, that his knowing took from the initial perception of it as holy to his understanding that it was not divinely sanctioned). Understanding John's use of the word "sacrament" in the *Liber florum*, and the way it does and does not replicate the usage in the *ars notoria*, is a key piece of this process.

Words that John uses in reference to his own prayers (as well as the knowledge delivered by them, and the sequence of revelations through which he composes them) include "sacrament," "mystery" (six times each), and "secret" (or "holy" or "heavenly secret").[1] All of these related words—sacrament, mystery, secret—are used in the various versions and textual components of the Solomonic *ars notoria* as well, to refer both to the mode of delivery of that art to Solomon and the holy secrets it imparts to operators. Julien Véronèse enumerates forty-three instances of various inflections of "sacrament" and "sacramental" in *ars notoria* B (not counting the gloss).[2] For "mysterium," I have found thirteen instances in *ars notoria* B, all confined to the gloss. Véronèse argues that the *ars notoria* uses the analogy and language of sacrament to distance the practice from necromancy and to highlight its filiation with standard liturgy.[3] I agree with this general point and would add that John's more particular usage, and indeed his manner of structuring his *Liber florum* as a whole, can be read, at least in part, as a response to the *ars notoria* that theologizes the filiation of his own art, in the *Liber florum*, more explicitly and carefully with sacrament.

At the same time, however, it seems important not to overread the word "sacrament" or to imagine that John should or would have seen any immediate problem with the use of this word, or understood it as intended to place the *ars notoria* either on a par with, or among, the sacraments of the Church. The loose and general style of usage in the *ars notoria* has ample precedent elsewhere, starting with the Vulgate. Instances of the word "sacramentum" are relatively higher in the New Testament than the Old, but the usage in both cases is similar. The word means "secret" or "mystery." In fact, the words "mysterium" and "sacramentum" often appear close together in the Vulgate and are used interchangeably. The word "mysterium" appears, in different inflections, twenty-nine times in the Vulgate, of which roughly two-thirds are in the New Testament; the word "sacramentum" occurs in different inflections sixteen times, of which just over half are also New Testament. There are fewer instances of either word in the Old Testament since the word "sacramentum" comes into the Bible as a translation of the Greek "mysterion," arriving in both forms only in the Hellenistic period in Tobit, Judith, Sirach, and 2 Maccabees.[4] It also occurs in the book of Daniel. Both Latin words—"mysterium" and "sacramentum"—may be rendered into English as "secret" or "hidden thing," or as "mystery," and in English translations of the Bible, these renderings are about equally frequent. See, for example, Daniel 2:47, where both words occur close together. This is the Vulgate followed by Douay Rheims, with my emphasis: "loquens ergo rex ait Daniheli vere Deus vester Deus deorum est et Dominus regum et revelans *mysteria* quoniam potuisti aperire *sacramentum* hoc"; "And the king spoke to Daniel, and said: Verily, your God is the God of gods, and Lord of kings, and a revealer of *hidden things:* seeing thou couldst discover this *secret.*" Some English translations render both italicized words in the above passage as "secret" (e.g., KJV, Webster's Bible, World English Bible, Jewish Publication Society Bible). The New American Standard renders both as "mystery."

It is an interesting feature of all of these words that, while gesturing at an ineffable knowledge in God, or beyond the grave, they also often indicate a knowledge that can be discovered here and now. The surrounding context often involves words of interpreting, revealing, making known, as in Ephesians 1:19: "*ut notum faceret nobis sacramentum* voluntatis suae secundum bonum placitum eius quod proposuit in eo"; "*That he might make known unto us the mystery* of his will, according to his good pleasure, which he hath purposed in him." In a similar vein, we have Ephesians 3:3: "quoniam secundum revelationem *notum mihi factum est sacramentum* sicut supra scripsi in brevi"; "How that, according to revelation, *the mystery has been made known to me,* as I have written above in a few words." Or again 3:9: "et *inluminare omnes quae sit dispensatio sacramenti absconditi a saeculis in Deo* qui omnia creavit"; "*And to enlighten all men, that they may see what is the dispensation of the mystery which hath been hidden from eternity in God* who created all things."

Beyond the senses immediately available through the Vulgate, an etymology of "mysterium" as a term for a "secret or hidden dispensation" was well known through Isidore.⁵ The general usage of "sacrament" as a word meaning "holy secret" is not confined to the Vulgate, but is in common use by many medieval writers in the later Middle Ages—notably, from John's perspective, including Gratian and Peter Lombard.⁶ Both words, "sacramentum" and "mysterium," also often get applied to non-biblical allegorical words, dreams or stories; like the words in the same family that function as modifiers ("mystical," "mystically"), it might be translated "something with a recondite meaning." All this we see in the *ars notoria* as well. Thus, while there are some problems around the peculiarities of usage in the *ars notoria* that may become apparent to a literate user like John of Morigny after serious and sustained engagement, there is no reason why he, or any other educated medieval reader, should have an immediate problem with finding the word "sacramentum" in a text from the time of Solomon, nor is there any reason that he would begin by assuming that it was a reference to any of the seven sacraments of the Church discussed by Peter Lombard.

Sacrilege, Disobedience, and the Devil's Appropriation of God's Throne

Despite this lack of specificity, the frame, appearance, and rhetoric of the *ars notoria* was designed to evoke, to call out to, a sense of the profundity of Christian mystery. True, the *ars notoria* had been connected by many influential theologians to demonic knowledge, and in this sense it represented a problem; however, the issue of its condemnation is clearly not here one of an unlettered lay practice being criticized as such by learned clergy. John *was* learned clergy, and to him, initially, and probably to the bulk of its users, the *ars notoria* did not represent a problem but the solution to one. If it was criticized by learned clergy, it was also learned clergy who copied, decorated, used, and transmitted it; and if it was connected to a category problematically magical, it was simultaneously connected, in its own terms, and presumably by many who set out to use it, to the sacred discipline of theology and to many legitimate knowledge objects that were constructed and represented within university curricula.

John describes his initial encounter with the *ars notoria* as the discovery of a sacred alternative to another magical means of knowledge acquisition, necromancy. John had been a Benedictine for about four years, when, as he tells us, he obtained from a certain cleric an interesting book

> in which there were contained many nefarious things of the necromantic art. I took a copy from it of as much as I could get, and after that I returned it to the cleric. I was noticed by the devil, and tempted, and blinded as the

temptation prevailed, I began to think how I might be able to acquire expertise in this nefarious science. I sought counsel about this from a Lombard medical expert, Jacob of Bologna by name. When I had consulted with him, he said to me: "Ask permission to use the school, and when you have obtained it, look for a book called the *ars notoria*, and from it you will discover the truth not only concerning this knowledge you are asking about, but all forms of knowledge."[7]

In this description, the *ars notoria* represents a means of access to knowledge that is not merely a pragmatically effective solution to a learning difficulty, but also a sacred alternative to a means of attaining somewhat similar goals by demonic magic. Further, according to John, it is a method that *works*.[8] John's claims for the efficacy of the *ars notoria* may serve as a good beginning point for understanding the broad appeal of the practice. John's ultimate rejection of it is consistent with an expected institutionally correct view, but none of this really gives an understanding of what John calls the "good part" of his intention, or the devotional needs that led him to the *ars notoria* in the first place; it does not tell us how he construed the goals of the *ars notoria* exegetically or theologically, how he set them against the category of *nigromancia*, or how he saw his own *Liber florum* as a better answer to the needs the *ars notoria* actually failed to meet in him. The background against which John came to grips with the *ars notoria* as the solution to a problem is important for understanding the purport of his own *Liber florum*.

At the outset, John emphasizes that the *ars notoria* is different from—and worse than—the art of necromancy by reason of its holy appearance, which makes it at once more subtle and more deceptive. His rhetoric about the *ars notoria* at the outset is extreme, though not original: it is drawn from Alan of Lille's diatribe against Cupid.[9] The notory art is "faith in a fraud, hope in fear, madness mixed with reason; a pleasant tempest, a lucid night, a dark light, a living death, mad rationality, erroneous prudence," and more oxymorons in this style.[10] In the context of the source, the tropes all describe the attraction of Eros: they are about being in love, the dangerous engagement with an object of compelling aesthetic fascination (the pleasant tempest, lucid night), and they also describe something that feels like knowledge but is not (mad rationality, erroneous prudence). In short, it is the very plausibility of its beauty that makes the *ars notoria* evil; or, to reverse the objectivities, it is the strength of John's desire for what it seems to offer.

One sees at least that the aesthetics of the *ars notoria* make it the very inverse of necromancy in principle. In its most well-known forms, the necromancer deliberately courts demons known to be of hideous appearance and nasty character. Medieval literature abounds with stories of sorcerers and sorcerers' apprentices, necromancers who are either ruined or saved from their demonic involvements at the last minute, by confession, repentance, and the intervention of Mary. Exempla concerning the dark arts were widely known because they were part of pastoral literature; as moral set pieces, romances of redemption, they would be readily remembered, their lessons easily learned. Not so with the *ars notoria* or other forms of medieval angel magic. Because these texts did not figure in this wider narrative transmission about the badness of magical knowledge, John needed to fill the gap with a compelling narrative.

For the evil of the notory art is not in anything immediately obvious in its construction or representation. Quite the reverse: John's problem is that it seemed most holy and beautiful in its presentation and goals. Its prayers—at least those in Latin—were of the highest order, an exquisitely lofty framing of petitions, incorporating biblical language and topoi, in a phraseology echoing the most beautiful parts of the liturgy of the mass. They are, as John's rhetoric suggests elsewhere, as sweet as honey. The attractiveness of these prayers is indeed the very reason for the notory art's danger, part of the acute moral paradox it presents. Its danger cannot be shown in its overt or stated intentions, but is instead only realized slowly and gradually in the experience of its use. For John, even though the *ars notoria* does not call upon demons, it nevertheless causes demons to manifest confusingly in frightening dreams that have a prophetic aspect. Yet it does other things, too, for God also appears when John prays for intelligence, sometimes after the driving away of demonic presences. In several loci—both in John's own visions, and in those of his friend John of Fontainejean—a message of divine origin and purport emerges from the use of the *ars notoria*. There is an apparent paradox in that the source of these visions, or at least their immediate prompts, derives from a text whose use is prohibited.

In the larger cosmic picture, however—the institutionally accepted knowledge that framed John's thinking—the paradox is not of a fundamentally different kind than the riddles that surround other parts of the dynamic of Christian salvation. Indeed, our whole earthly life is bound up in such riddles. In the last phase of his work, near the end of the New Compilation Book of Figures, John offers some comments that are helpful in understanding the kind of knowledge the *ars notoria* represents and its relation to the true knowledge he and others have received from it. In discussing why the figures of the Virgin should show her standing rather than seated, John notes that she should be standing, because a judge sits, but a fighter stands, and "in this world we must fight against temptations and against the airy powers; we cannot overcome . . . in this sort of thing by ourselves."[11] John goes on to note that the Virgin appears more often in the north part of the church than in the others, adding that no one need interpret this in a sinister way on account of the words "from the north shall evil break forth" (Jer. 1:14), because

> the Gospel is read in the north, for the purpose of confounding the devil and casting him down from his seat, which it says he places "in the mountain of the covenant, in the sides of north" to be "above the height of the clouds" and "like the Most High" [Isa. 14:13–14]. Thus, visions of this science [i.e., *Liber florum*], and the blessed Virgin also, are understood to appear in the north to the confounding of the devil and the casting down of his nefarious forms of knowledge, in which he placed his seat by teaching, and seated himself, giving to understand through his falsehoods that they are good and holy and like the forms of knowledge of the Most High.[12]

John's references to Isaiah and Jeremiah here show that his thinking is indebted to the interpretation of these passages expounded in the *Rationale divinorum officiorum* by the thirteenth-century liturgical exegete Guillaume Durand, who refers to the same topoi in explaining why the Gospel is read facing the north. Durand understands this as a protective movement, a counter to the evil that comes from the north. He writes,

> The Lector then crosses to the left hand side . . . and turns his face to the north . . . to show us that we ought to be armed with the Gospel teaching and that the preaching of Christ is especially directed against him who said "I shall place my seat in the north and I shall be like the Most High"; for according to the Prophet "every evil spreads from the north." . . . Again the Gospel is read towards the north according to the reading in the Song of Songs 4[:16]: "Let the north wind arise," that is, let the devil take flight.[13]

Like Durand's interpretation of the positioning of the lector, John's exegesis of the northerly orientations of his own visions presupposes an intensified need for divine aid in the quarter where the battle against temptation is thickest.

The explanation cuts two ways, though. On the one hand, John does, literally, have visions of Mary in the north parts of churches. But here, the image of the devil's seat metaphorically elides the "north" with the *ars notoria* itself, via the passage from Isaiah, in which the north is the region "on the mount of the covenant" (in monte testamenti), the location of God's throne, which the devil has tried to preempt to become like the Most High. For John, that throne is the sciences, "the forms of knowledge [scientiae] in which [the devil] placed his seat by teaching." In the narrative that guides John's thinking, when God's throne is appropriated by Satan (as has happened, in his view, through demonic corruption of the notory art), it is not merely possible but necessary, indeed inevitable, that God should cast him down and reappropriate his own seat: the narrative permits no other conclusion. In this particular exegesis, God is responsible for the destruction (or supplanting) of the *ars notoria*, the phantom throne, by its reality, a genuinely sacred knowledge for use by his own devotees. Thus, John continues,

> the blessed Virgin destroyed these forms of knowledge and all the arts of the devil and confounded him through the revelation of this science [i.e., the *Liber florum*], Although it was not permitted and may not be permitted to the devil and his angels it is indeed permitted to God and his saints. Indeed it is permitted and was permitted to the devil to appear in diverse evil things and shapes to those who keep his commands and rituals through nefarious invocations, as in necromancy, and through sacrilegious prayers, as in the *ars notoria*. Benignly, therefore, it is permitted to God also similarly to appear to his own holy people, who keep his commands through devout and holy prayers. Indeed I, John, often had doubts in the case of a vision experienced in this way before I grasped this mystery.[14]

John's comments on the restoration of knowledge further help to clarify the categories that shaped his thought around necromancy and the *ars notoria*. While (bad) necromancy involves "nefarious invocations" (conscious deliberate summoning of demons), the *ars notoria* involves "sacrilegious prayers"—an unholy mingling of sacred and profane categories that should have been kept apart.

While sacrilege could have looser and more specific meanings in medieval texts, just as it does now, John's hermeneutical habits make it worthwhile to examine the exegesis of its primary biblical locus in Daniel 5. The root meaning of "sacrilege," "theft of sacred things," was well known and transmitted through Isidore; however, as it was normally read, the sin of sacrilege did not only or even primarily concern literal theft, but extended the idea to cover a variety of modes of irreverence for, violation of, or injury to the sacred. The injury could involve not just physical contact with sacred things but also inward or mental violations as well as textual, verbal, or exegetical ones. The verbal and epistemological extensions of meaning seem to be clearer in exegetical traditions than philosophical ones.[15] Under the sin of sacrilege as described in handbooks of moral instruction, the scriptural *locus classicus* is the story of Belshazzar's feast from Daniel 5, where the writing on the wall appears to prophesy punishment for those who misused the sacred vessels from Solomon's temple.[16] Jerome's commentary on this story was influential, and the key parts on which I touch here also occur in the standard medieval reference book for biblical meanings, the *Glossa ordinaria*. Here is Jerome's commentary:

> As they drank from golden vessels, they were praising gods of wood and of stone. As long as the vessels had been in the idol-temple of Babylon, God was not moved to wrath, for they had evidently consecrated the property of God to divine worship, even though they did so in accordance with their own depraved views of religion. But after they defiled holy things for the use of men, their punishment followed upon the heels of their sacrilege. Moreover they were praising their own gods and scoffing at the God of the Jews. . . . Applying this figuratively, we should have to say that it applies to all the heretics or to any doctrine which is contrary to truth but which appropriates the words of the Biblical prophets and misuses the testimony of Scripture to suit its own inclination. It furnishes liquor to those whom it deceives and with whom it has committed fornication. It carries off the vessels of God's Temple and waxes drunken by quaffing them; and it does not give the praise to the God whose vessels they are.[17]

The construction of sacrilege as a moral error of words, of rhetoric, is quite specific. Jerome goes on to describe different ways in which the words of scripture can be misappropriated by intermingling them with other kinds of discourse, guided metaphorically by the metals of the sacred vessels: golden vessels are good doctrine corrupted by the use of earthly knowledge (*seculari scientia*); silver by rhetorical ornament (*eloquij venustate et rethorica arte*); and so on.

Two things are of interest here in regard to John of Morigny. First, we note that even in the idol-temple of Babylon the vessels were surrounded by an idea of sacred purity, of due solemnity, which kept God's wrath at bay; keeping sacred things in a space of purity, separate from profane things, is a gesture available even to people of idolatrous faiths. The sin of sacrilege is thus viewed, in the context of this exemplum, as something like a core violation of a universal divine and human code. Through this we can see a little way into the logic by which the *ars notoria* could be worse than necromancy in John's eyes. Necromancy, at least in the terms that guide John's thinking, keeps the holy and unholy distinct (with necromancy, one is aware of doing unholy things, at least), but the *ars notoria* mixes them. The way the *ars notoria* represents evil for John has to do with the way it represents a contamination of the sacred; its temptation to him, but also the very clothing of its hypocrisy, is its appearance of being set quite apart from the world, when in fact it touches it and is subject (like profane things) to demonic invasion.[18]

The other interesting feature of Jerome's reading of this text is that, in describing sacrilege as a misuse or misappropriation of the good and divine words of scripture, he makes available an idea of sacrilege that, like John's notion of "sacrilegious prayer," is primarily verbal and has aesthetic implications. Sacrilegious use of the words of scripture is likened by Jerome to drunkenness and fornication: it "furnishes liquor to those whom it deceives and with whom it has committed fornication. It carries off the vessels of God's Temple and waxes drunken by quaffing them." Each of his examples lays out a verbal (logical or rhetorical) idea of sacrilege. Here, perhaps, we have an analogue for John's understanding of the "honeyed venom" of the *ars notoria*; part of the wrongness identified by Jerome is similarly a misapplication of the beauty of scripture to wrap—and to sell—doctrine whose core is unsound. The problem has to do with the use of scripture as mere decoration, rhetoric, or to extrapolate from it a false logic. Through Jerome's reading it is possible to see that John's use of the word "sacrilegious" to describe the abuse constituted in prayers of the notory art forms a distinctive contrast to the abuse of necromancy. If the use of necromancy is wrong because it invokes demons knowingly, the use of the *ars notoria* is wrong because it does not respect—or creates a misapprehension of—the boundaries of the sacred. It is, at least in part, an abuse of *beauty*.

The way John parallels his visions of Mary in the north to Durand's gospel lector shows that his visions are also a mode of working out the part of divine dispensation which is his own personal part of God's greater covenant with humanity. Knowing what God wants is a tangled business, never instant or entirely simple. The knowledge that John gains through visions exists in a system that he works out through his conversations with Mary, learning as he goes, not only through her words and actions, but also applying his own knowledge of the Bible, theology, and the tools of exegesis to his visions. The learning process is mapped out both in his narrative and in his liturgies. John's role in this is simultaneously private or personal (inasmuch as John's own life is changed by his visions) and public (inasmuch as he also has the role of a teacher and pastor who ministers to the devotional needs of the Christian community, broadly speaking). If there were those in his community who required a correction for the use of the *ars notoria*, from John's viewpoint, the *Liber florum* was that correction. It contained a narrative arc that followed the course of John's own recovery from the notory art, and it passes John's processual and gradually accumulating learning on to his successors in a series of prayers, figures, and visualizations designed in some cases to imitate and in all cases to evoke the same kinds of visions that characterize John's bond with Mary.

In this sense, the *Liber florum* can obviously be seen to align itself with my first suspicions about it. Like the *ars notoria* itself, it is a mystical "technology." But with a difference: I now see that this mystical technology seeks to further a larger divine and cosmic process—the dispensational fulfillment to which the sacraments also refer, and which they also exist to further. In the sense that it is sacramentally affiliated, it may also be seen (in a sense similar to that developed by Talal Asad from Foucault[19]) as a "technology of the self"—a unified manner of disciplined thought and praxis working on body and soul, matter and substance, at the same time. No blinding revelation that takes place in the mind alone, abstracted from the body, John's theology is cataphatic, corporeal, and characteristically monastic. In its suspicion of what may lie beyond the letter and beyond the historical level, it may be seen as spectacularly mystical (in the medieval sense) as well.

The Rectified Process of Knowledge: Cataphatic Theology and Learning

As Denys Turner puts it, the cataphatic is "the verbose element in theology, it is the Christian mind deploying all the resources of language in the effort to express something about God." He notes in particular that such discourse need not be verbal; by his account, it is really essentially creative. The theology of cataphatic discourse emerges in "its liturgical and sacramental action, its music, its architecture, its dance and gesture, all of which are intrinsic to its character as an expressive discourse, a discourse of theological articulation."[20] Cataphatic expression is also imitative of the richness of divine procession. For John, who likes to quote Romans 8:28, "all things cooperate towards good for the man loving God," the proliferation of symbols and material allegories that he finds in the Church and the liturgy is an outpouring of divine gifts upon him, not merely a concession to his human incapacity—though no doubt that, too—but an abundant concession. His creativity in devising new liturgies, his proliferation of new patterns of devotional activity within these liturgies, and his exegetical practices around them are distinctive interactions with this richness. His prayers and the practices that accompany them, however idiosyncratic they may appear, must be seen both as constituting a form of praise and enabling a quite specific and theologically directed mode of contemplation of the divine.

I want to persist at least through this chapter in speaking of John's "mysticism." I do not mean by this to reduce his visionary autobiography to the set of things "mysticism" is typically taken to mean, nor to enter into an extended discussion of methodology; the difficulties and exigencies of speaking of an "experiential" category of religion in the Middle Ages have been adequately treated elsewhere.[21] However, I do want to press on the term a bit here and re-evoke what it means for religion to be "experienced," because this seems to me a necessary corrective to the broader tendency among scholars of medieval religions, as well as those of comparative mysticism, to divide magic from mysticism in a way that does not permit any conversation between them. Both "magic" and "mysticism," of course, are constructed largely through arguments about what they mean; they differ inasmuch as the discourses that have constructed magic are a long and deep part of our intellectual history. As I have pointed out elsewhere, medieval pro- and anti-magical arguments are formulated through the engagement of parties who were essentially in the same sociocultural and educational groups:

> If you were a medieval person who used, composed, or wrote down magic texts, you were quite likely also to be a monk, a friar, a doctor (a profession not necessarily excluding a religious vocation as well), or a university student (which also would include those of religious profession). This means effectively that the users of texts that fall into the category "ritual magic" in the medieval world were more likely also to be aware of the problematics structuring its condemnation; the more likely one was to think some aspect of a particular magical text or practice might be viable (or even to see it as necessary), the more likely one was also to be aware of why it was suspect. While there are always practices (magical or not) specific to certain sociocultural subgroups, learned magic was (problematically or not) the province of the intellectual elite who were also involved in theological discourse.[22]

Thus arguments about "magic" in the medieval intellectual sphere tend to arise among people on an equal footing who have different opinions about which rituals ought to be licit; the attempts to suppress forms of ritual magic cannot be seen as top-down oppression, no matter how the balance of power sways in individual cases. They are rather part of an ongoing conversation about orthodoxy and orthopraxis.

By contrast, there is no medieval conversation around, or recognizable medieval analogue for, the word "mysticism," certainly not in the sense understood as an experience involving the immediate or "direct union of the human soul with divinity."[23] Theoretically, in the context of medieval Catholic thought, all experience of divinity was necessarily mediate all the time for all living human beings. Indeed, the whole point of Catholic Christianity is mediation—the original mediation of the incarnation, followed by its extension in the mediation of the Church, the priesthood, and the sacraments. The Bible, too, is a mediation that encourages, as part of the exercise of climbing in and through the letter of scriptural books to their divine origin, the cataphatic outpouring of speech in allegorical exegesis. The exercise of interacting with scripture in this way can be seen as mystical in the primary medieval sense of that term: it crucially involves a mystery. In another sense, it was also experiential. But inasmuch as it is essentially an experience of *reading*, it could hardly be further from the modern sense of the term "mystical experience" as typically construed and understood.

Yet divine visions were recorded all the time. While such visions were theoretically mediate (that is, they almost always involved some sort of sensory mediation, such as visual or auditory signs, such that "spiritual perception" was always in some degree compromised by the embodied status of the experiencing soul), there is an equally strong sense in which such visions have to be understood as distinct from the mediations of the Church, even where they successfully interacted with it. John can be considered a mystic not simply because he was a visionary, and wrote of the visions that he experienced as more or less direct divine communications, but also because he stated that his visions constituted "mysteries." They were thus "mystical" in the same sense that the words of the Bible were mystical. They veiled secrets; they meant something beyond the letter of their representation; they required exegesis.

Two writers much better known as medieval mystics who were John's close contemporaries serve as a useful counterpoint: the Dominican Meister Eckhart and the Beguine Marguerite Porete. Both of them, like John, wrote in the ambit of Paris in the early fourteenth century, and both wound up being targets of condemnation by others, though for different reasons. These were writers whose theology ran in an apophatic track. Marguerite Porete, whose *Mirror of Simple Souls* was taken as speaking for the heresy of the Free Spirit, was burned at the stake in Paris in 1310. Meister Eckhart, who was occupied with taking a master's degree in theology in Paris right around the time when John began his work with the *ars notoria*, was not charged with heresy in his lifetime, but had forty-nine propositions from his writing examined and posthumously condemned by John XXII in 1329.[24] In the case of Marguerite, whether or not her subtle and difficult writing expressed all the antinomian views attributed to it, it is plainly marked by its meditation on the autonomy of the individual soul in its relation to God. The soul comes to God by an act of will—more precisely, by an abnegation of will to the divine, which allows the soul to experience heaven on earth, and in the same motion, it seems, to be free of the need for priestly or sacramental intercession even before death. Meister Eckhart was suspected of a tendency toward a similar quietism.[25]

John's theology is similar to theirs in its optimism as indeed in its respect for the central mystery of the dispensation, but he does not offer the shadow of a suggestion of *unmediated* transformation of the soul into a mirror of God, such as we see in Marguerite's writing or in Meister Eckhart's. John retains a strong investment in his own status as a priest, more specifically in the channels of the sacred instituted in the hierarchy of the priesthood and the body of the Church. The canonical mystics to whom he compares with least strain are from an earlier period. He has certain impulses in common with the Victorines and Hildegard of Bingen. Like them, John frequently uses the terminology of sapiential theology; he also quotes long swathes of Adam of St. Victor and Alan of Lille in his Seven Prayers and elsewhere.

Marguerite Porete and Meister Eckhart serve as a useful index of the sort of thing John was *not* doing, in part because their writings are more readily grasped now as a version of what medieval mystics were *supposed* to have been doing. That these two fourteenth-century authors have, with the invention of mysticism, attained a more or less canonical status as "mystics" to some degree reflects their accessibility to Protestant theology, for in a theological context where the sacraments themselves are suspected of magicality, a theology in which they are not seen as crucial to salvation has intrinsically less power to shock than it might have in the fourteenth century. In any event, the idea that the quest for attainment to God is ultimately a profoundly individual matter is certainly easier to see as viable now than it may have been in the time period when these two actually lived.[26] For John, the interpretive pendulum has swung in the opposite direction: all of the ways in which it might once have been possible to see him as an earnest Catholic thinker have turned into a suspicion of magic. This is not to deny that he was involved in things he himself understood as magic, or that his work was condemned on essentially magical grounds. What has become elusive for us, however, that obviously remained available to the operators of his work through the fifteenth century, is the way in which his engagement with magic is contiguous to, and congruous with, an unexceptional Catholic sacramental and dispensational understanding.

As a Benedictine, John was conscious of the need for ongoing practice and discipline to structure the life of the perfected soul on earth. The praxis offered by the *Liber florum* is intended as a lifelong mode of devotion for its adherents. It is synthetic and enormously learned, thought out in a manner that allows its existence within the already considerable devotional load of the specific daily ritual prescriptions of monastic life, though it is also clearly intended to be used by the laity as well.[27] John had a pastoral interest in providing, for all who desired it, a prayer program to be incorporated into a life of regular devotional activity, a set of meditative interactions with the divine that could be made more or less rigorous according to the needs and abilities of the operator. In being a devotional program aimed at lay folk, John's book has something in common with the earliest Books of Hours that had already begun to circulate in France in the thirteenth century. Not yet stabilized in their form, these books were an organic outgrowth of the *libelli precum* already circulating among monks.[28] John's book is similarly intended to help bridge the lay-monastic divide. The writing of the *Liber florum*, personal and divinely inspired as it was, remained for him indivisible from his activity as a monk and priest.

One of the ways John's writing differs most strikingly from that of the apophatic mystics is in his initial grasp of the *ars notoria* as a sacred text, as well as his ongoing fascination with the structure of the liberal arts as the initial phase of a path to God—a path with devotional implications. However, he is far from being a solitary exponent of the view that the liberal arts provided a framework for an ascent to God. We see the same impulse marked out in similar terms, mutatis mutandis, in Bonaventure's *Itinerarium mentis in Deum* and before that in Hugh of St. Victor's *Didascalicon*.[29] Indeed, it is no secret that monastic ideas about learning in general were consistent with, and followed from, ideas about the sacramental structure of the world, and hence with the devotional activity already in place for the monk.

In the first place, because even curricular knowledge is tied to the archetype of the world in the mind of God, the disciplines of learning the seven liberal arts, insofar as they help in revealing a shadow of this archetype in the human mind, may be taken up as part of a devotional program. In the second place, all devotional acts are also acts of learning as much as acts of homage: the aim of both was reformation of the whole self—the will, memory, and intellect—in conformity with God. Reading, especially scriptural reading, but to some extent all reading, was a discipline in which meditative and exegetical practices were simultaneously rooted. The attainment of the discipline of proper reading (of scripture, but also by extension of other things, or of everything else) allowed a better, more pure, more accurate recovery of the knowledge that existed already in the eternal template. But this could happen only if devotion was engaged with the aim of learning, and learning was engaged with the aim of devotion.

Hence the rhetorical habit in didascalic literature of the twelfth and thirteenth centuries of opening with homage to the topoi, both Neoplatonic and Christian, that mark out the body as an obstacle in the ascent to true knowledge, usually with a metaphor of the state of embodiment as a kind of cloud or shadow on the vision. The disciplines of learning and the disciplines of purgation of the body go together in the life of the scholar; the spiritual *informatio* of the liberal arts is cognitively possible only to the extent that the whole person is re-formed in the divine image. In the introduction to the anonymous *Philosophica disciplina*, it is said that

> philosophical discipline is desirable for users from three intellectual causes. One is the *informatio* of the human intellect insofar as it has been beclouded by the overshadowing of the body; which *informatio* indeed consists in the habit of the sciences as to the speculative part, and the habit of the virtues as to the active or practical one. The second cause is cognition of the magnitude, power, goodness, and wisdom of the Creator. For through philosophical cognition or discipline, we are moved to cognition of universal being; by its hidden power and operation, which the creator bestows on it, so marvelous that, once known, we are incited to the love, and fear, and reverence of so great a Creator in such great creations, admiring his infinite power, goodness, and wisdom. The third cause is the fittingness of the circumstances which it demands, and these are three: contempt of fickle affluence, desire for future happiness, illumination of mind.[30]

In the *Divisio scientiarum* of Arnoul de Provence, the implicit connection between the bodily cloud and the sin of the fall is made explicit:

> For just as shadowy air placed between the eye and color takes away vision, so the interposed body prohibits the lifting of the intellect to the First [Mover]. In the same vein the Philosopher says in the beginning of his *New Metaphysics*, "the human intellect aligns itself to that which is most obvious in nature, just as the bat's eye does to the light of the sun." The aforesaid seems to confirm Boethius in his book *On the Consolation*, in a certain verse suggesting the state of the soul in the body:
>
> For when it discerned the lofty mind,
> (that is, the soul [discerned])
> Equally it knew the sum and singular details;
> Now, assembled in a cloud of limbs,

> Not forgetful of itself entire,
> It keeps the sum, while losing singularities.

that is, it retains a confused and general cognition, yet has lost the discrete and particular one when weighed down by the bodily mass.

But the theological cause is posited as the fall of humankind in sin. For as Eustratius says, Adam, at the beginning [was] figure and image and similitude of the Maker or Creator, perfect in virtues and sciences; because he transgressed against the law of nature set for him, his intellectual eye was turned to shadow and error, and he became blind, and was despoiled of his virtues and sciences.[31]

Here, what is lost with the fall is memory of the *particulars* of the sciences, which are explicitly positioned as part of the original divine knowledge. If the failure of knowledge of particulars results from the cloud of sin, a remedy for it is the praxis of learning, or re-learning those particulars.

Learning viewed in this way could not occur without other aspects of discipline, specifically moral discipline, being set in place at the same time. Hugh of St. Victor's *Didascalicon* is one of the most important antecedents of these thirteenth-century "introductions" to philosophy, in which he writes that the good student

> ought to be humble and docile, free alike from vain cares and from sensual indulgences, diligent and zealous to learn willingly from all, to presume never upon his own knowledge, to shun the authors of perverse doctrine as if they were poison, to consider a matter thoroughly and at length before judging of it, to seek to *be* learned rather than merely to seem so, to love such words of the wise as he has grasped, and ever to hold those words before his gaze as the very mirror of his countenance.... This is the humility proper to a student's discipline.[32]

This is part of a discourse on virtue that runs through the *Didascalicon* and adumbrates an idea of learning as a part of a larger domain of practices whose primary aim is to reform the self. As we see later in the *Philosophica disciplina*, Hugh explicitly here distinguishes this goal from the worldly rewards that learning may also bring. The liberal arts may be secular learning, but they are nevertheless *prerequisite* knowledge for understanding of theology, for correct reading of scripture. They are part of the theologian's training, a knowledge necessary to John as part of his quest for a discipline that would bring him back to God. To a monk in the Benedictine tradition, the initial view of an illuminated *ars notoria* might seem to offer a route to learning and devotion at once—a natural coupling, which used a kind of averted vision to meditate on the way the liberal arts themselves sketched a sacramental mystery.

If learning is represented in the work of Hugh of St. Victor as furthering a sacramental process, so also within the same milieu, and in a parallel way, are the sacraments represented as furthering a learning process. At the heart of the idea of ecclesiastical intercession—inside and under it, holding it up—is the mystery of the divine dispensation that embodied all things, giving a specific body to God in order to enable the return of all souls to their point of origin, which is also their telos. The Church itself, the priesthood, and the seven sacraments of the Church[33] are all part of this structure, but in normal medieval usage the term "sacrament" may also refer loosely to the entire system of the dispensation, or to the key parts of it that are necessary to the execution of its end.

Near the opening of Hugh's *De sacramentis*, in chapter 2 of the prologue of Book 1, he offers a one-sentence summary of the subject matter of scripture. In the next sentence, he divides the first statement into two parts:

> The subject matter of all the Divine Scriptures is the works of man's restoration. For there are two works in which all that has been done is contained. The first is the work of foundation; the second is the work of restoration. The work of foundation is that whereby those things which were not came into being. The work of restoration is that whereby those things that had been impaired were made better. Therefore, the work of foundation is the creation of the world with all its elements. The work of restoration is the Incarnation of the Word, with all its sacraments, both those which have gone before from the beginning of time, and those which came after, even to the end of the world.[34]

Hugh's own book flows from this two-part distinction, sharing its two-part structure, hinging on the advent of Christ. As he explains even before we get to this passage, he has already written a guide to the historical reading of scripture, and this work is to be viewed as a guide to "the second stage of scriptural instruction, which is allegory."[35]

The pedagogical purpose of the *De sacramentis* as a whole, sprawling as it is, is tightly enclosed within the two-part schema of foundation and restoration, presented with the single purpose of serving as a guide to spiritual reading. This apparent singleness of purpose masks the great complexity that will ramify from it, due to the fact that God's writing is everywhere implicit in the structure of things. Because the view here is both sapiential and dispensational, the work of foundation appears, or emerges, in the natural or created world itself, as well as in the history described in the Old Testament; the work of restoration is ongoing in all who are living, as well as the history described in the New Testament. This makes learning to read an incredibly complex act since, with proper discipline, it must be an ongoing correlation of outer and inner, body and soul, world and text, all seeking conformation with the divine model. Effectively this is the only real learning. After describing the complementary relation between the rational soul and creation, Hugh continues:

> Wisdom was a book written within; the work of wisdom a book written without. But He willed afterwards that it still be written otherwise without, that wisdom might be seen more manifestly and be recognized more perfectly, that the eye of man might be illumined to the second writing, since it had been darkened to the first. Therefore, He made a second work after the first, and that was more evident, since it was not only pointed out but illumined. He assumed flesh not losing divinity, and was placed as a book written within and without; in humanity without; within in divinity; so that it might be read without through imitation, within through contemplation.[36]

In this complex parallel between the human and divine, the whole creation is the work of wisdom, which is already a book. The "second writing" is the incarnation, and the text that is written "without" is the flesh, the body, and is shared between humanity and Christ. This sharing was instituted in order to illuminate the text written "within" (in divinity here, but also in the human mind), creating a total book "written within and without"; the carnal outer text is "read" by imitation, in the human striving to create an obedient body, to remake the natural body into the flesh of Christ. The same text is "read" within by contemplation, in the striving to create a mental "body" in a divine shape.

The act of reading as depicted here thus encompasses much more than the act of "reading scripture allegorically" might normally suggest, but it also is the deep product of that reading, because it involves giving oneself to the book, allowing the whole person to be changed by what is written, to participate in the spiritual reformation the book exists to pull us toward. At the same time, we must bear in mind that this book is no ordinary book; from Hugh's sapiential-dispensational perspective, the book is the entire *system* that comprises the entire *cosmos*—the whole of time, all of humankind, God's restorative aim that takes it from beginning to end, the human self, and all knowledge we can have about the way these things interact.

The sacraments are understood to be systematic pieces of this dispensation. They are of a piece with God's working of himself materially into the process of the world, the "second writing": the sacraments of the Church collectively enable a view of the entire dispensation, a mapping of the individual life on the course of the dispensation, and a movement of the human soul toward the telos of the dispensation. As Boyd Coolman notes, Hugh's theology is distinctively practice oriented. Relatedly, it is also oriented toward the crucially interlocking nature of divinity and humanity in the dispensation, their essential *cooperation*. Coolman remarks, "re-formation involves active, cooperative participation by the rational creature. While in creation God acts alone, in salvation, as Hugh puts it elsewhere: there are 'two employed upon the work, God, and the man himself, and these two work together.'"[37] This dispensational process is essentially a cooperative knowledge project; the dispensation as it manifests itself in the two writings, the book and the world, shows as necessary all interconnections between human knowledge and divine Wisdom.

Hugh both draws on and transmits a long tradition in which Wisdom is part of the understanding of this interlocking structure that connects human and divine knowledge. Wisdom is, in a sense, the personification of the very communicability of God's knowledge, and in this way it always shadows Christ. The unfolding of the creation as a divine communication can be seen in a compressed form in Thomas Aquinas's prologue to his commentary on Lombard's *Sentences*, which is informed, like all of Hugh's writing, and like writing about the sacraments elsewhere, substantially and texturally by its interwoven quotes from the Wisdom literature, opening with a line from Sirach 24:40, "I, Wisdom, have poured out rivers," and continuing,

> Through the wisdom of God the hidden parts of the divine work are made manifest and the works of creatures are produced, and not only produced, but restored and perfected. I mean that perfection by which each and every thing is called perfect when it has attained its proper end. That the manifestation of divine things pertains to the wisdom of God is clear from the fact that God himself fully and perfectly knows himself by his own wisdom. Hence, if we know anything of him it must be derived from him, because every imperfect thing takes its origin from the perfect: whence Wisdom 9:17: *who can grasp your meaning unless you have granted him wisdom?* This manifestation is especially worked through the Son, who himself is the Word of the Father. . . . Rightly therefore is it spoken in the person of the Son: *I, Wisdom, have poured forth rivers.*[38]

As a work of Wisdom, the entire dispensation is viewed, here and throughout Thomas's prologue, as a single knowledge process. God's disclosure of himself in the creation and incarnation shows that God "fully and perfectly knows himself." All human knowing of God derives from this full and complete knowing. Implicit in this point is that, even if human knowing is incomplete, if human understanding starts blind from original sin and the burden of flesh, the purpose of God's full and perfect knowing is to communicate itself, to draw humanity toward it. Seen as a process, God's dispensation *intends to be known*. It is, in a sense, a machine for knowing, created in order that all parts of it might ultimately know their origin. It links humanity into the divine telos of perfection. Human knowing is both an obstacle to this process (one might say *the* obstacle) and a goal (one might say *the* goal).

The sacraments of the Church are instituted as a mode of praxis both for the battering down of this obstacle and the facilitation of this goal. When Hugh of St. Victor encapsulates the purpose for which the sacraments are instituted, he tells us that it is for three reasons: humiliation (*humiliatio*), instruction (*eruditio*), and practice (*exercitatio*—"exercise," as it is translated by Deferrari in this case):

> On account of humiliation, indeed, that, since man a rational creature by the precept of his Creator is subject to the insensible elements . . . he may by this very humiliation of his deserve to be reconciled to his Creator. . . .
>
> . . . On account of instruction, that through that which is seen without in the sacrament in the visible species the human mind may be instructed to recognize the invisible virtue which consists within in the thing of the sacrament. For man who knew visible things and did not know the invisible could by no means have recognized divine things unless stimulated by the human. And on this account while the invisible good which he lost is returned to him the signification of the same is furnished him without through visible species, that he may be stimulated without and restored within; so in that which he handles and sees he may recognize of what nature that is which he received and does not see. . . .
>
> Similarly the sacraments were instituted for the sake of exercise, that, while the human mind is exercised and cultivated by various species of works without, it may be made fertile for the multiple fruits of virtue within.[39]

Throughout this description, Hugh aligns external and internal processes to show how the sacraments serve as mode of instruction. The sacraments commemorate our distance from God in the very fact that our understanding must occur through *things*, which in turn bring us toward God because we must recognize and remember that their materiality represents something *beyond* them, and the iterations of our sacramental activity instill an active bodily memory of the fixed distance between inner and outer, truth and materiality, sense and sign—a distance we can only be brought across by *remembering* it. The sacraments, among other things, constitute a training that, when engaged, actively reforms the inner person by contemplation and interaction with their material substance. Talal Asad usefully summarizes Hugh's understanding of the purpose of these rites in a way that illuminates it as a learning model in a social matrix:

> Humiliation ensures that obedience as an act of will is at once a precondition, a continuous accompaniment, and the ultimate objective of Christian rites for restoring purity. Instruction ensures that learning to organize sensory evidence, to see what the untutored eye does not see, and to form desire, takes place by subjecting oneself to authority so that virtue (and truth) can be distinguished from vice (and error). And exercise ensures that the practice of differentiating is necessary to the formation of the Christian's will—that is, by learning what to follow and what to shun in accordance with God's law as conveyed by those who represent him. In the cloister, that representative is the Superior.
>
> His learning always encounters an element of resistance issuing from concupiscence. The process is therefore never mechanically assured, and that is what makes the developing self at once social and nonunitary. The self is irreconcilably divided, so the learning process depends on a permanent separation from what remains an essential part of oneself. . . . For Hugh, rites were aspects of the program for constructing obedient wills. Central to this program is . . . the sacrament of confession by which the Christian's will is tested and his works are judged and justified.[40]

In this section of *Genealogies of Religion*, Asad argues against an understanding of ritual or rite as primarily engaged in communicative and symbolic action; ritual, in Asad's way of thinking, does not exist merely to "express" some preexisting doctrine or mythology. It is an active practice, like an athlete's training, which molds and informs the disposition of the practitioner. Asad's interest is here in the construction of religious selves. He draws on Hugh of St. Victor's description of the purpose of the sacraments as a case in point of embodied discipline that is also an active technology of self-construction. He is not aiming primarily to show how humiliation, erudition, and exercise of the sacraments necessarily involve a learning process, but his reading of Hugh of

St. Victor relies on, and also helps make visible, many of the ways in which this has to be true.

I point out the ways the sacramental process is a knowledge process, and the systematic nature of the view of the dispensation obtained in and through the sacraments, because I want to put my readers into a position to resist somewhat the reflex that wants to seize upon the *ars notoria*'s liberal arts delivery in too simple a way as an *ars magica*, promising marvelous effects with no work. This is actually partly how it represents itself—a simpler and easier way to knowledge—but it is not an entirely accurate representation. It involved a considerable devotional load, one that few students nowadays would feel they had time to undertake in addition to their regular workload of reading and study. But to the medieval student, perhaps already having started on the path of a religious life, the *ars notoria* might be seen as worth the time away from regular study because the exercise it proposes would enhance the process of learning and bring the student more quickly to his goal. Otherwise put, for a monk like John of Morigny, the attractive feature of the *ars notoria* was surely not so much that it appeared to be magic, but that it appeared to be a specifically targeted form of devotion that would enable the necessary reform of self that allowed knowledge to be accessed and retained. This is consistent with its aspect as *primer*, already noted in regard to Bridget's reading lessons in chapter 1. Like Hugh of St. Victor, and knowledgeably informed by writings on the sacramental structure of the world, John of Morigny adhered to a theology oriented toward practice and rooted in an idea of divine-human cooperation. In many respects, for a medieval witness encountering the *ars notoria* for the first time, the text could appear to have certain fundamental things in common with the knowledge-project of the sacraments. John's error was not so much in failing to recognize the magical and diabolically contrived nature of the *ars notoria* initially, but in persisting in its practice long after he had reason to know better.

I do not wish to excuse John from his error of complicity any more than he excuses himself. I only want to draw attention to a set of possible reasons for John's initial pursuit of it, as well as his ongoing embrace of its central purpose in his own work. The view of the action of the *ars notoria* as magical is of long standing, and complicated, but not perhaps exactly the same for us now as it was for the medieval clerics, who felt the force of its recalling of biblical precedents, understood that it wanted to be sacramental, and objected that it was theurgy—neither a *covenanted* mediation, nor a form of learning *natural* to humanity, and not even *comprehensible* in its language.[41] At the same time, the *ars notoria* is a discipline of practice. It is performed over a space of months, and its effects are, as Asad says of the sacraments, "never mechanically assured." As with the sacraments, so also in principle with the *ars notoria*, the effects of grace (and make no mistake, learning is an effect of grace here) depend on the disposition of the recipient. Ultimately they must become part of the entire process of self-reformation that the sacraments of the Church also entail if they are to have any effect at all.

And so too, ultimately, and more interestingly perhaps, with the prayers and figures of the *Liber florum*. As will be more fully demonstrated in upcoming chapters, John's understanding of his own process is sacramental in the strong sense that the Book of Prayers and the Book of Figures are intimately connected to the entire dispensation, map onto it structurally, and are designed to further it. The next chapter will be concerned with the most important individual sacrament governing John's work as it is viewed from the vantage of the Book of Visions: the sacrament of penance, or reconciliation.

3

PENANCE:
THE SACRAMENT OF THE MIDDLE OF LIFE

The Eucharist is well known for its role in triggering visions in the Middle Ages, but confession and penance seem to have received short shrift in the scholarly discourse surrounding visionary experience. Yet in the later Middle Ages, as Miri Rubin describes, these two sacraments could hardly be dissociated:

> Communion and confession were bound together in the attempt to create an effective focus for examination of conscience and for the imparting of new knowledge. . . . the initiative which boosted confession, as both dependent upon and confirming sacerdotal mediation, was matched and ultimately surpassed by another, which designed the eucharist and communion so that eventually confession became essentially a form of preparation for communion. . . . The interaction between learning and confessing was complex, and in the rhythm of instruction one was meant to be led through edifying and effective preaching, towards confession and penance, as "dire," in Berlioz's words, led to an ultimate "faire dire." The confessional, then the penitential and finally the sacramental moods conceptualised and sealed a cognitive and sensory whole.[1]

John of Morigny's Book of Visions manifests a preoccupation with penance, a sacrament with which several of his most important visions are primarily concerned. The visionary reflection of acts of penance and confession is interesting to me, in this context in particular, because of the way confession also is a kind of visible hinge between the institutional knowledge of canon law and the interiority of individual consciousness.

In tracing the history of confession through the thirteenth century, where an increasing market for penitential manuals responded to an increasing demand for more frequent confessions after the fourth Lateran council, Joseph Goering has brought out references to the "inner" and "outer" forums of canon law, terms with wide enough currency to be used in Dante's *Paradiso* as in Thomas Aquinas. As Goering notes, "In general, the external forum is concerned with public and manifest transgressions of the Church's law or of divine law, while the internal forum is the court of conscience ('forum conscientiae') where even secret crimes and sins are considered."[2] But the secrets of the internal court and laws of the external courts are also two aspects, inner and outer, of the same knowledge; they are closely related sciences, for "canon law was not just a system for lawyers, judges, and administrators, but a body of learned jurisprudence that affected everyone, in the most intimate ways, in the confessional."[3] Both inner and outer courts are dynamically concerned with the encoding and deciphering of truth in relation to God's agency on earth.

John was also an expert in the confessional, and thereby in the discipline of this encoding and deciphering, from all these angles. He was a Christian and made confession; he was a priest and heard confession; and he was trained in canon law, and knew what confession and penance were supposed to do. All of these aspects of his experience and expertise are reflected in his visions in various ways. Although the Eucharist is obviously not absent from his liturgical life, and is an element in his visionary life too, as will be seen, nevertheless in general the primary focus of the Book of Visions is rather on contrition and confession, a sacrament that is useful in being friendly to narrative. If, for a medieval Christian, baptism is the purgative and initiatory sacrament that marks the beginning of life, and extreme unction is the sacrament that marks its end, penance is *par excellence* the sacrament of the middle of life. It is repeatable, and as a precondition for communion, it helps link the soul back to God—in short, it has the power to keep the story going that otherwise might founder on human sin and error, just as it is vital in furthering the longer dispensational history of redemption which otherwise would have ended with the fall.

John makes it explicit that his book concerns—and shares in—penitential action. Early in the Book of Visions, John writes, "All things written in this book are categorized under the sacrament of penance—that is, so that they may be categorized among the seven principal sacraments mystically."[4] There is a slight ambiguity here, in that it is not clear whether John means by "this book" the *Liber florum* as a whole, or the Book of Visions in particular. Penance certainly describes the main action of the autobiographical Book of Visions; however, the autobiographical parts of John's work are refracted by the prayers, which are penitential as well. In several places the Seven Prayers recall or evoke John's penitential visions quite specifically, blazing a penitential path for operators to follow. Even the Thirty Prayers are almost without exception concerned in some manner with purification of the soul and so are meant to incite penitential thoughts in the speaker. Thus, it seems fair to see the entire *Liber florum* as a meditation on—as well as a modus operandi for—penitential action.

John's penances, at least the ones he tells us about, are performed very much in the interior arena of vision and imagination. While he engages with all the normal monastic bodily disciplines, severe or extreme mortifications of the flesh are not his style. When he describes penitential behavior for us, it involves confession, meditation, prayer, and vows of renunciation to the Virgin. In the one episode where John describes a physical punishment, it happens in a dream. This punishment, enacted in vision 11—the culmination of part 1 of the Book of Visions, in which John is given an ultimate and absolute mandate to turn away from the exceptive or magical arts—was foretold by a divine voice in vision 10:

> When God, the Creator of all, saw that fear of him had not recalled me from evil, he decided to recall me by force, through strenuous ecclesiastical discipline. Thus, one night in an ecstatic sleep, I saw a man robed in a red toga or surcoat coming into the solar where I was, along with some others clad in similar costume. He sat down there in the throne like a master. And seeing by the revelation of the Holy Spirit in my heart, I knew this to be the lord Jesus. Coming before him I sought mercy, prostrate, as the religious custom is in chapter before masters of the order. And then the lord Jesus, my master, ordered one of his associates to beat me harshly. One of them got up and began to hit me hard with his fist, saying, "Take that, because of the things you have done and are doing that are contrary to your Creator." And he beat me very hard, so much that I woke up because of the extreme pain and suffering I was enduring. I was much amazed, being in pain in my shoulders and the other places where I had been beaten, and I smarted for almost the whole of an hour. And thus the chastening Lord chastised me and did not deliver me to death.[5]

Although the structure of John's punishment here is external, modeled on the monastic discipline of the obdurate,[6] the vision is internal. In the dream, Jesus takes on the role and function of the abbot, and at the end, John invokes the biblical language of paternal chastisement that recurs in reference to God. The concluding sentence of this episode, "the chastening Lord chastised me and did not deliver me to death," quotes Psalm 117:18, a psalm on which John draws elsewhere in his prayers (the next line is "Aperite mihi portas," a phrase recurrent in the angelic prayers), but this sentiment is also a New Testament leitmotif, echoed again in 2 Corinthians 6:9: "As dying and behold we live: as chastised and not killed."[7] God's chastening is simultaneously a sign of love and the desire for redemption of the souls belonging to him (e.g., Heb. 12:6, "For whom the Lord loveth he chastiseth: and he scourgeth every son whom he receiveth"). It also sets the precedent for penitential action (e.g., Rev. 3:19, "Such as I love, I rebuke and chastise. Emulate me, therefore, and do penance").[8] Prostrate before the abbot Jesus, John seeks mercy. It is important that this beating *is* the mercy that he requests: it is his redemptive medicine.

The biblical precedents make it clear that the situation in which Jesus takes up a position as abbot is a divine literalization as much as an earthly metaphor—that is, it literalizes the abbot's divine agency, bringing God into the abbot's position. It also emphasizes the presence of God in John's monastic life and practice. Psychologically, the bodily experience of pain might be seen as a mark of John's awareness of his failure to do God's will, yet the pain is miraculous, too: it is a real chastening from a real God that leaves its imprint on John's waking body, real pain resulting from the dreamt blows. The monastic structure and the cosmic structure dovetail here precisely because of the way in which John's body is involved, and here (as elsewhere in John's work) the focus is on God's intervention in the world through a particular intervention in John's life. Through contrition and penance, John gains and regains the ability to restore a right relation to God, to "emulate" his chastisement, and thus to cooperate in God's plan for his restoration.

It would hardly be possible to find a clearer instantiation than this vision of the way John's self-construction is linked both to his own body and to the embodied disciplines of monastic institution. Some further observations by Talal Asad help bring this point into focus:

> In answer to my earlier question about the role of bodily pain in spiritual sickness, I now venture that the body was not merely an obstacle to the truth . . . but was primarily a medium by which the truth about the self's essential potentiality for transgression could be brought into the light, so that it could be illuminated by a metaphysical truth, a process in which pain and discomfort were inescapable elements. Foucault in effect makes us aware that it is not the traditional symbolism attributed to ascetic pain to which we must finally look (chastising or mortifying the body) but the place occupied by bodily pain in an economy of truth.[9]

Against Foucault, however, Asad emphasizes the social rather than the solitary aspect of monastic discipline: "In the dominant form of medieval monasticism (cenobitic as opposed to eremitic), the technology of the self, which lies at the heart of the combat of chastity, is itself dependent on the institutional resources of organized community life. The inspection and disengagement of the will, which Foucault describes, takes place within the stuff of monastic life guided by the abbot."[10] He adds, "It must be stressed that monks were living an enclosed life in order to exercise virtues, not in order to be beaten into submission."[11] John's vision of the external divine chastisement (which is also an internal penance—the two can hardly be distinguished here) make visible how this is so. In the dream, sociality and divinity mirror one another, and it is through this divine (but also personal, willing and willed) chastisement that John experiences in his dream and in his body that his reformation becomes possible.

Self-formation is both a subjective and social act. Nowhere is this more clear than in the regulations and practices governing penance. What I mean is not that sociality *determines* self-formation—this is not what is borne out by the evidence—but that social reflections of self (such as we see occurring in John's dream) are *necessary* for self-formation, or in medieval terms, for the cultivation of a healthy soul. Depictions of God and depictions of penitential action are mirrors of the self, inscribed both on the ordinary human corporeal body and on the social body. I do not mean that the self is a communal project; I mean that knowledge of self, when it feels like it is working properly, must be. Knowledge becomes knowledge when it is reflected as such in the social body. Knowledge is a communal project, and in some sense communally held. That does not mean that everyone has the same knowledge (obviously), but that knowledge whole is everyone's knowledge, in the same way that the Catholic Church is (literally, in its original Greek sense) everyone's church, and Christ is its head.

This can be seen equally clearly in the two visions that are recounted just prior to this one (visions 8 and 9, both of which concern the divine demand that John renounce the *ars notoria* specifically). Both are dramatic instantiations of this type of institutionally reflective divine and human mirroring. These episodes detail John's visions of conversion away from the *ars notoria* and collectively constitute the more or less gradual turning point for John's understanding, and hence for his story. Both visions involve different molestations by the devil. Both are also woven into specific prayers in John's introductory or preparative liturgy, the Seven Prayers, so that the divine-human institutional mirror is subject to another translation, from experience into ritual. In what follows we must necessarily consider the visions and the prayers together, since the visions offer a personal view into John's life, while the prayers open out this view, adding a social perspective as the elements of John's visionary life are incorporated into ritual action for performance by others. In the Seven Prayers, John's primary experiences of conversion away from the *ars notoria* are scripted and transmitted in a directed way that is obviously intended to bind John's community of operators together.[12]

Vision 8 takes place after John has been practicing with the notory art long enough to learn all the magical or exceptive arts, including necromancy. He tells us that one night he sees an angel of the cherubim, dressed in a black garment, coming into his chamber. The angel orders him to "go downstairs."[13] Prepared to do the angel's bidding, John pauses at the top step, thinking that the angel had something to say to him, and abruptly he is given a shove between the shoulders by the angel and falls all the way to the bottom, where a devil appears and grabs him. Allegorically, the stairs become a sort of descent into hell, a pathway that John has resisted, but evidently not hard enough; John is aware, and suggests at the outset, that the reason behind this "fall" is his continued use of the *ars notoria*, which was revealed to him in visions 7 and 8 as containing diabolical corruption in the prayers involving outlandish tongues.[14]

At this point the devil, keeping a tight hold, walks off with John, leading him away into the town, making threatening pronouncements, telling him that he cannot escape, and looking for an opportune place to kill him. John writes, "I thought to myself that if I could find a confessor, I would confess and repent that I had sinned and done these things, and that I would not do them after this or sin any more. And as soon as I had this thought, lo, the enemy let me go and betook himself away from me somewhat."[15] No longer held fast by the enemy, John blends into a crowd of people in the town square, where he meets a bishop and confesses his sins. After doing this, John says, he no longer fears the devil at all, and at this point the dream turns from a nightmare into an ecstatic experience. John wanders away from the bishop and comes to a church. His description, as always, is careful about the direction and positioning of objects in the vision:

> When I was leaving the said confessor, I entered the church by the south side; and there, next to an altar that was on the north side, upon the steps of the altar of the said church, stood the sweet and undefiled virgin Mary, mother of God, adorned in the very whitest robes. Her beauty was so great and of such a kind that no human tongue would be adequate to the vision and declaration of her. And I was struck with wonder, and justly so, since indeed the sun and the moon marvel in her company. Next to her stood the blessed John the evangelist, dressed in Jacobite garb, marvelously beautiful beyond measure. After seeing these things, all thoughts remote, my heart exulted in such great happiness that I never felt the like.[16]

John approaches the divine figures, and he exchanges kisses with them, each in turn instructing him to sin no more. John now moves into the choir area of the church[17] to find the high altar, where someone is celebrating mass: "And it was during the Canon of the Mass,[18] and around the altar were the four evangelists in white clothes, and lo, one of them, who had the head of an eagle and a man's body and limbs, came to me and I embraced him. I sat down there holding him in my lap, and as he sat he spoke with me, and I was put into such a state of peace that I straight away woke up."[19] John's confession has made it possible for him to entertain the notion of taking communion, though in his description of the vision it is not stated that he does so. However, the close embrace of John the Evangelist in his bird-headed form suggests a mystical event[20] experienced at the altar while the ceremony surrounding the Eucharist is going on. The four living creatures with which the evangelists are associated occur in the visionary prophecy of Ezekiel 1:4–10 and are iterated again in Revelation 4:6–8, in both cases surrounding the throne of God. Here in John's vision they take up similar positions around the altar on which Christ's body lies; reading exegetically, John sees the altar (on which God's body is being consecrated) as it appears in the sight of God. The identity between earthly and heavenly altars—the idea that the true place of the ceremony is actually *in heaven*—is suggested in the very words of this prayer from the canon of the mass specifying the altar as linked to an "altar on high" in God's presence: "We suppliants beseech you . . . : command that these things be carried by the hands of your angel to your altar on high in the presence of your divine Majesty; so that we who, by this partaking at the altar, shall receive the sacrosanct body and blood of your son, may be filled with every heavenly benediction and grace."[21] The transformation of the evangelist from the human form (in which John of Morigny saw him a few moments before on the steps up to the high altar) to the animal-headed form encountered here signifies a leap of vision: John's newly illuminated sight allows him to see with heavenly eyes, to view the mass taking place in God's presence, through the mystical portal of the church into which he walked as a dreamer, and the sacraments that are part of its dispensation. The import of the confession and absolution that he underwent prior to entering the church is precisely that it makes this view possible. It signifies a purification of his sight, a cleansing of his vision. Again, John participates mystically in an event where there is an institutional mirroring of human and heavenly worlds: he experiences a heavenly communion, sharing a seat with John the Evangelist and embracing on his lap the historical person, here figured in his beast-headed form, who wrote the last canonical gospel. It seems that John has come very far from the demon who pursued him so frighteningly in the first part of the vision.

Indeed, in the account above, what initially causes the devil to recede slightly is not even the act of making confession but the mere *thought* of doing so; it is the inkling that confession might be necessary that immediately loosens the devil's grasp.[22] In fact, the very thought of confession actually allows him a preliminary auditory perception of heaven. "And as soon as I had this thought," he writes, "lo, the enemy let me go and betook himself away from me somewhat, and I immediately heard angels singing so sweetly and melodiously that in all my life I never heard the like. But I was unable to see them."[23] The fact that John mentions his inability to see the angels seems to suggest the notion of a visual part of the experience that is still missing, to be filled in later. But even if it is only full confession and absolution that purges the faculty of vision, even the initial thought, the very recognition that he has an error to confess, allows the song of angels to become audible. Like the beating he received from Christ in vision 11, this confession and absolution are imaginary or spiritual in the sense that they are entirely internal to John; there is no real bishop, only a visionary one, and the absolution must therefore be internal as well. The contrition occasioning the act of confession is presumably sufficiently real, since it is internal anyway.

A parallel renunciation and triumph over a tormenting demon occurs in a vision already discussed in chapter 1, in which John told how his sister Bridget, after she had been using the *ars notoria* for awhile, began to be troubled by apparitions of a demon standing near her in her bed, threatening her physically and constraining her so that she could not move or cry out, terrifying her so much that she was afraid to sleep alone. John admonished her to "say an Our Father and the Creed and Hail Mary," but even when she had said these prayers, the spirit did not recede. John began to feel his own compunction at this point, silently, as he said, incurring "great pain and fear, thinking that she endured these things on account of the work of the *ars notoria*." He suggested that she must renounce the *ars notoria* in a solemn vow before the statue of the Virgin in church. The spirit then gradually receded, and the next morning Bridget followed John's advice.[24]

A complex and familial penitence operates here: it is partly John's, who knows her involvement with the *ars notoria* is his fault, since he was her teacher in it, and thus he experiences his own compunction, as he thinks this might be the reason for her torment. At the same time the demon itself is clearly hers; John comments, twice, that he does not see it. Standard prayers—the Creed, Paternoster, and Ave Maria—do no good. Yet even his suggestion that she confess and promise before the Virgin to sin no more has at least preliminary results, as in his own vision: she feels an immediate loosening of the devil's grip. Later, after Bridget has formally disavowed the notory art, she gains dominion over the devil, beating him and trampling him underfoot whenever he appears.[25]

Bridget seems to have been more immediately successful in meeting the requirement of conversion than John was at first. Though by vision 8, God has unambiguously expressed a prohibition against this ritual practice, John tells us that he did not in fact completely dismiss the *ars notoria* in its wake: "and then," he writes, "I truly knew that the said *ars notoria* was deeply evil, and I put it away from me somewhat, but not entirely."[26] One might expect a more complete conversion after such a dream, but divine illuminations do not automatically create perfect people. In any event, this is not a hagiographic narrative; it is a *confessio*.

We know that the vision was nevertheless profoundly important to John because he tells us that he wrote a prayer in response to it: "And rightly amazed, I gave thanks to God, who deigned to show such great secrets to me. And in perpetual memory of this vision, I composed and fashioned the prayer which begins *Ave, salve,* et cetera."[27] *Ave, salve* is the incipit to prayer *4,[28] whose rubric offers an opening instruction for a visual meditation that recollects John's vision: "Here imagine that you are entering a certain church from the southern side" (*4.1). Other meditations going with the next three prayer subdivisions have instructions that recognizably replicate the staging of the first divine part of John's vision. You are invited to imagine that

- (*4.2.a) you are in the same church watching the glorious Virgin with the blessed John in human form, adorned in white garments
- (*4.2.b) it seems to you that you are being embraced by the glorious Virgin; the holy virgin Mary is looking at you
- (*4.2.c) the holy virgin Mary is smiling at you
- (*4.3.a) you are watching the blessed John standing in the same church beside the virgin Mary, embracing you and talking with you
- (*4.4) you are watching the glorious Virgin speaking with you in the same church.[29]

Clearly John does not aim to replicate the entire vision precisely, and he does not include the ecstatic conclusion, in which he holds John the Evangelist on his lap. (Indeed, in the first meditation, it is explicit that you are to imagine John the Evangelist in his human form, not the eagle-headed one of the communion vision.) But the visualizations serving as prompts for the operator clearly echo his own visionary experiences.[30]

The reminder goes beyond the meditations, for John evokes his own personal experience in the words of the prayer as well. In the rubric to prayer *4, he tells us that he composed this prayer after the Virgin came to him for the first time (that is, after vision 8), and that "it should never be said unless the blessed Mary herself has appeared in dream." As we know also from its rubric, the immediately preceding prayer (*3) is likely to evoke a vision of Mary.[31] Prayer *4 is thus a prayer of thanksgiving for any vision occasioned by prayer *3, and prayer *4 is intended in part to memorialize and amplify the effects of that vision.

Prayer *4 itself is in four parts, addressing Mary and John in turn, meditating on their roles as cosmic intercessors, and requesting that their intercession continue in personal ways. John says that he composed this prayer himself, although, at least in later drafts, some parts of the blazon of both Mary and John in the prose sections of the prayer derive from Alan of Lille's *Plaint of Nature*, while other parts, in poetry, rearrange a well-known hymn, "Ecce ad te confugio." Yet John interweaves his own words with those of his sources to ensure that his personal experience is remembered. This address to Mary gives the flavor of the interpersonal complexity of John's imagination in the interesting refraction of his own experience through the words he gives the operator to speak:

> O lady of ladies, queen of queens, virgin Mary, my beloved and mother.... You have drawn me—.N., a wretched sinner, inflamed and kindled by love of your beauty and desire for your loveliness—towards you. You have most violently pierced my heart and my soul with your glance, *cast as it were sidelong over me—and over John, the composer of this book*—by your eyes (most sweet thieves striking and enjoying the lover's heart) as though by two very sharp and graceful darts.[32]

This prayer, like the others in the book, retains throughout a strong sense of John's personal part in the divine action that he occasions for the operator, and that initially happens through him in a penitential mode. Despite the fact that John was unable fully to engage a change of life at this point, he understands the vision as important enough to invite other operators to share, both in its images and its implications.

The penitential vision that truly turns John away from the *ars notoria* is vision 9. Like the previous one, this vision concerns confession and absolution, but it differs from vision 8 in terminating on an apparently less ecstatic note. As with vision 8, however, language internal to the vision is reused in an important prayer (prayer *1, "O Rex regum"), which, though written late in the sequence of the Seven Prayers, is placed first in the final known version. I quote the chapter containing John's account of this vision in full:

But after this I saw the ninth vision. There came to me a great trouble, and while this trouble was going on I saw many horrible visions every day. One day I wanted to find out what they meant, and in order to know this I uttered a prayer from the aforementioned book of the *ars notoria* which is said for memory, as the custom is. And lo, in the night following, I saw this vision. It seemed to me that there was a malign spirit lying beside me in my bed. Rising instantly when I saw him, I chased him away fiercely with a drawn sword; I struck him, and he withdrew. After he fled, I suddenly saw a man entering my chamber, quite tall, and with a long face and a long aquiline nose, clothed in a robe not exactly white but as though it had been burnt—that is, his robe had the color of ashes—and he called me and said to me, "You are to interpret a vision for me." At that point I recalled why I had said the prayer earlier, and I said: "O sir, but you are to interpret for me!" He responded: "That's to no purpose. And don't go meddling in such matters any more, because they are not pertinent to you—if you go on doing it we will make you be silent."

Having said this he spoke to me again: "Come here, because I want to confess with you." And taking me by the hand, he led me to the bench next to my bed and we both knelt on the bench in the manner of people confessing. He began to confess, saying, "I am a great man, strong and powerful, and I have dispensed mercy where I should have dispensed justice, and I want you to absolve me of this." I said to him, "It seems to me that this is not a sin," and he said, "My conscience chides me. Absolve me quickly." So I said, "Then let me absolve you of that for which your conscience chides you." But when I wanted to absolve him with the common words of absolution, he said to me, "Don't use those words, but open your mouth and I will fill it." When I opened my mouth I uttered these words of absolution to him, as if I had seen them in a book: "King of kings, prince of princes and lord of lords, man, God, son of Mary born of a virgin." And after I had spoken this last word he exclaimed in a loud voice saying, "O cursed Jews," with me speaking thus and absolving him: "May He absolve you from those things which you have now confessed to me, for which your conscience chides you." And when I had said this, he went away from me and I immediately woke up. And then I understood, I knew without doubt, and I had proven by experience, that the book of the *ars notoria* was entirely malign, that it did not please my Creator that I should operate through it any more, and that what I had done in it displeased him. And because of this, from that point on I wholly put away the work of the said nefarious book or art, and I made confession and repented of what I had done.[33]

John is here uncharacteristically nonspecific at first about the identity of the tall ashen man dressed as a penitent; indeed, it seems that he does not recognize the man at the start, or if he does, his conversation does not show it. In vision 8, John immediately named Mary and John the Evangelist when he saw them; in vision 11, where the key figure is perhaps less iconically identifiable, John tells us that he "knew from the holy spirit" that the master dressed in red was in fact Christ. In this case, however, he never mentions Christ by name at all. Our realization that the man is Christ must thus (if we are sufficiently alert) dovetail exactly with John's own. The revelation probably began for him when the ashen man said, "open your mouth and I will fill it"—a phrase echoing God's identification of himself in Psalm 80:11: "I am the Lord your God who led you from the land of Egypt; open your mouth and I will fill it." The ashen man is unambiguously identified as the incarnate Christ in the words with which John's mouth is filled: "Rex regum, princeps principum et dominus dominancium, homo Deus filius Marie natus ex virgine." These words, which he is forced to speak like a prophecy, supposedly in absolution of the ashen man (but obviously these are not words of absolution), in fact must be read as John's own confession of the power of Christ. The "absolution" of Christ here illuminates how the divine power passes through John as a priest even in his error. After the words are out of his mouth, John does not name Christ further.

If the reader should remain in any doubt about the identity of the penitent here (as I did myself at first, both because the vision is so odd, and because John has reported false visions of God earlier), it is not possible to remain in doubt about it once one reaches the first prayer of the book, prayer *1, "O Rex regum." Indeed, the sublimity of the occasion, so muted in the visionary record, is fully illuminated in the prayer, which is a meditation on the incarnation. This prayer incorporates the words with which John's mouth was filled in its opening lines in a direct address: "O king of kings, you are the strongest prince of princes and the most excellent lord of lords, a most powerful man, God, just and true judge dispensing justice and judgment."[34] The phrase "O rex regum, dominus dominancium" (which also occurs in the *ars notoria*) draws on Revelation 19:16: "Rex regum et dominus dominancium" (king of kings and lord of lords), a blazon written on the cloak and thigh of Christ as he appears in the vision of heaven opened. More strikingly, the prayer's amplification of this phrase iterates the substance of Christ's confession to John—that he has dispensed mercy where he should have dispensed justice[35]—as an attribute of the Son, one of several attributes evoking Christ as Wisdom in the prayer:

> Beginning without beginning, end without end, blessed leader of all, most wise and incomprehensible and eternal, you who created all things

from nothing, you are the ineffable wisdom of God the father, and spotless mirror of the majesty of God, and image of his goodness, begotten from eternity without time. Lord Jesus Christ, most clement son of God the almighty Father, you are my savior and my redeemer, *a great man, strong and powerful, you dispensed and dispense mercy and grace where you ought to have dispensed judgment and justice.* From the supernal citadel, from the lap of the Father, descending as an *ave* for the sake of our salvation into the womb of the blessed and undefiled most glorious virgin Mary, conceived by the Holy Spirit, you saw fit to assume precious flesh here.[36]

Visual meditations accompanying the prayer invite reflection on the life of Christ, taking operators all the way from the annunciation through the passion to the apocalypse and God reigning in the Trinity. In other words, the cosmic cycle of the new dispensation is fully represented here, both in the visualizations and the prayer itself, from the annunciation to the end of the world. But the prayer reflects the vision too, as John ties his penitential experience in the vision to the prayer's opening, repeating the key phrases spoken to him by Christ in vision 9. Even the exclamation, "O cursed Jews," that comes from Christ's mouth in the vision—which I suggest must be seen as a metonymy of the passion—is refracted through a typically late medieval anti-Semitic symbolic link in the part of the prayer about the passion:

> *Imagine here that you see the passion of our Lord, Jesus Christ:*
> Oh how medicinal, curing and healing, pious and just, memorable and pitiable, the death and passion of so great a man; but to impious Jews and other infidels who believe it not, terrible and damning.[37]

The Jews are here too invoked as the medieval Christian prototype of the "failure to know." At the most critical point in the vision, Christ's cursing of the Jews thus stands in both for the crucifixion and for John's own disobedience, which, like the Jews' failure to know, proleptically occasioned the crucifixion.

Christ's public and cosmic role as creator and redeemer is thus tied to John's personal life. Christ is "creator of all" and "our savior" but also, clearly in reference to the vision, "my savior" and "my redeemer." His manhood, articulated in the words of the dream vision, "you are a great man, strong and powerful," is juxtaposed with his aspect as the eternal Wisdom, "spotless mirror of the majesty of God." God's dispensing of mercy instead of the justice that was due is clearly represented as the incarnation itself. The knowledge John gains from the vision is both internal and external: the vision seems to have offered a complete view of the dispensation, having at its heart a God apparently repenting his own act of redemption. "And then I understood," says John, "I knew without doubt, and I had proven by experience, that the book of the *ars notoria* was entirely malign, that it did not please my Creator that I should operate through it any more, and that what I had done in it displeased him."[38] This view of divine penance occasioned a fuller knowledge than John had had before, as evinced by the fuller (though not yet complete) change in John's life and habit, but also by the way it is inscribed on the entirety of the dispensation in the prayer.

But not all questions are answered by this exegesis. Let us move back to the vision for a moment, and consider what may be its oddest moment: the conversation about absolution reported between the ashen man, still appearing simply as a penitent, and John: "'I am a great man, strong and powerful, and I have dispensed mercy where I should have dispensed justice, and I want you to absolve me of this.' I said to him, 'It seems to me that this is not a sin,' and he said, 'My conscience chides me. Absolve me quickly.'" That God first of all should walk into John's chamber dressed as a penitent, and second ask to make a confession to John—even as it is revealed in hindsight—must surely have been as unexpected for John as it is for us. It also remains an open question why this vision should succeed in converting John away from the *ars notoria* so immediately and thoroughly when the earlier, more ecstatic vision did not. I remark the extreme oddity of the visionary action carefully, because surely, for John, the unexpectedness of the revelation of this man's Godhead was part of the vision's forceful effect. The tension intrinsic to the situation will not be possible to resolve completely; the suggestions I am about to make by no means exhaust the possibilities of its interpretation, but rather are meant to chase the tail of my points about divine pedagogy and the institution of the sacraments.

One way that Christ's behavior can be seen to work pedagogically here is by modeling, first, the unwanted behavior John has been engaging in up to now, and second, the desired behavior. This modeling is also a mirroring. For if the monk's duty is to make himself over in the image of God, so far as he can, through obedience and humility, what happens if he fails in obedience and humility, as John has done? At a minimum, the image of God that he sees in the mirror of himself must become distorted, if indeed he is capable of seeing the divine in himself in any form at all. The vision that John sees suggests a solution to the problem of the "dirty mirror": the actions of the ashen man show both how God is distorted by the dirty mirror and how John's behavior has to change—how he himself must become the penitent—to rectify the mirror's image. One might say that Christ thus, as he did at first, bends down to show himself as a human being to a human being. A certain enigmatic deformation is acquired by his taking on or mirroring the form of the human being he seeks to teach ("You are to interpret a vision for me"). For God to require an interpretation from the dreamer who invoked him for purposes of divination is a self-evident absurdity, which in turn, once the divine identity of the apparition is made known, illuminates how John must reshape his own behavior. In this case, he must stop using the *ars notoria* prayers. Additionally, in order for God to appear properly in the mirror of himself, John must confess and undertake penance, as illustrated by Christ in the vision. The apparition of Christ here demonstrates in microcosm the purpose of the sacraments as they pertain to John in particular, the dimensions of humiliation (in God's bending down to engage John as a priest), erudition (in the pedagogy of divine self-modeling), and praxis (in the ashen robe). The vision offers a knowledge model that links divine wisdom and the dispensation to John personally. It seeks to locate the point of connection between John and Christ, through which John can once again move toward God, or at least begin to shape his behavior toward the re-creation of the divine in his own behavior.

Not all questions are answered by this exegesis, either. Indeed, this is a risky vision for the exegete, for if we consider the vision simply as a narrative, its point inevitably appears to be that Christ repents of, and seeks absolution for, some act of mercy toward John. If we consider the prayer, which interprets the vision cosmically, Christ seems to repent and seek absolution for the act of mercy *represented by the incarnation itself*. How could either of these things be? The difficulty of this request for absolution in the visionary context is alleviated by the prayer, which is about the divine wisdom that decreed the incarnation in the first place; it reminds us that Christ's passion can be seen as precisely the same kind of divine/human cooperative penance—the penance of God in his man form, or man in his God form, for the sins occasioned by the shared flesh of humanity. Yet even if this divine and sapiential perspective is helpful, it does not completely erase the paradox implicit in the moment: how could God *seek to be absolved* for his own infinite mercy? The exegetical risk is that the vision might encourage us to understand God as passible, capable of regret, his very integrity dependent on John's acting one way or another, as though God were susceptible to diminishment through human disobedience, or augmentation through human cooperation.

It would be a correct move in this language game to say that whatever may *seem* to be the case here, all parts of the dispensation are known only to God, who has understood eternally *in advance* what all consequences of all moves would be. This is John's move, when he writes his prayer from the perspective of the divine Wisdom, the perspective *in aeterno*. Yet from the human perspective—the perspective *in saeculo* that we are granted by the visionary narrative itself—there certainly *appear* to be immediate consequences for the dispensational outcome, which shows itself to be still developing, still dependent on human actions. In the problem as John's ninth vision renders it visible, the sacrifice of the passion will only redeem John if he can interiorize the knowledge it was meant to pass on. But this also means that John himself is part of the dispensation—indeed more vitally so, as a monk and a priest, than a layperson might be: he is part of its *administration*. Even if we understand this penitential theurgy as wholly internal, acting only on the human soul, even so, unavoidably, the vision renders visible an *entanglement* of human and divine action. For how can the imperfection of humanity not leak into God in a system so obviously shared by both? This vision offers a unique and potent window into the theurgic problem.

In an earlier essay, published in 2012, in which I examined the valences of the word "theurgy," I looked at this term as it is currently being developed by several scholars in different historical areas.[39] Of these, I argued that the usage of kabbalistic scholar Moshe Idel is in many ways the most idiosyncratic; I also think it is in some ways the most interesting. Idel uses the term "theurgy" or "theurgical" to refer to, in his words, "operations intended to influence the Divinity, mostly in its own inner state or dynamics, but sometimes also in its relationship to man."[40] This is idiosyncratic in the sense that, by "theurgy," Idel does not primarily mean to indicate—as other scholars of theurgy outside late antiquity often do—a set of *practices* analogous to Late Antique theurgy. As I wrote in 2012,

> the word "theurgy" points, in Idel's usage, first and foremost to an idea or proposition about God: the proposition that the divine is a dynamic entity in need of human action in order fully to inhabit its correct relation to itself. In the subsection of chapter 7 [of *Kabbalah: New Perspectives*] titled "Augmentation Theurgy," Idel discusses the interrelation between human acts and the augmentation of the divine *Dynamis* (*Gevurah*) as a key concept of rabbinic literature. Idel focuses on the assumption present in certain classical Jewish sources that the power of God is weakened or diminished by human transgression and augmented by the proper performance of the commandments; as an illustrative locus, he quotes the *Pesikta de-Rav Kahana*: "Azariah [said] in the name of R. Yehudah bar Simon, so long as the righteous act according to the will of heaven, they add power to the *Dynamis*.... And if they do not act [accordingly], it is as if: 'you have weakened the Rock that formed thee.'"[41]

Idel demonstrates that later kabbalistic writings enhance and expand the suggestions and problems implicit here in this early midrash about the interlocking of human/divine powers—the problem of *entanglement*—which is clearly embedded also in the issues surrounding Christian theurgic or sacramental thinking in John's vision. Within the intra-divine system, it certainly looks as if human action must have consequences for the system as a whole. John's right action at this juncture will further God's purpose (as if adding power to the *Dynamis*); John's disobedience, if he does not repent of it himself, must be imaged as God in an ashen robe (like a weakness in the rock). John's vision makes graphic the principles of augmentation theurgy as outlined by Idel.

The aspects of the vision that make John's mode of apprehension and praxis resemble augmentation theurgy are not themselves particularly Jewish (except in specific and limited ways, since Christian sacramentalism has been mapped onto Jewish law from the beginning), but rather a structural feature of theurgical/sacramental thinking in general. Idel's definition of theurgy, idiosyncratic as it is, helps give form to this problem. As I argued in my earlier essay,

> [i]n one sense, it may be said that Idel positivizes the radical aspect of the theurgic idea that others try to escape from when they seek to justify it.
>
> In another way, however, Idel's definition of theurgy addresses, if idiosyncratically, a difficulty that everyone else sees too: the difficulty of conceptualizing the human relation to God that is implied by religious action when that action is conceived as necessary to *anyone*. . . . If theurgy is defended as a divinely instituted action put in place on account of human necessity, acting upon the human soul alone, the problem appears susceptible to resolution. But it is not a perfect resolution, inasmuch as, from either a Jewish or Christian perspective, it is evident that any human being can choose not to be saved—can break the commandments, live an impure life, and ignore all God's work on his behalf. There is bound to be occasional anxiety about the effect of these failures on a system in which God and humankind appear to be so closely linked.[42]

To put this another way, if the human soul is a functional piece of the intra-divine system, then nothing can act on the soul "alone." Indeed, nothing can ever be wholly independent of God, but this is especially so, perhaps, where it is a question of the soul. John's vision helps bring the point home by virtue of the mirror language in which Christ shows John both what he is and what he must do. Where one gets close to the core of the sacrament of penance, in actual recognition of the gravity of error, there may be an anxiety that turns on a view of the intra-divine process as humanly contingent. It is not enough to recognize the ashen man as Christ; there is a corollary action required by John's sin, which, if it is not made, seems to leave the entire system in its debt. If John's use of the *ars notoria* has made God a penitent, then John must help supply the corrective, not by absolving God—an absurdity—but by his personal reformation, trying in the future to live more carefully, to construct a self in accordance with what he knows the divine will to be. John's self-formation is thus also God formation. Faith can make possible lucid and even dazzlingly beautiful renditions of the system in which this occurs, but until the perfect are truly perfected, nothing can make it easy.

The Thirty Prayers of John's *Liber florum* are all about this system; John's preliminary set of Seven Prayers starts with prayer *1, effectively a microcosm of the entire remaining six and the Thirty Prayers that follow, reflecting on the structure of the entire divine plan that ramifies through the incarnation. Deeply embedded in the unity of the divine plan is an idea of wisdom and perfect knowledge, which includes the liberal arts, philosophy, and theology. As the whole set of prayers is introduced by prayer *1, so it is closed by prayer 30, which is described as "the end of the prayers and a complement to them and for all the sciences."[43]

Opening with an echo of the incipit of Saint John's Gospel, prayer 30 meditates again on the beginning and end of the world, the whole cosmic cycle of procession and return, affirming the completeness of God both in eternity and in time:

> Word in the beginning and Word with God and God the Word, mystery inexplicable to human senses and wits, and ineffable sacrament, Father, Word, and Holy Spirit, heavenly witness, altitude incomprehensible, Trinity indivisible, essence unchangeable; Eyehye heser, eyheye,[44] lacking nothing before the beginning of the world, but being sufficient to yourself and remaining always in yourself and rejoicing: eternal deity, Alpha of all creatures, you who in your Word created all things from nothing at the beginning; Omega in whom all things will receive the terminus and end of mortal corruption, so that they may reassume you, the beginning, immortal and incorruptible in heritage and perpetual stability.[45]

The prayer goes on to request again the wisdom and knowledge sought by the whole art, making much of the abundance of divine grace and of human lack and sin, always in such a way as to emphasize God's completion and restoration of the defects by which human beings fall short of being all they are meant to be. John's request to be cleansed and restored comes (as it were) in one breath with his request for knowledge. Love and purification and knowledge are all one effect of grace, all one corrective for sin:

> How much more wretched is it possible for me to be, who was conceived in sin, born and nurtured in sin and all day every day I do not ever cease to sin. For that reason I want and desire to be cleansed. . . . wash me, Lord, from all my iniquity, and deign to clean me from all my contagion. . . . deign today kindly to infuse into the innermost parts of my mind the softest sweetness of your most pleasurable love and the riches of incomparable manifold wisdom and of your multiform grace; so that I may be perfectly understanding, unfailingly mindful, wisely eloquent, swift and elegant, praiseworthy and fluent in science, philosophy, theory, ethics, and logic.[46]

At this point John invokes the Tetragrammaton three times, his prayer stressing that Christ's redemption of humankind is what fulfills the mystery of the Tetragrammaton. In fact, John suggests, in fulfilling John's prayers for knowledge, God will be carrying forward the mercy begun by the incarnation, continuing it by enabling for John and other users of these prayers "the final gift of knowledge." Here, as before, John reinscribes the Trinity on the divine name, moving from the four-letter name to the tripartite JE EV VE:[47]

> Hear me lord Jesus Christ . . . you who are justly called by this name: Joth ✠ He ✠ Vaw ✠ Heth ✠ Je ev ve ✠ Jahweh, whose help today I have invoked upon me, and I have spoken this name as a help for my infirmity, whose mystery you have fulfilled by redeeming us from death. Give glory to your name and not to me, and act not towards me according to my sins nor apportion to me according to my iniquities, but according to your mercy, with which the world is full. Have mercy on me, grant me, through your ineffable grace, the ultimate gift of knowledge, you who marvelously deigned to bestow the gift of all sciences on king Solomon and on your holy apostles, through which I may clearly recognize the gift of your generosity towards me, so that by means of it I may be able to restrain myself from the impious way and walk more devoutly along the paths of your light.[48]

The completeness of knowledge, in particular the establishment of the curricular knowledge of the university in the individual, is here seen, rather interestingly, not as a reward for the perfect, but rather something that enables triumph over sin and temptation. It is part of the divine virtue that will enable John and others like him to carry forward the work of the dispensation.

The second and final part of this prayer returns once again to the Virgin. After Mary is invoked with a wide-ranging array of traditional epithets (she is the mother of her Father and daughter of her Son; she is Hester and Judith, conqueror of Satan and the stone that killed Goliath, and so on), John goes on to name her, via a complex metaphor of a tree bearing fruit of gems, as a variety of knowledge domains, including the liberal arts:

> You are the loftiest tree, adorned with gems of every virtue, whose fruit is a precious stone, the carnelian of charity, the topaz of knowledge, the jasper of judgment, the chrysolite of reverence, the onyx of domination, the beryl of power, the sapphire of virtue, the carbuncle of clarity, the emerald of virginity; whose roots are the lodestone of conjunction and the adamant of firmness; whose trunk is the marble of solidity and whose branches are the pearl of wisdom. You are the suitable understanding of grammar, true memory of the argument of dialectic, the ordered rhetoric of eloquence, the scales of geometry, the accumulation of arithmetic, the concord of music, the speculation of astronomy; the cognition of philosophy and the contemplation of theology; the knowledge of the mechanical arts, the operation of the exceptive ones; the recompense of vows, beseechings, and of all virtues, and the perfection, end, and glorious consummation of wisdom and knowledge.[49]

The blessed Virgin has a special and particular responsibility for the restoration of knowledge in John's account, connected not only to her role in delivering John's book (the specific remedy for the *ars notoria*) but also to the already long-established association of Mary with Wisdom, *Sapientia*, from which arose a natural link with the liberal arts and learning.[50] Mary's connection with the liberal arts is evidently so familiar to John that he makes her executrix of the prayers: as Mary delivered the book, now she must activate its power. As without Mary no enfleshment would have been possible for the Word, so without Mary no extension of divine mercy can be obtained by the Thirty Prayers. It is Mary who engages the operator's words with the divine engine that gives them agency:

> With your help, your book is finished by brother John, a monk, composed and fashioned at your license and directive in honor of your son, our lord Jesus Christ, and you, and the whole heavenly court, both for the salvation of my soul and of all those who enjoy and use it in a good way. And

now, lady and beloved, give honor to yourself and not to him, and watch over your word, promised by you to him, although unworthy, so that you do not permit the great prayers of this book spoken and pronounced by me to be brought to nothing, lest the devil . . . rejoice in it, perhaps thinking on this account that I seek from him what I can mercifully obtain, if it pleases you, from you and through you. Give power therefore, sweetest lady and my beloved, virgin Mary, to the book's holy words in the prayers spoken and uttered by me.[51]

This prayer, which may seem to steer dangerously close to threatening God with a failure of the dispensation if he does not comply with the operator's request, nevertheless articulates a dispensational understanding behind the book's knowledge goals. In this prayer, Mary represents the archetypal human intervention in the process by which the divine returns to itself. In a parallel that will become clearer and more explicit in the parts of the text to come under analysis in the next few chapters, John sees his book as an extension of the same salvific mechanism delivered through Mary initially by her parturition of the divine in Jesus Christ. The ritual of return embodied in John's book of prayers similarly represents a compensation for human error, an anagogical aid to the purgation, illumination, and perfection that both God and the operator intend to happen, but cannot be attained without grace. As an intervention harnessed to the mechanism already built to deliver grace into the world, John's book is like the Word delivered by Christ through Mary for the salvation of humankind; but it is a Word restored to words, enfleshed by individual operators, enabling them to take up the work of Mary, and follow Christ to heaven. John closes his thirtieth prayer with a sequence of brief addresses to Mary, the Trinity, and Christ, praising God and requesting intercession in words drawn from the liturgies of the feast of the Holy Trinity, Pentecost, and the Nativity of John the Evangelist.

John's Book of Prayers clearly embeds a strong theological narrative. Theology must understand divinity as perfect; however, it must also mediate human life, which cannot be. It must guard the sense but also the mystery at the heart of the Christian dispensation by adumbrating the closed system of divine perfection while remaining available, as a working discipline of knowledge, to mediate the stresses of an imperfect world. John's thirtieth prayer seems both conclusive and expansive in this sense. It is a cataphatic spilling forth of words that touches on and refracts all the personal, ritual, and theological ground just traversed and imagines it perfected. It gathers up everything he desires, envisioning it complete and perfect, part of the forward motion of the divine plan. It is a lovely final move in the liturgical language game.

Yet as final as this last piece of the Book of Prayers might feel, the *Liber florum* is not finished. Indeed, even as John is at work composing the set of ritual instructions for the Book of Prayers that he presciently calls the Prima Practica or First Procedure (already suggesting that there will be more than one such "procedure"), he is thinking about the next installment, which is to be a Book of Figures that will provide visual meditative anchors to be used with the prayers—a "second procedure," as he sometimes calls it. As he began to conceive it in 1308, this installment of the developing *Liber florum* looked more ambitious than anything he had written yet.

As it turned out, the path to knowing constituted in the Book of Figures was more difficult and beset with more unexpected twists and turns than John had any reason to suppose at the outset. A few scant years after the Book of Figures was completed, it was condemned—devastatingly, against his expectation—by certain "Barking Dogs," unnamed parties who were evidently ecclesiastical officials, probably from outside Morigny, of whom more later. The Book of Figures was then subject to a hasty rewrite connected to a new set of revelations from the divine. Is John's theology flexible enough—is it enough of an open system—to deal with the ecclesiastical condemnation of his work? How will the divine space itself open up to the task of making the necessary revisions?

The following chapters deal with the theology behind the renewal of John's sacred narrative in the Book of Figures, the twists and turns his knowing took, and the twists and turns of my own knowledge connected to the discovery of key parts of John's Old Compilation in the Bodleian Library. None of this could be straightforward, because each new revelation continued so stubbornly to be just what one did *not* expect.

Part 2 | RESTORATION

4

ERRORS OF INTELLECT, ERRORS OF WILL:
I ENCOUNTER THE BOOK OF FIGURES

The truth cannot force its way in when something else is occupying its place.

To convince someone of the truth, it is not enough to state it, but rather one must find the *path* from error to truth.

—Wittgenstein, "Remarks on Frazer's *Golden Bough*"

/(Tolstoy: the meaning (meaningfulness) of a subject lies in its being generally understandable.—That is both true and false. What makes a subject difficult to understand—if it is significant, important—is not that some special instruction about abstruse things is necessary to understand it. Rather it is the contrast between the understanding of the subject and what most people want to see. Because of this the very things that are most obvious can become the most difficult to understand. What has to be overcome is not a difficulty of the intellect, but of the will.)/

—Wittgenstein, "Philosophy: The Big Typescript"

One cannot avoid being wrong at least some of the time. It is the plague and the privilege of studying manuscripts that if one persists, one also cannot avoid *discovering* that one has been wrong at least some of the time. One finds that one's errors always involve both intellect and will because understanding and desire are not ever separate; the link between them is captured in the very idea of *quest*.

In a new area—in a case like John of Morigny's *Liber florum*—when the only prior interpretation is a brief, secondhand description of a condemned text, where the researcher starts only with the most basic tools of data gathering (dictionaries, indices) beyond the text itself, it happens that one must invent for one's self all the machinery of finding out. It is exciting to do this, but one can hardly help leaving the traces of one's initial wrong assumptions behind. One tries at once to admit and correct these errors (one ends up doing considerable penance for certain things), for one must, as Wittgenstein says, find the *path* from error to truth. But in so doing, in order to construct a coherent narrative, one is forced in some cases to bracket some of the missteps, or wash over them with forgiving generalities, as I shall do presently with my own work in *Conjuring Spirits*. This is not so much vanity as an exigency necessary to keep the narrative clear enough to comprehend.

The discovery of one's own wrongness is helped along partly because manuscript books are all unique—no handmade book can be an *exact* copy of another—so that even though part of what you discover on rereading anything connects in some degree to the specific ripeness of your mind at that precise moment, reading a different manuscript copy of a text is more informative than rereading a printed one. More is laid bare because there is more variance among the copies, each of which has been filtered through a slightly different human consciousness. Because one enters the system at a random point—there is no way to "choose" the first point of reference of one's discovery of some new text in manuscript, as one might do in building the syllabus for a class—there is in a certain sense more to be wrong *about* than in the study of texts already interpreted through printed books. Also, however, there are more corrective forces.

To put a geographic analogy into play, the game is like finding stepping-stones (solid data) over a bog (the ground one has a long view of, but does not yet know by walking on it). One aims to be strict in the essential disciplinary matter of not indulging what Wittgenstein suggests are "errors of will"—beliefs upheld by the desire for certain things to be true, or alternatively by the desire for certain things not to be manifested as *un*true (things regarded as "common sense," or things consistent with a pet theory about something else; this is why he calls it an error of "will"). The trick is that, where information is minimal, an imaginary stone may uphold one's weight just as well as a real one. Sometimes indeed one *needs* imaginary stones because one cannot get from A to B otherwise. These are speculations: facts that seem to fit with other data, but cannot be proven or disproven. Historical work is full of these inevitable and necessary made-up facts. Think of them as traverse points. One designs them on purpose to cross the bog, but one aims always to tread lightly and regard them as provisional. Occasionally these imaginary stones turn out to mark what is more or less solid ground underneath. Other times one indulges the accidental belief—the supposition that appears relatively green against a landscape of green, and that, because of this, one ends up treating as if it were solid ground when it is not. It stands in the way of the truth, taking up an imaginary space that looks real from a distance and is even to a certain extent weight bearing. If you don't pass that way very often, and go relatively quickly, and are not carrying too heavy a load, it can endure as solid on your mental map of the territory for quite some time.

In this second half of *Rewriting Magic* I will be looking at some of the parts of John's text that were initially quite difficult to interpret, and in which, as it turned out, some of my initial traverse points were set in rather undesirable locations. Otherwise put, I made vexing interpretive mistakes. Not coincidentally, this part of this book also looks at the way John himself came to know and rectify his most vexing early errors. For him, there could be no question of effacing these early traces of error, for the manner in which the book was circulated—by installments, each pushing forward a work already in the hands of his audience—meant that the text could not be other than a single book the whole time it was being written.[1] Each new installment must therefore not efface but complete the earlier parts of the story. However, beyond the simple needs of his narrative, the experience of finding himself wrong was actually far too important to John—too emotionally, spiritually, and intellectually formative—to cover up even if he had wanted to do so. He cannot maintain an untruth against all the evidence he has already provided about what happened; consequently, the *Liber florum* as a whole cannot do other than commemorate a process of finding, in some sense, the *real* truth of what happened. The *Liber florum*, or at least the parts of it that we have found so far, provides insight into one man's process of finding "the *path* from error to truth." It also compellingly shows the entwined and symbiotic processes of constructing a self in and through the construction of a book. We are privileged to see into John's knowledge as it leans, topples, and recovers, each recovery more difficult but also more bountiful in its yield.

The process feels familiar. For the manuscript scholar, the bracing experience of observing large sections of one's carefully built historical-theoretical scaffolding topple with the discovery of a single new manuscript is not all that uncommon. It is even possible to become somewhat addicted to that sense of shock to the system, so that one is always in some way seeking or at least hoping for that moment when one feels the thing that is "taking the place of the truth" begin to move out of the way. It is the scholar's addiction, a kind of intellectual bungee jump. You cannot die of it, or course, but the adrenalin is there because something at the very core of the self nevertheless *feels at risk*. Yet it is not, for the truth of the new thing upholds you as you put together a new self that can encompass the new knowledge. Part of the excitement is having no idea what will come next, beyond the dim but certain sense of the shape of something massive, something unquestionably real, actually *pushing* against the fragile vessel of one's own knowledge. What happens, when it results in new knowledge, also in some manner forces or catalyzes a transformation of the self.

I felt the warning tremor—the foreshock—of such a shift on a hot and humid day in July 2004 on opening the Oxford manuscript Bodleian Liturg. 160, which contained the first and still only known copy of the text accompanying what John called the "Old Compilation of Figures." In order to appreciate the simplicity of my knowledge prior to this discovery, I quote here some of the least wrong parts of my own conclusions and speculation about the "Old Compilation" from my 1998 chapter in *Conjuring Spirits*:

> John makes reference to "a compilation of figures made and published by us in the beginning." It is unclear what this "compilation of figures" is, at what point (or at the beginning of what) it was made, or whether it was intended for inclusion in the [book] or not. The fact that it was published "in the beginning" . . . suggests at least that it may have been prepared before this text, and separately circulated. There are no figures, diagrams or drawings associated with the [book] in Clm 276 (John refers at one point to a figure in the form of a ring associated with "the prayer of investigation of Scripture"—but that figure does not seem to be included in this manuscript). Tantalizingly, however, the condemnation in the *Grandes Chroniques* refers to images which John included in his books—chiefly, it would appear, images of the Virgin. . . .
>
> There remains some chance that the unexamined manuscripts will actually contain the figures that may have been intended for use with this text. However, for the moment, I would direct the reader's attention to the way this reference to "a compilation of figures made and published in the beginning by us" suggests John had some sort of public life even prior to the composition of [this book]—that he was writing, compiling and even circulating other works, to however small an audience, either during the period of lapse after his first set of revelations, or possibly even earlier, at the time when he was occupied with "chasing after the exceptive arts."[2]
>
> A little farther on, John refers again to an "antiqua compilatio" as well as "nova compilatio." . . . Here the "antiqua compilatio" is referred to, not (apparently) as a collection of figures, but as another ritual text, also claiming a visionary basis, and written before "this book" in a manner that "prefigures" it. By saying that "God himself and the Blessed Virgin Mary" were responsible for the completion of "this book," John suggests that the old compilation is in some manner the origin (perhaps a preliminary draft?) of this one.

> ... Certainly, as I have already shown, the redactions of the [book] already available to us show the influence of the Solomonic [*ars notoria*] in many aspects of its structure and arrangement, and John has explicitly acknowledged that he has drawn "good and divine words" therefrom. It is tempting to speculate that the "antiqua compilatio" included a collection of images drawn from or inspired by those in the Solomonic Ars Notoria, and with a similar function.[3]

I was basing this analysis on the scant and partial chapters from the end of what turned out to be a defective text in Clm 276. The framing materials of the *Liber florum* prayers in this manuscript are extremely brief and idiosyncratically arranged: not only is the entire Book of Visions missing but so also is most of the last third of John's book (i.e., most of the First Procedure and the Book of Figures), of which only a few mangled scraps and snippets are preserved. No "Book of Figures" is announced; the end matter skips from the opening paragraph of the First Procedure to the last three chapters of the Book of Figures,[4] after that jumping directly back to chapter 1 of the First Procedure, which it leaves unfinished in the middle of the page. In the end, Clm 276 preserves only about 7 percent of the book's final matter, and only about 50 percent of the New Compilation text as it survives in the most complete manuscripts.[5] The passages on which I drew to substantiate my speculations in *Conjuring Spirits* actually came from the part of the work that is, in other manuscripts, designated as the New Compilation Book of Figures, though I did not know it at the time. If I had been able to do a full comparison of Clm 276 to Graz University Library 680 I would have known more, but the printer's devil was at the door, and when *Conjuring Spirits* went to press I had no idea how much new information was waiting to be discovered at the end of the Graz manuscript text.

Despite the slender and partly opaque nature of my window onto John's work in 1998, I had deduced a few things correctly. By the time we completed our new transcription of the full text in the Graz manuscript, it became clear that the Old Compilation of Figures *was* the origin of the New, evidently an early version of it (though as it later turned out, the New Book of Figures is so completely different from the Old as to make the term "draft" quite wrong). Certain other things John pinpoints with habitual specificity—dates, for example. He writes that he began the New Compilation of Figures around vespers on the Ides of August, 1315.[6] Several other similarly precise internal dates scattered through the text make it evident that he finished perhaps late in 1315, or not later than early in 1316, so the whole New Compilation Book of Figures as it survives in the best manuscripts was written in just a few months—in great haste, compared to his normal rate of composition. As for images, the New Compilation of Figures was intended to contain seven images of the Virgin; the Book of Prayers was to hold as well an image of Christ as described in the Apocalypse, with two swords coming out of his mouth, illuminating the first letter O of the first prayer in the book, "O Rex regum." Careful specifications for the content of all these images are given in all complete copies of the Book of Figures; the main elements of the images of the Virgin include, centrally, the Virgin standing, holding her child in one arm, and in the other a specified plant or flower. In the last four images, a bird above or near the plant is also specified. The seven plants were a lily, a rose, a vine with grape clusters, an olive, a palm frond, a cypress branch, and a pomegranate. The birds in the last four images were a dove (over the olive); a phoenix (over the palm); a pelican (over the cypress); and an eagle (over the pomegranate).[7] Executed images of the program described here are extant in two known manuscripts.[8]

A more unexpected thing became clear at this point as well: the New Book of Figures was John's response to a *condemnation* of the Old. This was the first indication we had that the 1323 burning recorded in the Chronicle was not in fact the first brush John had had with more critical readers of his work. But in this regard the New Compilation Book of Figures raised as many questions as it answered. The evidence scattered throughout the book for the theological and legal grounds of the accusation is very interesting, and it will be more closely considered in the following chapters, yet the *dramatis personae* are veiled. The accusers remain unnamed; they are simply called "Barking Dogs"— an old and generic term of opprobrium for troublemakers, carpers, quarrelsome persons, heretics.[9] How the work came into their hands is not made clear either. These passages from the opening chapter of the Book of Figures of the New Compilation lay the ground for what we know:

> After I obtained a license in canon law at Orléans (with the blessed, glorious virgin Mary aiding and predicting figurally in dreams that I would receive it, and firmly promising me that I would obtain it without doubt), I heard and considered certain ones of the seed not of Judah but of Canaan who were growling with rabid bite in the fashion of barking dogs. They were inveighing against the figures of this science composed by me with the counsel of the glorious Virgin and afterwards confirmed by her, as appears in the Old Book of Figures and is more fully contained there; detracting from this knowledge and from the holy figures; gnawing with poisoned tongue at the grace of the Holy Spirit; receding from God, and saying to him, "Go away from us, we do not want knowledge of your ways"; seeing good things and despising to learn them.

Then, because they were saying that these figures had been composed in the manner of necromantic figures, because of the crosses and circles on them; and then too because considerations of planets and daily cycles were established in these figures and in the prayers that had to be said . . . a sort of scandal arose as a result of this science. . . . And so, by my own counsel with the mandate of the glorious Virgin, I considered—not only to avoid the aforesaid scandal now risen, since it was brought about by dogs and not by the faithful, but rather because of the difficulty of uttering the prayers with the figures, because it could scarcely be managed by anyone—how to change the said figures that were previously in the cross and circles—the images of the glorious Virgin only. . . .

Because already, with the Devil gaining ground among the children of disobedience, he so much prevailed that people seeing me shook their heads in mockery; they spoke against me saying, "There goes the Dreamer [Ecce, Sompniator]," believing that I did not know their hearts.[10]

While John never names the Barking Dogs, scattered pieces of evidence from other parts of *Liber florum* make it seem unlikely that the attacks originated at the Abbey of Morigny. As noted early in the Book of Visions, John had a responsible position as *prepositus* or provost, the person who managed tithes and rents for the monastery—an appointment he would not have achieved without the trust and respect of the abbot.[11] Second, from textual evidence that emerges later in the book it appears that the Barking Dogs had training in canon law. This makes it unlikely on the face of it that John's monastic peers were responsible for launching the critique, since John would not probably have been sent to Orléans to study law had there been many resident legal experts already in place at Morigny (i.e., John *was* the legal expert at Morigny). The likelihood is thus that the attack came from parties outside John's community, and indeed the rhetoric transmitting John's anger and distress—the description calling the Barkers the "seed not of Judah but of Canaan," saying "we do not want knowledge of your ways"—could also be read as suggesting an attack brought by outsiders.

Who they were can only be a matter for speculation. Condemnations were hardly an uncommon feature of intellectual life in early fourteenth-century France, as John is clearly aware. Nobody was immune to them.[12] Yet in order for a work to be condemned it has to get some attention. It is possible that John's circle of correspondents, the operators and copyists of his work, had expanded widely enough for the book to have attracted such attention outside Morigny,[13] though it seems to me now, given the number and complexity of the original figures, that it would not have been able to spread very fast. In the passages just quoted, John himself speaks of how difficult the figures are to use with the prayers, and it looks as though there were complaints from operators about their original form that would probably have meant slow distribution. Yet if the prayer book had circulated widely enough beforehand for users to be discussing the problems about the figures among themselves, it might have attracted attention for this very reason. Perhaps John had an enemy who called for the book's investigation by outside authorities; perhaps, on the other hand, it was not enemies but friends of John who initially brought the developing book to the attention of an expert theological reviewer in hopes of getting approval for its broader distribution, and the attempt backfired.

Whatever may have been the cause of the initial attack, once John's work was known to have been criticized, others more local to the situation must have chimed in. John asserts that people who saw him mocked him with the epithet "Sompniator" ("dreamer," and perhaps "magician"), though the structure of this passage may have been designed for rhetorical effect.[14] Such a potent charge is quite likely to have affected John's fellow monks and others in the environs of Morigny in ways he did not anticipate. Elsewhere John mentions trials and tribulations connected to the scandal, which may have included mockery, gentle or otherwise.

It is interesting how strongly and with what assurance John presses forward against this first difficulty, and the manner in which he does so is interesting, too. The opening announcement of his successful attainment of his own degree in canon law—a degree, like the book itself, backed by the virgin Mary—establishes his authority to speak as an equal to the attackers on the dual grounds of his advanced education and visionary capacity. He is obviously taken aback by the charges—enough, at any rate, to begin changing some of the images, though it seems quite likely that complaints about the complexity of the text offered a real reason for revision as well.[15] This initial move ultimately becomes an entirely new version of the Book of Figures that evolves rapidly under the advice and guidance of various visionary authorities, including Mary, the archangel Michael, even God the Father. Throughout the book, however, John remains forthright and adamant in his defense of the orthodoxy of the work and the authenticity of his visionary contact with the virgin Mary.

But many questions hang fire, not answered by the New Compilation of Figures, especially as concerns the Old Compilation itself. What did the figures of the Old Compilation look like? How did they differ from the New? How many of them did the book contain? Most perplexingly, what did the Barking Dogs actually mean by "necromantic" in this context? It is odd here that the *ars notoria*, so important to the 1323 condemnation and the whole later history of the work, is not mentioned at all. John himself is preoccupied with distinguishing his own work from the *ars notoria* throughout the *Liber florum,* even from the period of the Thirty Prayers, so that one would hardly expect a charge of "reviving the *ars notoria*" or "using *ars notoria*-like figures" to go unreported by him if anything like this had been said. While for some people in the Middle Ages the *ars notoria* might sometimes be subsumed in an idea of "necromancy," for John, a distinction tended to be maintained. At the very least, "necromancy" was a generality, a category designating an assemblage of practices comprising many texts, whereas "*ars notoria*" was specific: it was *the* text and practice the *Liber florum* sought to replace. Thus it seems to me that it could not have been the primary intent of the Barking Dogs to suggest that the book had *ars notoria*-like features. What the figures actually looked like remained a mystery.

Which brings me back to that hot July afternoon in 2004. Scanning through manuscript catalogues prior to my visit to Oxford, I had stumbled upon the description of a manuscript that certainly contained writing by John of Morigny and needed a look, Bodleian Liturg. 160. The catalogue description runs thus:

> Visions, prayers, and rhapsodies of "Johannes de Carnoto, monachus de Morigniaco," i.e. of the Benedictine abbey of Morigny (Maurigniacum), near Étampes, composed in 1301-4, but here copied about a century later.... The whole composition is of a mystic kind, and consists chiefly of "orationes," half didactic ("ad omnes artes sciendas," fol. 41), half religious, with many sub-titles and divisions—a summary is given on fol. 68, where also the Hebrew and Greek alphabets are written.[16]

The last bit about the "summary" on fol. 68, where "also the Hebrew and Greek alphabets are written," did strike me as odd; there was no such thing in the copies of the text I knew, neither summary nor alphabets, in fact, but my assumption to begin with was that another text had been tacked on to the end of the *Liber florum* in the manuscript, and the cataloguer, careful as he was, had somehow missed this. The byname "Johannes de Carnoto" (John of Chartres) was also unique, though perfectly reasonable; John is explicit about his schooling there. The dates 1301-4 were unusual (most manuscripts we had seen read 1304-7 in the spot where dates of composition were given), but might be a copyist error. Thus I went to Oxford prepared to explain away all the small indications that *this* book was different.

In the Bodleian I was handed a small codex just over six by four inches, the script proportionally small in scale. It had been rebound very tightly and it only opened to about 90 degrees. Especially after the brightness of the summer day outside, the lighting in the Bodleian was such that my normal reading glasses (magnification 1) did not cut the murk enough to decipher the script. It was only after I fished out my second pair of spectacles that I really grasped what I was seeing. The text was familiar, but the image was not. The figure in the lower right quadrant was one that I had never seen before, neither in other copies of John's book nor anywhere else. It was the iceberg bumping gently against the hull of everything I thought I knew. The figure was neither large nor clear; I here show it at somewhat larger than its actual size (fig. 1).

Fig. 1   Bodleian Library, University of Oxford, fol. 1r.

The whole of that first page was somewhat rubbed and faded, but as noted earlier, the text was more or less familiar. I recognized the prayer above the figure, which combines an invocation of the Tetragrammaton with a gloss tying the four letters of the divine name to the incarnation and passion. The prayer was in our other manuscripts too. It runs:

Ioth: God of intellect and understanding;
   (Jesus Christ, beginning of life)
He: God of perfect retentiveness and memory;
   (You who through the yoke of the cross)
Vau: God of reason and eloquence;
   (Through the death of the Passion)

Heth:[17] God of stability and perfection and perseverance, fount of all grace, of wisdom, knowledge and prudence;
(Became the life of all:)
Begin now, set, perfect, fashion, fulfill in me, you who are as I have spoken above. Amen.[18]

This prayer appeared twice in the book as I knew it, once at the very end of the *Liber florum*, at the close of the Book of Figures, and once on the page meant to open the book, the Ritual Prologue. In some copies this page comes at the head of the Book of Prayers, but here in the Oxford manuscript it appeared on the page before me, at the front of the whole work (as it is clearly meant to do, and does in some of our New Compilation manuscripts as well).

But here it appears with a twist, for although the New Compilation retains an instruction in the Ritual Prologue, "hic debet esse figura" (here there should be a figure), no manuscript I had yet seen retained any figure. In the last part of the New Compilation of Figures, John explains, "in the Old Compilation this prayer had its own figure, but not in this one. . . . Whence, when you say it, let the form of a ring be mentally visualized."[19] Even without looking further into Bodleian Liturg. 160, the fact that there was a complex figure—not an instruction for a mental visualization—associated with this particular prayer was strong evidence that this was a copy in the tradition of the Old Compilation.

Despite the worn condition of the page, I was able to work out some of what was going on in the image because the letters were obviously initial letters of words that occurred in the prayer itself. My notebook shows a crude drawing of the image, with the letters transcribed and their associations extrapolated. The letters in the four small circles are Latin versions of the letters of the Tetragrammaton: *I* (ioth) at north, *He* at south, *W* (vau) at west, and *Ht* (heth) at east. The letters nearby in each case are the initials of the intellectual powers associated with these letters in the prayer: IN (*intellectus, intelligentia*) at north, MR (*memoria, reminiscentia*) at south, EF (*eloquentia, facundia*) at west, and SP (*stabilitas, perseverantia*) at east. The middle letters were harder to make out, but included an *M* (perhaps for "Maria") and what might have been letters from the operator's name. The figure struck me not only as being obviously different from the style of figures in the New Compilation, but also, and at the same time, not really consistent with what I knew of figures in necromancy (despite the cross with circles on it), nor indeed really consistent with the *ars notoria* figures either[20]—though in all cases reminiscent enough for the whole puzzle to be worth further thought.

There was one more anomaly on this first page which made the whole ritual operation a little more complicated than the one we find in the New Compilation: the figure is preceded by a *cogitatio* unique to this manuscript, not all of it legible, but enough to work out most of the intended image: "Imagine here, after these things have been said, that <you are at the ga>te of paradise and that an angel is opening it for you."[21] This instruction does not occur in any of our New Compilation manuscripts, though it does further the first visualization, meant to be used with the prayers of the Ritual Prologue in both texts: "Imagine that you are on the road to paradise." In effect this is a second stage to the ritual, one that is meant to be put in place after the prayers are said, in which the visualization is evoked just after the figure has been inspected, or perhaps while the operator is still looking at it.

It is hard to see how this meditation in practice would not end up conflating the figure with the visualization, into an amalgam where the figure becomes part of the gate of paradise—trying to hold both in mind, or in the transition from one to the other, it is possible to imagine a gate shaped something like the figure, or with something like the figure inscribed on it. This would not be inappropriate, of course, since the prayer itself depicts a complex in which lines respecting God the father (represented by the Tetragrammaton, associated with the faculties of memory and so on as aspects of Wisdom) are interwoven with lines respecting Christ's passion, the salvific engine of the dispensation, ending with a plea for the fulfillment of that dispensation with respect to the person of the operator. The figure, in short, is or represents a kind of gate to paradise, by its initial letters, and by the sign of the cross that structures it, insofar as these things—the passion in particular—contain all that the operator seeks that is relevant to the restoration of soul to make it congruent to paradise. Otherwise put, the diagram is of a soul-making or soul-regenerating machine, in which the foundational skills of learning are embedded in the pattern of divine disclosure that enables the ascent to heaven.

While the *ars notoria* figures might have had similar goals in pragmatic terms (that is, they aim at the restoration of the operator to the Adamic state, by virtue of which all knowledge is to be laid open in the mind), one does not find there any instruction for a visualization quite this complicated, nor any figure whose signification is quite this legible in its compression, or quite this Christocentric. When one grasps the connection between the figure and the gate to paradise in John's book, and thereby grasps the sense in which the figure is meant to be used, it becomes hard to see the figure as looking "necromantic." It seems like a devotional meditation. (Again, despite the cross and circles—it is vexing that one can pretty well imagine what the figure might have looked like to the Barking Dogs, even while one is rebelling against their understanding of its purport.)

Having worked out the relation between the figure and prayer to my own satisfaction, I went out to do what I always did when I found something engrossingly interesting in a John of Morigny manuscript: sought an Internet cafe in order to consume coffee while writing an email to Nicholas. I described the figure and transcribed my own notes on it as best I could. I remember his caution (a scholar's caution): was I absolutely certain, he asked, that it was not another writer interpolating a figure into our standard New Compilation text? After all, we did know versions redacted by other compilers, more than one at this point. Then too, there is actually an instruction to put a figure there in the text. I actually *was* certain that it was John's work, had been so in fact from the moment I opened the book. I could see his mark was on it, recognized it, just as one can walk into a seventeenth-century gallery in any museum and pick out a painting by Rembrandt from a distance, or as one can hear Mozart without knowing what work of his may be playing on the radio. But I also knew that I had not actually transcribed enough of the manuscript to prove it.

Back in the Bodleian, I wasted no more time at the beginning of the text, which seemed similar to the books we already had, but went leafing quickly through to the end to see what the Book of Figures looked like. I found a rubric for it on folio 55. Clearly, the following folios were intended to contain a sort of procedural or instructional manual for the use of John's varied array of devotional devices: "Here begins the Book of Figures of the blessed and undefiled mother of God, Mary. How one should operate through all the prayers, figures and visualizations of this art of the blessed Mary for all the arts to be known and obtained through the prayers of the selfsame Virgin."[22] In this part of the book I found what was obviously a different text and yet ample evidence to support authorship by John of Morigny. There were more interesting visions and cross-references to the *Liber visionum* in evidence here and there. I transcribed what I could get. Unfortunately the book seemed disappointingly lacking in figures as such (though the Greek and Hebrew alphabets mentioned by the cataloguer were definitely present, definitely part of John's book and not something else). One other figure did jump out at me though, on folio 66r, just three leaves before the end of the book. This was a pentangle with a cross at the center holding a monogram for Jesus Christ, IHV XPI, in alternating red and black letters above and below the horizontal arm. The words radiating down from the top letter *M*, "Mater misericordie," undoubtedly stood for Mary,[23] though I did not at first see her name in the confusing braid of letters on the figure, here again reproduced somewhat larger than its actual size (fig. 2).

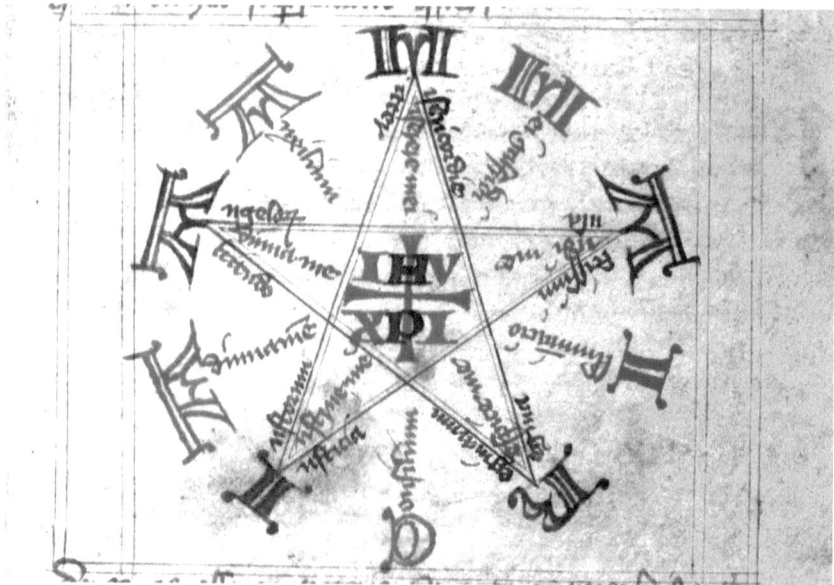

Fig. 2 Bodleian Library, University of Oxford, fol. 66r.

At first glance this figure might also seem to bear a resemblance to classic figures of necromancy.[24] Certainly the pentangle has floated around in magic texts of all sorts since antiquity. It does not necessarily denote necromancy, of course, and indeed many medievalists know it as the esoteric symbol on the front of Gawain's shield in the Middle English poem *Gawain and the Green Knight*, where it is closely associated with Mary as well; as the poet explains, the five sides of the figure signify Gawain's faultlessness in his five wits, the unfailing grip of his five fingers, the five wounds of Christ, and the five joys of Mary. An image of Mary herself is depicted on the verso of the shield, where Gawain alone can see her. She is tied to the pentangle through the design of the entire object, which is a shield in more than one sense—an apotropaic device with both physical and spiritual protective functions.[25]

The figure in John's text is also tied to Mary, but it represents her not through an image, but through letters, also intertwined in a complex manner. I did, after a bit more scrutiny, figure out where her name was in the figure. The capital letters at the tops of the points are done in black. Starting with the *M* on the northernmost compass point, they spell the name MARIA. The capital letters between the points are done in red (thus allowing the viewer who has the image in color to track their interlacing with the letters of the name MARIA). Starting with the *A* immediately due west of the *M*, they spell AMICA. Taken sequentially, reading clockwise twice around the circle, the letters read something like "Mary, beloved" or "Beloved Mary," depending on whether one begins with the red or the black lettering.

The letter play does not end here, for the words radiating from the endpoints of the pentangle each begin with the letter that tops the point, forming a prayer, and there are words also radiating from the letters between the points, which are part of the prayer too. These are the Latin words of the figure, reading clockwise from the *A* just left (west) of the *M* at the top (north) of the figure; italics indicate rubrication.

   Auxilium
/ Mater | *Miserere mei* \ Misericordie
   Mei Galfridi
/ Aula | *Audi me* \ Altissimi
   Illuminatio
/ Regina | *Respice me* \ Reginarum
   Consilium
/ Iusticia | *Instrue me* \ Iustorum
   Adiuuamen
/ Altitudo | *Adiuua me* \ Angelorum

As noted earlier, the central cross contains a monogram, IHV XPI, for "Ihesu Christi." Because the prayer is transcribed elsewhere in the text, it is possible to see its syntax and know that all the letters in the figure are parts of the prayer: that one "reads" clockwise around the points to the center of the figure, and then clockwise around the spaces between the points. "Ihesu Christi" is meant to be repeated after each line. No letters are unused. In English the prayer runs: "Maria, mother of mercy of Jesus Christ, court of the most High of Jesus Christ, queen of queens of Jesus Christ, justice of the just of Jesus Christ, altitude of angels of Jesus Christ, friend, support, of me, Geoffrey; illumination, counsel, assistance: have mercy on me, hear me, look on me, instruct me, assist me."[26] The pentangle inscribed here is called the "general figure of the experiment for having a vision," and in the text associated with the image, John describes a ritual involving this figure that helps recover visions when they have been lost due to disobedience. The action of the figure is thus represented as instrumental, in a certain sense; however, since the whole ritual is also an act of purgation, to be done following a conventional penance, it is hardly any more (or indeed any less) instrumental than any other penitential rite. The ritual of the pentangle is likewise designed—like any other purgation—to work on the soul of the operator, in part by focusing the operator's mind on key aspects of the divinity he strives to emulate. The figure with its interwoven words represents, and contains a plea for, Mary's intercession; Christ's monogram is positioned so as to occupy a womblike space in the pentagon at the center of the figure. If the pentangle, used along with its prayers, furthers the instrumental goal of obtaining a vision or recovering a lost visionary capacity, it also centers the Christian viewer cognitively, visually, formally in the flesh of Christ embedded in the mercy of Mary, both implicated in (perhaps also complicated by?) the letters of their names. One needs to remember that if a vision follows, it happens as a result of God's will after the operator's internal and spiritual cleansing, not as an automatic result of the figure, which itself is no more than an aid in the process. In this sense, although it may be mysterious initially, the intent of the deciphered figure is surely legible as genuinely Catholic and authentically devotional.

Obviously there remains a vast range of things I did not know then, and still do not and cannot know, about John's Old Compilation practice, absent the rest of the figures. Every layer of each configuration of letters and symbols has meaning, and much of that meaning is visually conveyed. It seems probable that a good deal of the ritual instruction went missing with the figures, too; in any event it is clear that there was more instruction at one time, since John sometimes references instructions in parts of the book that are not there in our copy. Yet despite these gaps, a few more things about the figures can be deduced from other matter in the book.

In one place, near the midpoint of the Book of Figures, under the rubric "Chapter concerning the letters and writings on the figures," there is a list of "letterings" for inscription on individual figures that conveniently serves as a list of figures as well.[27] When one adds up the list, combining it with the seven figures of the Virgin, the seven planetary figures, and the twelve zodiacal figures (whose lettering is said to be described in another location, "after them, in the book in which they are contained"[28]), it becomes clear that the Old Compilation originally contained ninety-one figures.[29] John offers descriptions of the first fourteen of these, the seven figures of the Virgin and seven planetary figures, in enough detail to have allowed their reconstruction by operators.[30] He also mentions figures of the twelve houses, though these are not described.[31] Another chapter makes it clear that not only were all the figures intended to contain two initials of the operator's name, but the first twenty-six figures (those with the images of Mary, the planets, and the twelve houses) were also supposed to bear a more complex form of lettering, which would have taken some time to do. Here is an extract from John's instructions:

The figures are lettered with the operator's name mixed with the name of the blessed Mary, and with the letters of the names of the property of the figures, and situated in the figures in the form of a cross, thus: one letter (namely the first) is taken from the name of the blessed Mary; and of the next name according to the property of the figure, and the next from the name of the operator, and they are conjoined and situated in the figures one after another; thus, in the form of a cross; and it must be done in this way using the other letters in the name of the blessed Mary, and the names of the properties of the figures, and the operator's name, always repeating the letters of the operator's name as many times as there are letters in the name of the blessed Mary and in the names of the properties of the figures. And this is to be understood concerning the figures at the beginning all the way to the figures of the twelve houses. But in the other following figures, two letters of the operator's name with the name of the blessed Mary and the name of the figure's property suffice.[32]

Clearly, the braid signifies the interrelated nature of the operator, Mary, and the aspect of the cosmos represented by the property of the figure. As far as I am able to reconstruct the pattern, the letter braid described in this passage would have looked something like the bold letters crossing each other in the figure below, where the gray letters with the names Mary, John, and Luna (the "property" of the figure of the moon, presumably) are meant as a reference to show how the braid comes together (fig. 3). The shape formed by the letters—a cross—signifies the passion of Christ and the event of the incarnation more generally. The letters mingling Mary's name with the operator's thus become the "flesh" of the cross, the flesh shared between the operator and Christ through Mary.

Such letter games are not without precedent in the tradition of *carmina figurata*. While these significations are undoubtedly implicit in the lettering, it is also true that the mixed form of the letters moves them away from immediate legibility; although the letters are there only because they have meaning, they are not, in the context of the figure, *meant to be read*. The figure moves the signification of the characters to the very limit of what is speakable and legible. In this sense the letter braid seems as if it has a meditative function similar to the *ars notoria notae*, which likewise contain words and characters at the limit of the legible, intended not to encourage rational thought but to dissipate it. Yet a strong difference does exist between John's letter braids and the *notae* of the *ars notoria*: the rationale behind the obscure signs and characters is never explicated in the *ars notoria*, which throughout advertises the mystery and inscrutability of its symbols rather than their exegesis. John seeks to make the

Fig. 3 Letter braid.

mysteries of his text in some sense *transparent* through his writing. Their obscurity *in situ* is a by-product of the mode of praxis, not a principle of its action, which is legibly Catholic. The thinking behind it draws on a working theological understanding of the whole dispensation; it is not intended as mere mystification (though that may be the effect it has on the noninitiate).

Only the shallowest and vaguest sketch of the turbid complexity of these figures was I capable of rendering when I went back to that Internet cafe to tangle with Nicholas's objections again. While there were all sorts of influences moving around under the surface of things here that I could hardly see into at all, it was patent that the figures were too idiosyncratic, as well as too deeply enmeshed with all the other extant parts of the *Liber florum*, to be anyone's work but John's. Even so, Nicholas took some convincing, and I remember finally reaching a zone of frustration in which I felt compelled to tell him point-blank, "it *is* the Old Compilation, Nicholas, it really is!" What I could never have suspected about this work before I had a chance to see it, aside from its idiosyncrasy, was its theological and devotional seriousness. I found both aspects of this text quite difficult to convey in those first emails. Of course it was not quite like any form of devotional praxis I'd ever seen before; nevertheless, I was sure I had been wrong in my *Conjuring Spirits* article to suggest that the Old Compilation might contain anything at all like the *notae* of the *ars notoria*. It wasn't; this was another animal entirely. The original Book of Figures was so much its own thing that no one but John could have done it.

If Nicholas had any lingering doubts about the authenticity of this work after our conversation, he came round fully as soon as he saw the book, which happened a scant few weeks later, before the digital reproduction had been finished or delivered to us. The visual impact of that first page somehow lays all doubt to rest. There was much more than this that passed between us in a stream of emails over the next few months, a mass of excited findings of details differing between this manuscript and all our others. In his own time in the Bodleian, Nicholas, paying attention to slightly different parts of the book, picked up masses of new data about the prayers, finding that they lacked all the visual meditations, that there were many more evidences of revision, and that in a few crucial cases, there were clearer and obviously more correct readings of passages that had been corrupted in the tradition of our New Compilation manuscripts—cruces that we'd been puzzling over for years were suddenly capable of resolution. This was exciting, though it also led to a temporary but thorough devastation of our editing process. First, it obliged a complete re-realization of the New Compilation Book of Figures (which we had only just finished). Second, it put our editorial method into crisis: Nicholas wanted to draw on the clearer and better readings of the prayers offered by the Oxford manuscript, and I (at least some of the time) wondered whether it was right to mix textual traditions that seemed so clearly to be unrelated to each other. Suddenly, it was as though we had a *double reading* of everything, or more precisely, as though overlapping views of early and late versions were merging into a three-dimensional image as we sought urgently to hold both in focus at once. How to keep all this clear? The impression of occasional disjointedness we had gotten originally from the New Compilation copy, which we'd once suggested might be a result of haste or carelessness on John's part, now translated into an impression of the very reverse of haste: a symptom of excessive care and long handling, of revision upon revision.

That this was a work that had been rewritten not once but many times was patent not only from the evidence of successive strata in the prayers and the Book of Visions (the entire Old Compilation text had obviously been revised at least once before 1315), but also from John's careful documentation of the process of composition as he interacted with the Virgin over the Old Compilation of Figures. This process, too, was other than one might expect, because it shows from the first an unaccountable *resistance* to the project of the figures on the part of the virgin Mary. In the first chapters of the Old Compilation Book of Figures, John relates a series of visions that took place in 1308 (this is about four years after the *ars notoria* had been laid aside and the licensing vision for the

Book of Prayers was received, probably in 1304). In recording his repeated unsuccessful attempts to obtain the Virgin's consent for the Figures preliminary to this project (resulting only in a somewhat ambiguous gesture of interest, her "negative assent," as he calls it), John relates Mary's short speeches verbatim, like a lover the more anxious to preserve the beloved's words in memory because they are ambiguous. (Has she broken with me? Or not?) The first of these visions gives the flavor of his account:

> After I composed the prayers written down above, with a sort of particular or introductory or preparatory procedure for them, as noted already, I set to work on getting the license and backing of the glorious Virgin for composing the figures. And for this composition I sought license from my lady and beloved, the glorious Virgin, by praying and supplicating very devoutly, with my heart perfect and clean. And I, John, was put in an ecstasy. She appeared to me in our church of the Holy Trinity at Morigny on the altar. And I said to her, "My lady and my beloved, will I now be able to complete the book I have begun?" Smiling, she responded most sweetly, "No." And she held her foot out towards me so that I might kiss it. And I kissed it, and immediately woke up.
>
> And wondering and fearing, I said in my heart, "Perhaps she has denied me at first, not so that I won't undertake the book, but so that while composing it I might ask her more ardently about it. And the sign of this to me was that she was smiling when she denied me. And because of this I will set to work on the book as well as I am able, while always asking her for it." And so I did. But in point of fact, there are two pertinent meanings here; one of them I have already given, and the other follows, but I did not understand it right away, not until a long time afterwards. And it is this: the blessed Virgin spoke the truth to me when she said that I would not be able to "complete" my book, namely in regard to the *bringing to effect* of all its operations, not the *writing of the composition*—because as to that, she was intending only that I should seek more ardently. But for the effective completion of this art, the operator must work through all its operations to all the arts and sciences, and for all these I did not work through the book for the reason that is described above before the Prayers in the last chapter of the Visions; and thus she spoke the truth to me in both meanings.[33]

The form of the question John puts to the Virgin is interesting; it is notable that he does not ask in specific terms for license to compose a new "Book of Figures" (as he did, for example, with the Thirty Prayers).[34] Rather, he asks only generally if he will be able to "complete the book he started." His subsequent comments make it clear that by "the book" he means not the Book of Figures in itself but the entire *Liber florum*, including all the prayers, as suggested by his reference to "working through all of the book"—which he did not do in order to gain all the arts and sciences, because he had already done this with the *ars notoria*.[35]

At this stage, then, the "Book of Figures" in John's mind is not a new or additional work, but the final part of the *Liber florum*, a complement to the prayers, necessary to fill out the liturgy already in place. From this perspective John may well have been puzzled to find the Virgin denying him a request to "complete" the project—a book that she had approved to start with, at least in principle, and on which she had shown a general willingness to collaborate up to this point. His feeling that she denied his request because she wanted him to "ask more ardently" is not an unreasonable hypothesis under the circumstances. It has a precedent in monastic custom, as prescribed in Cassian and summarized in the Benedictine Rule, chapter 58: "Do not grant newcomers to the monastic life an easy entry, but, as the Apostle says, *Test the spirits to see if they are from God* (1 John 4:1). Therefore, if someone comes and keeps on knocking at the door, and if, at the end of four or five days he has shown himself patient in bearing his harsh treatment and the difficulty of entry, and has persisted in his request, then he should be allowed to enter and stay in the guest quarters for a few days."[36] This is also the model of "testing the spirits" that seems to be in play at the beginning of the chapter of the Book of Visions in which he teaches Bridget to read (I.iii.1), where it would appear that he denies her at first only in order to make sure that her will does not falter and that she is truly serious about the project. John notes, too, in the general advice about the Virgin's modes of apparition and behavior, that "sometimes at first she denies the requested or sought for things, not so that [the operator] may not obtain them, but so that after that he may seek them more ardently; and later she concedes them when they are solicitously sought."[37] The rule of interpreting initial denial as a kind of test is a familiar pattern of thinking for John, and even though his model is from the Rule, he applies it to situations both in and out of his monastic life.

He thus goes forward as he said he would, putting the Book of Figures together while continuing to seek approval from Mary, who does eventually offer what seems to be a somewhat palliative form of acquiescence:

> The virgin Mary appeared to me painted on a sort of pillar and suddenly transmuted into the likeness and form of a beautiful woman. I asked her to give me a license for the composition of the book of her figures, which

> I had already begun to put together. And she said to me, "I tell you that I will not give you license. But when you have made the book, I will willingly look at it." And it seemed to me that my sister Bridget was near me when the virgin Mary spoke these words, and my sister said to me, "What the virgin Mary said should be enough for you; go ahead and make your book, and when it is made she will look to see if it is well done or not, and she will respond to you accordingly." And I thanked the glorious Virgin again and woke up, and I brought this book all the way to the end of its composition aided by her support.[38]

The Virgin did not give the "license" John was waiting for, and he could not have been completely happy with the muted form of her approval or he would not have needed Bridget's reassuring comment, "what the virgin Mary said should be enough for you." Yet Mary's new willingness to look at the book "when done" is certainly a step forward, and no doubt he very much hoped that she would be interested when she saw it. It is not hard to sympathize with this view, catching only a glimpse of the care and detailed workmanship of the extant figures. Later he shows her the book both in a draft (which she called "well enough done") and a revised form (which she declared "very well done").[39] Her ambivalence, however, could not have been entirely erased, since John records a later vision in which Mary counsels him that it is really his internal orientation that is important: "I'm telling you," she says, "I do not want prayers nor figures nor visualizations without your heart!"[40] Signs that she does not really countenance the figures, but merely permits them, become clearer as the story continues.

There is another side to this, however. For if the Virgin does not seem deeply invested in John's project at this point, his monastic colleagues seem to have been quite eager for information about his conversations with Mary, as John notes in the vision describing his request for another type of license, this time for preaching. This is in the fourth vision of the sequence opening the Book of Figures:

> The virgin Mary appeared to me again on account of my preaching. For I, John, was often asked by my companions about the aforementioned visions; in fact even by our abbot it was bid and enjoined upon me that I should preach publicly in our chapter, from which I excused myself many times. But they were insistent, asking me all the time, and the abbot bidding me as well. I acquiesced, as though being good and obedient to their will and inquisitive bidding; and yet without license from the glorious Virgin, I did not dare to enter upon this important office—I still knew

too little about these things, about how much I should or could preach publicly.... Finally she appeared to me in a dream, painted on a pillar of the same church, and I said to her, "My lady, I seek to know if it pleases you that I should enter upon preaching." She responded, "It pleases me; preach." And I woke up and with confidence on that account entered into preaching with her grace helping me.[41]

A couple of interesting things are evident from this narrative. First, John is evidently not precipitate in undertaking to preach about his visions; he does not do it at the request of his fellow monks, and he acquiesces only after repeated requests from the abbot himself and a confirming conversation with Mary. His slow, patient refusal and then his capitulation after a suitable interval, and out of fear of seeming recalcitrant (the abbot is the superior to whom he owes obedience), offer a window onto John's navigation of the various tensions pulling on him between humility, courtesy, obedience, and self-disclosure.

I was (and still am) struck by the zeal of John's colleagues, and particularly his abbot, to know more about John's visions. There is clearly support within John's community for his conversations with the Virgin and presumably for his book project as well. Preaching about the visions would have made the entire project public within the confines of the monastery of Morigny, at least. Perhaps not everyone embraced it; some monks may not personally have liked the book, or cared for the attention John was getting on account of his visions, but in any event his writing could not have been a private, hole-and-corner matter. The *Liber florum celestis doctrine*, even the Book of Figures of the Old Compilation, has to have been a public, communally understood and officially countenanced undertaking up to the point where the Barking Dogs intervened.

The sense of general approbation and encouragement that John must have felt at this time, along with the easy and inspiring flow of visions and the new license to preach about them, all become part of the backdrop against which we must see John's claims to prophecy. He first starts to write about receiving the gift of prophecy in the second half of the Old Compilation of Figures.[42] In a string of visions itemized in chapter 25, he sees himself winning a battle against the devil, as a playmate of the infant Jesus, and ultimately as present with the crucified Christ:

> Put in ecstasy after the gift of the spirit of prophecy I saw the devil in our cloister in the likeness of an ox, and I fought against him and I won. Again, I saw that I gave a wreath of roses to the blessed Mary, and she set it on her head saying "My sweet beloved gave me this, sweet and kind." Also, I saw myself lying and sleeping on the breast of the virgin Mary,

and she put her breast in my mouth, and I suckled and slept. . . . Also, I saw myself playing ball with Christ as a boy. And I saw that our lord Jesus Christ kissed me on the mouth, and on the morning after that I entered into the office of preaching. Also, I saw that the crucified one was above my cup and drops of blood from his feet ran into my cup. Also, I saw that I was climbing the cross where the crucified one was, and the blood from his feet flowed over my head.[43]

As medieval visions of the holy family go, these are not unusual; however, they gain a new dimension in the remarkable passage with which John concludes this chapter. Via a rapid series of biblical and exegetical allusions, Mary's milk becomes first a figure for the angelic food that sustained Elijah, and then a figure for the book itself:

Seek the prophecies of all these visions in the Book of Prophecies of the blessed Mary.[44] Here otherwise we do not write them down by reason of brevity, and because they are not part of the visible body of this art, although they may be part of its invisible operation. Whence if anyone asks how I knew these things and where I got what I have written and am about to write, with my thoughts and visions having been considered and studied, I thus answer: from the sacred spiritual kiss of the blessed feet of the glorious virgin Mary, which is reconciliation; and of her holy hands, which is reward; and of her mouth, with its blessed embalsamed honeyed scent, and her selfsame son, our Lord Jesus Christ, which is contemplation. And at this point from something more, namely from the sacred fount of the breast of this same Virgin on which spiritually I reclined and slept, and from the emanation of the milk of spiritual grace and the holy mercy of her nipple with which Christ was nourished and I was spiritually nourished and comforted. In the strength of this spiritual food, I journeyed all the way to the mount of God, Horeb, and thence I drank what I have written and am about to write, the sacred flowing words of this book.[45]

Briefly, the three kisses alluded to here are a topos in commentaries on the Song of Songs, an elaboration of the reading of the kiss of the mouth as a figure for Christ's incarnation and for the delivery of spiritual grace in general.[46] Though normally addressed to Christ, not Mary, the three kisses are, as here, typically aligned explicitly with ideas of reconciliation, reward, and contemplation; they implicitly evoke the work of penance, aligning with the anagogical uplift of sacramental action. The idea of sacred nourishment suggested by

Mary's milk provides the link to Mount Horeb, for here John references a passage from 3 Kings 19:8, which tells how Elijah was sustained by food given him by an angel; only because of this could he reach the mount of God after forty days in the desert. John's sequence of transformations along the thematic line of spiritual food forces a corollary extrapolation about the matter of his book: the prayers and visions flowing through John, having the same source as biblical prophecy, are a spiritual food on their own account, allowing the operators who are John's successors to raise themselves from earthly things into the zone of heavenly knowledge. Standing with John on Mount Horeb offers us perhaps the best view of how monumentally important the work of this book was to John. The work of figures at this point is a big part of it.

Despite his assertions that the Barking Dogs are carping, despising good things and spitting out the knowledge of God, there is no doubt that they and the ensuing scandal cause John some anguish and are key in his decision to cut out most of the operations with figures and streamline the book to the seven images of Mary. He ceases to advocate use of the more "necromantic"-looking figures (though as we have seen, a sympathetic reader might see in them an intent more devotional than that word suggests). Nevertheless, John can hardly escape the conclusion that despite all his work and good intentions, they are not right. Here we must ask: did John simply fail to take the Virgin's politely worded cautions seriously enough? Did she in fact *never want* the figures? More seriously still, was he actually drawing inspiration, visually or intellectually, from works that he actually understood as really belonging in the category of "nigromancia"? If so, how could he possibly have imagined that he had Mary's approbation?

In the New Compilation Book of Figures we are allowed a glimpse into the process by which she and other spiritual guides lead him patiently toward the new version of his book. He needs such guidance now more than ever, and he is painstaking in the care with which requests instruction, because the dilemma here for John—the part that he must negotiate most carefully—is not really about the scandal, nor about the loss of all the work that went into the figures. It is rather about John's own perception of himself as being involved in a process of sacred transmission. How does he leave behind the self that created the first Book of Figures without also abandoning the God who opened the way and the Virgin who authorized and encouraged him? How can John absorb so immense a shock to the system? How can he *go on* tracing this work as sacred history? At the same time, how can he *not go on* doing so? This is really the crucial question, for to err is human, as it is said, but nevertheless John's mission is from God. No more than the biblical prophets can he abandon the work entrusted to him just because he is a sinner, because he is human, or because he made a mistake.

The next two chapters will tease out the knowledge process key to John's reconfiguration of his book. Chapter 5 will reconsider John's attitude to necromancy, offering more precise suggestions about attitudes to it that were available to John, and will examine some of the texts and images that may have informed the thinking about his own figures. Chapter 6 will look at his late-stage reinterpretation of the entire process in the last part of the New Compilation of Figures, the phase of his work in which he defends the book in its sacred integrity, mapping his own original Book of Figures onto a model of spiritual childhood, his reconstructed work onto a spiritual maturity, and the scandal itself onto the passion of Christ. The transit to spiritual maturity thus becomes consonant with the transit at the moment of the passion into the dispensation of grace.

5

MAGICAL OBJECTS OF KNOWLEDGE:
CATEGORIZING THE EXCEPTIVE ARTS

While the *ars notoria* constitutes the most important and longest-running part of John's extracurricular liturgical practice, it is undeniable that he knew and used necromantic texts as well. Immediately after laying aside the *ars notoria* forever (which John tells us that he does after vision 9), he descends for a period of unstated length into the necromantic arts.[1] From these arts he is dissuaded by a divine voice saying, "You fool, you fool, you fool!" while he is in the process of fashioning the fourth of the *Four Rings of Solomon*, a work whose extant manuscript versions openly engage with demons.[2] The last vision of this sequence, in which Christ has John beaten for his misdeeds, has already been described in chapter 3.

After John has finally laid aside all magic arts, and penance for these activities is engaged both on the material and spiritual planes, John begins to have visions that, as he says, "come from God."[3] It is not always possible to ascertain whether the visionary experiences in this section of the book were brought on by specific prayers of solicitation or were "spontaneous" apparitions; however, for a monk, the difference between spontaneous visions and those that came as a result of prayer might well seem nugatory. Clearly John does have some unsolicited experiences of the divine, where God breaks in on his activities unexpectedly (the voice crying "you fool!" as he fabricates the ring is a good example). John also speaks at times of waiting for apparitions of Mary, as though it were her volition and not his own that occasioned her appearances to him. This is in no way inconsistent with a practice of prayer being employed—not only because the monastic life is predicated on daily prayer, so that at no time of day would John have been very far from prayer, but also because it is clear that he was using his own Seven Prayers to solicit dreams during this period. Yet since John's prayers, too, are meant to be said repeatedly and daily, and an answer is never guaranteed, the apparitions always remained at Mary's discretion even when John was praying for them regularly.

In the case of the first vision that John says "comes from God," the vision has an internal setting that suggests John was probably soliciting Mary's attention in some fashion, though the questions that he ends up asking seem more circumstantial, more a puzzle produced by his immediate life experience than anything he had thought to seek a visionary answer for:

> It seemed to me that I was in the great church of the blessed Mary at Chartres, in front of the high altar of the church, and I was petitioning the glorious Virgin there. And when I had been asking for a little while, lo, the silver image, having been transformed carnally and corporeally into the selfsame Virgin, descended from the altar and came to me. Taking me by the hand, she led me to the middle of the steps in front of the altar and said to me, "Stand here, and worship God, and give Him thanks." And though I was going to pray with the common prayers, the blessed Virgin said, "No, do it this way; just say 'thank you.'" And when I was there with knees bent and hands clasped, the whole choir was singing "We praise you, O God," because of the miracle that the blessed virgin Mary had fashioned in my person in the sight of all. While they were singing, I meditated in my heart and said, "Mary, if books of that most nefarious art of necromancy are discovered to belong to me, will it be said that this is no miracle, but by means of that art that I made your image descend and change? And what shall I do with the books of this knowledge? Shall I remove and hide them from my colleagues?" While I was thinking these things over, I woke up. And in memory of this vision I composed the prayer "Glorious flower of heaven" and the other that follows it, "Thank you."[4]

When John hears music in a vision, it always means something good. We recall the sound of angels singing that followed his sense of contrition in vision 8, discussed in the last chapter. Here, too, music follows contrition as John is accepted back into God's graces. John's situation overall has parallels in many medieval exempla of magicians, necromancers, and sorcerers' apprentices. The best known of these tales in John's day may have been the story of Theophilus, a deacon who sold his soul to the devil; the pact with the devil, implemented through a magician, was snatched back by the virgin Mary, who returned it to a penitent Theophilus to be burned. The story of Theophilus was a popular one and well known to John, who quotes it and refers to it regularly in his prayers.

Yet John's account here offers some twists on the Theophilus theme. First, unusually for an exemplary penitent, John worries that if the members of his community discover his necromantic books, they might decide that the apparitions of the Virgin he has been reporting to them, the miraculous speaking statues and moving images, were necromantically contrived. Through this comment we may glimpse the extent to which John has been pursuing his conversation with the Virgin through and around magical activity that he here patently acknowledges to be forbidden.

Second, nowhere in the standard exempla do we find the necromancer wondering in this way about what to do with the books of necromancy he still has in his house. In the story of Theophilus, the material equivalent of the necromantic books is the pact with the devil, which is quickly burned once retrieved from the devil's hands. By contrast, we never actually find out what happens to John's books; unlike Prospero, he makes no declaration about destroying them. We do know from an earlier part of his narrative that among these books is one he has been writing himself, a *nova nigromancia*.[5] The Virgin—wisely, it seems—offers no advice here, for if it is difficult to reclaim a pact with the devil, it may be even more difficult to convince an author to dispose of a book in which he has invested his manual and intellectual labor.

I do not mean to reflect in one way or another on the quality of John's repentance over his forays into *nigromancia*. Indeed, there are many reasons to think that he was a true penitent, but the process of redemption, like any knowledge process, is complicated and may take unexpected twists and turns. All knowledge, but especially difficult knowledge, becomes integrated into personal history and memory in ways that cannot simply be excised. So in this case the necromantic books appear as a kind of dream metonymy for all the knowledge they contain—a knowledge that flows through and around every node of John's story, permeating his visions, which, in turn, inform his adaptations of the books he reads and writes. The question I want to address here is how John's use of *nigromancia*—a vehemently prohibited art—might have influenced or been reinterpreted through the construction of John's own redemptive and sacral art of knowledge, the *Liber florum celestis doctrine*.

It is a delicate matter to look at the way ideas or modes of operating drawn from *nigromancia* may have influenced John's book, for in fact he denies that there is any influence or similarity at all. Nevertheless, there is a certain amount of evidence that deserves further consideration. As noted earlier, in chapter 2, John's story opened with the copying of a necromantic book that he had only been deterred from trying by a Lombard doctor who had said, "look for a book called the *ars notoria*, and from it you will discover the truth not only concerning this knowledge you are asking about, but all forms of knowledge."[6] The episode is noteworthy, not only because it shows that the two types of text—necromancy and the *ars notoria*—are categorically connected as "magic," but also because the two types of texts are categorically connected as *knowledge*. The *ars notoria* is presented as a means to "the truth of all forms of knowledge"; it is a fuller, better, and more complete kind of knowledge that in fact subsumes (rather than excludes) necromancy.[7]

Though it is not mentioned again, later visionary events, including the vision quoted above, strongly suggest that this original book of necromancy had never left John's chamber. Moreover, it was obviously augmented by others, certainly including, but probably not limited to, the *Four Rings of Solomon*. John's use and possession of necromantic books has consequences elsewhere in the *Liber florum*, and there is reason to look more closely at the entire work for what it can tell us not only about *nigromancia* but also about fourteenth-century knowledge categories more broadly. In this chapter, I aim to assemble the evidence available in the *Liber florum* for what *nigromancia* meant to John, and at the same time to use John's work to refract the status of *nigromancia* in the broader intellectual culture that was his habitus.

Good, Bad, and Ambiguous Necromancy

At one point, John tells us that he learned all the liberal and magic arts from the *ars notoria*, including *nigromancia* "in both kinds."[8] The general intellectual background for a dual sense of necromancy that became available to late medieval literati has been laid out by Charles Burnett.[9] Burnett charts uses of the word "nigromancia" in works by Petrus Alfonsi and Gundissalinus, among others, to label a benign or at least not necessarily very bad form of knowledge that could be understood as philosophical or scientific rather than diabolic. Burnett notes as well that "nigromancia" was used to translate "sihr," the Arabic word for magic,[10] and in some usages it thus began to acquire a more neutral range of connotations. Instances of such neutral or positive usages are clear in the image magic compendium known as *Picatrix*, for example.[11]

At the same time, the normal definition of necromancy as a dark and demonic practice—sometimes, though not always, inflected through the classical sense, divination by the dead—continued to be operative. As the number of available types of magic texts increased, particularly as more Arabic image magic texts came into the West in Latin translation and spawned artful rearrangements and spinoffs, there was also increased controversy about distinguishing exactly where one kind of *nigromancia* left off and the other began. Part of the problem was that many types of magic that seemed in some locations to draw on natural astrological forces also included invocations in other places, so the distinctions that existed in principle were riddled with ambiguities in practice. While some might acknowledge the idea of a more or less benign necromancy, it was nevertheless hard to defend many of the actual texts circulating that contained instructions for making astrological images.

Because of this difficulty, it was not uncommon among intellectuals to shy away from suggesting that there was any genuinely licit kind of *nigromancia*, but nevertheless to distinguish between *strongly* (or mortally) sinful kinds, which involved explicit pacts with demons, and more ambiguous, *weakly* (or venially) sinful kinds, which might or might not involve the questionable use of signs or figures, but did not invoke demons explicitly. An important touchstone for this array of distinctions is found in the *Speculum astronomie*, a frequently referenced mid-thirteenth-century catalogue of texts whose author was concerned to lay out principles for distinguishing between licit and illicit forms of image magic. The Magister Speculi divided texts into those which explicitly invoked spirits (abominable), those which might use characters and unknown names but did not explicitly invoke spirits (less abominable but still detestable), and those which worked naturally (this ended up being a very small category indeed). Nicolas Weill-Parot has noted that the first two categories are distinguished by what he terms an "addressative" element,[12] and I follow him in seeing this as a useful term of art to cover the primary index that distinguished magical texts and practices as objectionable.[13] Weill-Parot goes on to note a further distinction that could be made by medieval authors between the "implicitly" and "explicitly" addressative.[14] This distinction is important in that that it allows us to grasp the way intentionality operated in dividing mortally and venially sinful magical practices; it also helps in separating out from intentional necromancy the Augustinian logic by which the use of signifying elements which are not explicitly or obviously addressed to anyone at all (as abstract figures, or *voces magice*, or the jumbles of sounds sometimes occurring in charms) may nonetheless be characterized as involving a demonic agreement or "pact." In order to get a better view of the way this notion of a median, questionable, but not mortally sinful type of magic is consistent across an array of different medieval disciplines and cultural habitus, I want to draw out the sense of the passage from Thomas Aquinas clarifying an earlier, more ambiguous notion of demonic "pact" that arises from Saint Augustine. Thomas does this by breaking the idea of pact into two branches, "tacit" and "explicit."

Briefly, in several frequently quoted sentences from *De doctrina christiana*, Augustine suggests that *all* superstitious signs, whether or not they involve explicit or knowing demonic commerce, or summon demons intentionally, actually rest on a kind of "pact" or agreement with demons. For example, he writes, "And so all arts of this kind, whether of trifling or harmful superstition, from a certain diseased association of humans and demons, a pact, so to speak, constituted of faithless and guileful friendship, are thoroughly to be repudiated and fled by the Christian."[15] This notion that any superstitious signs involved a "pact" or agreement with demons was absorbed early into the encyclopedic literature on magic, reappearing in canon law collections by Burchard of Worms, Ivo of Chartres, and Gratian.[16] However, the idea of demonic "pact" here has little to do with the notion of a legal pact that became common later in the literature on *maleficium*, nor even the signed legal document that was returned to Theophilus by the Virgin. Rather, it is rooted in Augustine's sign theory: for him, since the connection between given signs and their meaning is arbitrary with respect to the signified, all language implicitly rests on a kind of "pact" or agreement between the people who use that language—an agreement that language shall be used for certain purposes, and that certain words shall mean certain things. From Augustine's perspective, magical effects always depended on the interception of signs by demons and hence became the basis of a linguistic "pact" between demons and the human beings who chose to use such signs. This did not mean that humans were in fact contacting the demons intentionally, or bonded with demons in a knowing or fully complicit sense. Rather, they were allowing demonic intervention by implicitly treating unclear or ambiguous signs as meaningful.

Thomas Aquinas, however, noticing that the "pact" spoken of by Augustine in this context does not refer to an intentional pact or legal-style contract with demons (which was also understood to exist, even by Augustine), refines the category.[17] For Thomas, *nigromancia* refers only to magic that involves a clear, open, explicit commerce with demons, intentionally invoked, bound, and dismissed. He distinguishes this both from astral images and the *ars notoria*, which he treats in separate but contiguous sections of the *Summa Theologiae* (II^a II^{ae}: *nigromancia* is discussed under "divination" in Q. 95 and the *ars notoria* is discussed under "observances" in Q. 96, where he also talks about astral images).[18] In Q. 95, article 1, Thomas says that while there are many subspecies of divination, there are three overarching divisions or types. One type of divination is that done by open invocation of demons, to which he gives the general term "nigromancia" (subsuming classical necromancy with any more current practices of invoking demons), and two are done without open invocation of demons, including what he calls "augury" and "lots."[19] While he does not refer to "tacit" pact here, it is already implicit in this article that, for Thomas, divination which does not openly or consciously summon demons does not come under the rubric of *nigromancia*.

Thomas goes on to say more about the distinction between tacit and explicit demonic commerce in treating the questions on the natural power of image magic in article 2 of Q. 96. Here he argues that artificial shape is not a principle of natural action, since its immediate cause is the conception of the artificer; hence artificial forms cannot obtain power from the stars the way naturally made things do. On demonic involvement in astral magic, Thomas says,

> the sign of this [demonic involvement] is that it is necessary that certain characters be inscribed on [the images], which do not operate naturally at all; for a figure cannot be a cause of natural action. But in this respect astrological images do differ from necromantic ones: in necromantic images there are expressed certain invocations and magic signs [praestigia] which pertain to *explicit demonic pacts;* but in the other images there are *tacit pacts*, through certain signs of figures or characters.[20] (my emphasis)

In this passage, Thomas offers a philosophical way of distinguishing image magic texts along the same lines as the Magister Speculi: he divides astral images into those which involve "explicit" invocations and those involving what he calls "tacit pacts" through cryptic signs. Though both types are called "nigromancia" by the Magister Speculi, Thomas uses "nigromancia" to cover only those practices where demons are being summoned intentionally and *explicitly*, yet all the practices he discusses here are understood to be essentially illicit. They are all addressative and correspond roughly to the Magister Speculi's categories of abominable and detestable.

I do not want to suggest here that John of Morigny was necessarily familiar with the idea of the "tacit pact" in the writings of Thomas Aquinas or even the Magister Speculi. However, a common set of distinctions certainly underlies the writings of Thomas Aquinas (speculative philosopher), the Magister Speculi (natural philosopher), and John of Morigny (liturgist). As will shortly be seen, it is found in the *ars notoria* as well. In this triple set of distinctions, there is not only the major watershed that exists between illicit (addressative) and licit (non-addressative) forms of astrological magic, but also another watershed between mortally sinful *nigromancia*, which involved intentional demon summoning, and a median category of magic, not ever quite confessed to be good but also perhaps not so bad, that involved signs and figures of a more ambiguous kind. Since it was quite difficult (perhaps impossible, as Weill-Parot and others have suggested) to find actual texts which unambiguously met all the criteria of purely natural or philosophical magic, it is the existence of this ambiguous and indeterminate category, the questionable, the "perhaps bad or perhaps not so bad," which virtually guaranteed that a variety of different types of magic texts would need to be retained in the libraries of philosophically oriented magicians for further consideration and perhaps testing.

It is against this background of conceptual *gradations* of illicit magic that John of Morigny's ongoing engagement with necromancy must be seen. John's advanced degree in canon law would have made him quite familiar with the Augustinian prohibitions against addressative magic (indeed he quotes them, via Gratian, in his New Compilation Book of Figures, part III). It is clear that he had absorbed an idea of *nigromancia* that had a dual valence. It remains an open question how he navigated the middle ground of the *nigromancia* that is perhaps less illicit, perhaps indeed not sinful in the same sense. He speaks only on that one occasion of *nigromancia in utraque specie*. Elsewhere in the *Liber florum* he seems to acknowledge only one form of *nigromancia*, and it is very bad indeed. Yet at the same time it is clear that his period of reading, writing, and practicing of *nigromancia* has not left the *Liber florum* untouched.

Categories of Magical Knowledge in the *Ars Notoria* and *Liber Florum*

The opening of the New Compilation Book of Figures, which dates its inception to the Ides of August, 1315, describes how John rewrote the third part of his book because the original Book of Figures had been attacked by certain "Barking Dogs." The figures (according to the Barking Dogs) seemed to be composed "in the manner of necromantic figures" (more figurarum nigromancie), "on account of the crosses and circles in them, and on account of the consideration of planetary and daily cycles in the figures and prayers."[21] It is not clear what stance (if any) was being taken on the issue of tacit and explicit demonic pacts by the Barking Dogs. It is possible that they were accusing John of summoning demons explicitly, but they need not have been. The reference to planetary and daily cycles suggests that their concerns may have been for a visual evocation of the figures of astrological image magic, much of which fell into the large "ambiguous" category of necromancy. In any event, the astronomical references suggest that John's detractors were not much concerned at this point with the possibility that John was reviving the *ars notoria* by imitating the *ars notoria* figures (which, though strictly ordered to the lunar calendar like other Christian liturgies, do not employ, as John's original Book of Figures evidently did, planetary images or characters).

That John clearly distinguished the *ars notoria* from necromancy is a point that may need reinforcing, since there are later medieval treatments of necromancy and the *ars notoria* that *do* lump the categories together. When this happens, however, it necessarily involves the Augustinian logic that does not distinguish between explicit and tacit demonic pacts, because it is actually impossible to elide the *ars notoria* with necromancy following Thomistic logic. One example of such "lumping" should serve to make the point. In the middle of the fifteenth century, Johannes Hartlieb, in his well-known guide to bad magic, a *speculum principis* titled *The Book of All Forbidden Arts*, sets the *ars notoria* in the category of necromancy. Yet it is clear that for Hartlieb, any work that involves figures, characters, or any ambiguous signifiers at all is a candidate for the "necromantic" label. He writes,

> Under this heading [i.e., of *nigromancia*] is another art, called the "notory" art, that enables one to learn all the sciences by means of all sorts of words, figures, and characters. This art is not devoid of alliances with evil demons, because the unknown words function to create a compact between humankind and the devil. Even if this method is associated with fasting, prayer, and a pure, chaste life, it is forbidden anyway, and a sin, because the evil demons are hidden by this beautiful appearance in order to seduce and lead men astray.[22]

The Augustinian logic is quite recognizable. Hartlieb here clearly acknowledges that the notory art does not involve *explicit* demonic invocation, and the demonic "alliances" are of a tacit kind. The *ars notoria* involves recognizably sacred practices; it is associated with "a pure, chaste life"; demons are hidden by its "beautiful appearance." The problem is that the text is ambiguously addressative. It includes "all sorts of words, figures, and characters." Demons can make their way into its operation through the "unknown words," the ambiguous signifiers that are the primary Augustinian index of magic in its broadest sense.

Like Thomas Aquinas, John of Morigny largely reserves the word "nigromancia" for explicit and intentional demon conjuring. And like Thomas, he understands that people may become entangled with the demonic in ways that are neither fully explicit nor fully intentional. Further, and still like Thomas, he does not conflate the processes of the *ars notoria* and necromancy, but sees them (and the evils they represent) as distinct and separate. In his personal history, he distinguishes the period of his involvement with necromancy from the period of his involvement with the *ars notoria*; they are sequential, not entwined. His conversion away from the *ars notoria* (which happens slightly earlier, at vision 9, I.i.11) is also distinguished from his conversion away from necromancy (detailed later in visions 10 and 11, I.i.12–13). In the lengthy set of flourishes by which he condemns the evil of the *ars notoria* at the outset of his autobiography, John never charges the notory art with being, in essence, necromantic; he *does* suggest that it is more subtle and more deceptive than necromancy, and also, as already noted, that "nothing can be accomplished in necromancy without it."[23] However, this is a way of relating the two categories, not lumping them. Nowhere in his opus does he refer to the *ars notoria* as a necromantic practice.

John does make a number of things explicit about *nigromancia* that enhance our picture of what the word meant to him and how it related to figures. One clear feature of the category in John's work is that despite all the care and caution that enfolds it, nevertheless he understood it as an area or branch of knowledge that fit into a larger schema of knowable things, of arts and sciences and virtues. While the *ars notoria* also requires knowledge, or at least a skill that is learned by study (John says that it took some time for him to learn how to make it work[24]), it is primarily seen as way of opening the mind to knowledge in general, not as a branch of knowledge in any specific or curricular sense. As Benedek Láng puts it, the notory art is a "metascience."[25] It represents something both more specific and more absolute than necromancy. John seems to subsume the *ars notoria* implicitly in the general category of "exceptive arts" (a category comprising, more or less, the traditional magic arts, of which more below), though he does not give any explicit information about where it would fit in.

On the other hand, *nigromancia* is explicitly included as a branch of (or area within) the *artes exceptivae*. Toward the end of the New Compilation, we find a set of tables that includes the exceptive arts laid out in a curricular scheme owing a clear debt to the *ars notoria* (fig. 4). Figure 4, which pairs each of the seven gifts of the Holy Spirit with one of the seven liberal, exceptive, and mechanical arts, is included in some form in all manuscripts containing John's New Compilation *Liber figurarum*.[26] The liberal and mechanical arts, of course, are well-known categories. The term "exceptive arts" is idiosyncratic—it does not occur outside the *ars notoria* tradition. The term is absent from Latin dictionaries and does not occur in any *locus classicus* for the discussion of magic in the major encyclopedias or the catechetical literature. Hugh of St. Victor includes a disquisition on magic arts in an appendix to the *Didascalicon*, where he discusses magic as false or unreal knowledge, "excepting" it in that sense from the order of knowledge properly speaking; but even so, Hugh does not use the word "exceptive."[27] Despite this lack of any external gloss or referent, however, the content of the term "exceptive arts" in John's table is clear enough from the table itself: the category subsumes the traditional magic arts. We see that necromancy heads the exceptive arts, paralleled with intellect (in the gifts of the Holy Spirit), grammar (among the liberal arts), and weaving (among the

Gracie Spiritus Sancti	Artes Liberales	Artes Exceptive	Artes Mechanice
Intellectus	Gramatica	Nigromancia	Lanificium
Fortitudinis	dyaletica	aeromancia	Theatrica
Consilij	rethorica	pyromancia	fabrilis
Sciencie	arismetica	ciromancia	Venatica
Tymoris	geometria	geomancia	Agricultura
Sapientie	Astronomia	geonegia	Medicina
Pietatis	Musica	ydromancia	Nauigatio

Fig. 4   Arts and gifts.

mechanical arts). After necromancy come aeromancy, pyromancy, chiromancy, geomancy, *geonegia*, and hydromancy.

Outside the *ars notoria* itself, the closest parallel I have seen to this categorization of magic arts, in a group of seven meant to parallel a standard curriculum, is in the fifteenth-century work whose description of the *ars notoria* has already been quoted above: Johann Hartlieb's *Book of All Forbidden Arts*. This work is arranged according to a curricular model under seven headings. The first six of these correspond to the exceptive arts in John of Morigny's table: necromancy, geomancy, hydromancy, aeromancy, pyromancy, and chiromancy.[28] The seventh art found in Hartlieb, however, is different from the seventh exceptive art in John's table; it is listed as "scapulomancy" (a term indicating divination conducted with bones, especially shoulder blades). John's seventh art points us to another anomaly, another word idiosyncratic to the *ars notoria* tradition, and again not found outside of it: the word "geonegia."[29] Hartlieb's adoption of the relatively more well-known term "scapulomancy" for the seventh art highlights the singularity and relative inscrutability of this term even to its medieval audience. Like the *artes exceptivae*, *geonegia* is conspicuous by its absence from medieval Latin dictionaries, and while John does not offer us many clues as to the content of the category, fewer still are offered in the *ars notoria* itself, which is, if anything, even more idiosyncratic in its presentation of these arts.

It is a singularity of the *ars notoria* that in most manuscripts of both A and B traditions documented by Julien Véronèse, the exceptive arts are elided with the mechanical; that is, the mechanical arts are not actually listed, and instead, the *ars notoria* includes John's seven magical arts under the heading "mechanical" or (following Hugh of St. Victor) "adulterine" arts. More precisely, the notory art includes six of John's magic arts: necromancy, hydromancy, pyromancy, chiromancy, geomancy, and *geonegia*. It omits the seventh, listed as aeromancy in John of Morigny's work, instead using another *hapax legomenon*, "neonegia"— a word also unknown and unrecorded elsewhere. The only clue to the meaning of either of these terms in the *ars notoria* is that an association with astronomy is suggested for one or both of them.[30] It would seem from John's separation and rearrangement of these categories that he saw the ars notorial list of mechanical arts as a model he could adapt and modify to suit his needs, as others (probably including Johann Hartlieb) did later.[31]

The model provided by the *ars notoria* has other aspects that informed John's ideas, however creatively he may have handled them. It is notable that, according to the *ars notoria*, *nigromancia* has two parts, one that is sinful and one that is not; from it we learn that by means of *nigromancia* "the ancient masters were accustomed to comprehend certain mysteries without sin—whence Solomon decreed that any righteous man may read five books of this art without sin."[32] In the gloss we get amplification:

> Among the mechanical arts is one called *nigromancia*, concerning which it is not licit to operate . . . on account of the sin which is done by sacrificing to malign spirits. But nevertheless Solomon said that in there are seven books in the art, of which five can be read with less sin, and through them the science of *nigromancia* can be worked. But two of them are deeply prohibited to work with. . . . And whoever offers sacrifice to demons from human blood or other bodily things offends God. . . . Because of this, these two books are specially prohibited, and although there may be sin in working with those in which there is no need to perform a sacrifice, yet there is less sin in these than the others—but I will skip over how to work with the five books concerning which there is no great sin . . . because concerning that knowledge it is not good to mention it to anyone, and especially in this book in which there are pure and mysterious things of God.[33]

In his discussion of necromancy as a liberal art, Charles Burnett makes note of a similar bifurcation in the work of Petrus Alfonsi (though Petrus speaks of nine parts, not seven). The idea of dividing *nigromancia* into better and worse parts is the same: "First you should know that the art which is called 'nigromancia' has nine parts. Of these, the first four of these deal with the four elements <showing> how we can operate in them physically, but the five remaining ones <show> how one cannot operate with them except through the invocation of bad spirits ('*maligni spiritus*'). These bad spirits are called devils by men."[34] As Burnett notes, Petrus's description here seems to align with a tradition of "nigromancy according to physics" documented in Gundissalinus.[35] The *ars notoria*, too, evidently harks to a tradition of construing necromancy as divided into more and less licit parts—an important feature to note here, because it shows that the philosophical divisions we have observed in Thomas Aquinas and the Magister Speculi as well as Petrus Alfonsi, in which shades of sinfulness were mapped onto the magical tradition, were adopted and propagated similarly within the magical traditions themselves. This feature underscores the fact that we are really in the same intellectual world in the *ars notoria* as in the *didascalica* and other works concerned with constructing hierarchies and categories of knowledge.

It may be noted further that the master of the *ars notoria* (at least the glossator of the B text) is not really less ambivalent about the "sinless" nature of the nondemonic parts of necromancy than the more philosophical and theological writers, for even though it is suggested that this branch of necromancy is not sinful, it is also stated that it is not really an appropriate thing to discuss in a work on divine mysteries such as the *ars notoria*. Thus, the *ars notoria* itself clearly distinguishes between ambiguous and bad necromancy, on the one hand, and its own sacramental and salvific practices on the other. From this source, if no other were available, this triple set of distinctions would have been absorbed by John of Morigny.

Within the liturgy of John's metascience, it is also possible to see a careful gradation of relatively appropriate and inappropriate forms of magical knowledge. To understand its shadings, we must look further at the ways he breaks down the content of the exceptive arts. The magical curriculum and its correspondences delineated graphically in his table are reflected in many places in the liturgical parts of John's work, in both the New Compilation text and the Old, making it clear how deeply embedded they were in John's scheme. In later drafts of the Book of Thirty Prayers (this passage is missing from the earlier version of the text preserved in the Oxford manuscript), the exceptive arts, including *nigromancia*, surface in the prayer for philosophy, which invokes all the cherubim by iteration of their offices. Each office is a branch of knowledge, and the cherubim of the exceptive arts are invoked after the mechanical arts and before the virtues, thus: "Cherubim of weaving, Cherubim of the theatre, Cherubim of metalwork, Cherubim of hunting, Cherubim of agriculture, Cherubim of navigation; *Cherubim of necromancy, Cherubim of aeromancy, Cherubim of pyromancy, Cherubim of chiromancy, Cherubim of geomancy, Cherubim of geonegia, Cherubim of hydromancy;* Cherubim of patience" (my emphasis).[36] That this part of the prayer is added later means that the inclusion of the exceptive arts here was a considered decision on John's part, most probably in fact a by-product of the need for systematization of all forms of knowledge in his production of the figures to go along with the prayers—though a note suggests that for the operator, reciting the names of the cherubim for the exceptive arts is optional, not required: "The names may be omitted from 'Cherubim of weaving' to 'Cherubim of patience.'"[37] Each petitioner is left to make up his own mind whether or not to include the exceptive arts in the quest for knowledge.

Clearly there is an ambivalence around the exceptive arts that is not there for the liberal and mechanical arts. While the exceptive arts have a definite status within the order of knowledge—indeed, they have an unequivocal status as *heavenly* knowledge, part of the divine archetype, witnessed by their representation among the offices of the cherubim—it remains a knowledge set apart from the salvific knowledge that is a functional part of the divine dispensation, legitimate and wholesome for human use. The exceptive arts are knowable, but their soteriological status is ambiguous. Like the demons themselves, perhaps, they could be considered good as to origin, but not as to present action.

More information about John's understanding of the content of the exceptive arts is offered in chapter 19 of the Old Compilation Book of Figures; this is the chapter with the list of "letterings" that yields our primary information about the number and intention of the figures in John's book. The list includes a set of seven figures for taking all four types of knowledge listed on the table. These figures were apparently multipurpose, for though there are distinct prayers for each of the liberal, mechanical, and exceptive arts, a single figure evidently comprises a complete set of related sciences. That is, the lettering for each figure lists the allied mechanical and exceptive art, the allied gift of the Holy Spirit, as well as one of the seven planets and one of the seven virtues. All the inscriptions also contain the name of the operator (in the case of the Old Compilation text in the Bodleian, the operator was a certain Brother Geoffrey).[38] The words of the inscriptions are elusive, but they do make it clear that the knowledge table above articulates correspondences that are stable in John's thinking from the Old to the New Compilations. For example, the heading "Inscription of the figure of Grammar and the arts contained under it" is underwritten with these words: "Y e v e God Mary spirit of *intellect* of Geoffrey. And of *grammar* of Saturn of Geoffrey. And of *weaving* of Saturn of Geoffrey. And of *necromancy* of Saturn of Geoffrey. And of *patience* of Saturn of Geoffrey."[39] The four types of knowledge are implicitly allied in the figure that would have contained these words, and it appears that one figure has the ability to access all the sciences across one row of correspondences in the spiritual archetype of knowledge represented in the table—in this case intellect, grammar, weaving, and necromancy. The seven cardinal virtues have been added to the set in this grouping, and patience is here included in the figure's lettering as well, all being linked to the dominion of Saturn (suggesting the astrological features of the design that troubled the Barking Dogs).

As noted, each figure is to be contemplated with a prayer, different from the inscription, but likewise to be imagined in the heart, John says, not uttered with the tongue.[40] John gives a list of brief prayers for each liberal, mechanical, and exceptive art. The prayer for astronomy, for example, is laid out as follows: "Visualize these words for astronomy: May I understand the *Treatise on the Material Sphere*, and know Alfraganus, Arthabicius, the Toledan Tables, judgments, the astrolabe, the courses and places and natures of the planets, the twelve figures and twelve houses."[41] Where the prayers contain lists of books or authors, as here, they give a good idea of works or authorities commonly studied in university curricula. However, the knowledge sought by the prayers is not always textual. Most often the prayers are for a mix of texts and skills, but in some, such as the prayer for the mechanical art of theatre, the operator seeks only a more practical, "how-to" knowledge: "Visualize these words for the art of theatre: May I know and understand the whole theatrical art, how to dance, to play in all sorts of ways, to fight, to leap, to drum, to caper, and to remove all tedium and melancholy through games in theatres and elsewhere."[42] Like the prayers for the liberal and mechanical arts, the prayers for the *artes exceptivae* request specific subspecies of knowledge, and sometimes knowledge from specific texts. The prayers for the exceptive arts stray from the form of the other arts only in one respect: the operator asks only for theoretical or speculative knowledge. Practical or working knowledge is explicitly excluded. Here is the prayer for necromancy: "For the art of necromancy, these words are dwelt upon in the heart: May I know and understand, *but not perform*, all arts of necromancy, including sacrificing, suffumigation, and auscultation."[43] All prayers for exceptive arts similarly request speculative or theoretical knowledge only, excluding the practical.[44] Yet they are represented in the figures and prayers just as they are in the table. It seems that, unlike Hugh of St. Victor, John does not see the magic arts as excluded from the order of knowledge in principle, at least not wholly so—except that something may be known but not practiced, itself a complex manner of exclusion. (For how much does one actually know without practice of a discipline? Is speculative knowledge of magic really knowledge at all?) Yet the exceptive arts are at any rate important enough to compose prayers for and to place among the offices of the cherubim. If this is exclusion, it leaves open the notion that this knowledge has a legitimate place in the divine idea and is a working piece of God's providence.

Content of the Category *Geonegia* According to John of Morigny

The most interesting subdivision of the *artes exceptivae*, because there is so little information about it anywhere else, is the category of *geonegia*. In this prayer, John offers a list of texts (something he did *not* do in the prayer for *nigromancia*, above). For *geonegia*, he writes, "Visualize these for the geonegic art: May I know and understand (but not perform) all the arts of geonegia, the books *On Images* by King Ptolemy, *Book of Talismans of Abel*, *Book of Seven Senators*, *Book of Twelve Firmaments*, and *Book of the Semhemforas*."[45] This is a fascinating though somewhat inscrutable grouping of works, not all of which can be identified with extant or known texts, though some of them can at least loosely be categorized among texts that are known to exist. Books on images attributed to Ptolemy are widely known and have been found in multiple manuscripts.[46] The *Book of Talismans of Abel* can probably be identified with a work that circulated as the *Liber planetarum ex scientia Abel* (Book of Planets According to the Knowledge of Abel), an image magic text including a book for each planet, of which at least several seem to have circulated separately.[47] I cannot identify John's *Book of Seven Senators*. The identity of the *Book of Twelve Firmaments* is not certain, though there are several works in the magical tradition involving twelve orders of spirits with which John may have been familiar.[48] The final book in the list, the *Book of the Semhemforas*,[49] is well attested; the work is a treatise on divine names that discusses methods of forming and using them. It circulated with some versions of the *Liber Razielis* and is referenced by Hartlieb among the "works containing figures." A version of the *Liber Semhemforas* is shown by Jan Veenstra to have been embedded in the mid-fourteenth-century compendium by Berengario Ganell, the *Summa sacre magice*.[50]

The identifiable works in the group come together to suggest that John intends the category of *geonegia* to capture the genre of texts broadly concerned with magical images, talismans and figures designed to trap divine and stellar powers and put them to practical use. Many such texts are preserved, and some might fall into the spectrum of texts considered under the category of *nigromancia* in the Thomistic and explicit sense of that word. As a whole, though, they also capture the full range of moral ambiguity in the category that I have been trying to describe. They operate within a strongly articulated framework of divinely governed cosmological correspondences, which Sophie Page has referred to as the "harmonious universe" of image magic.[51] The works may include addressative elements, and even express invocations of spirits, but the spirits themselves may have ambiguous status, or be referred to as angelic as often as they are demonic. The texts also contain discussion of topics that certainly had the capacity to be construed as "scientific."

Perhaps most importantly for my purposes, such texts are actively invested in a similar lofty and divine idea of curricular knowledge, seen as an aspect of Wisdom, that I have remarked in the didascalic literature. It is sufficient to make the point generally that even works concerned with very workaday instrumental uses of magical images (such as repelling pests or advancing love or enmity, common goals of image magic) inscribe their powers in a structured hierarchy of knowledge with a divine origin and *telos*. Thus, the *De imaginibus* ascribed to Thabit begins by establishing a curricular hierarchy in which astronomy is the highest of the liberal arts and the science of images is the pinnacle of astronomy. It winds up with assertions of the work of images as part of the divine plan:

> And know that these images circulate in all things which the sons of Adam are disposed [to use], namely concerning reparation and destruction, and health and infirmity, and love and hate . . . if their author is prudent and skilled in the work and in the complement of planets. Therefore take care of these things, because they are from the secrets of the planets and hidden things of the wisdom of philosophy; and this is a great wisdom which God the most high was willing to open up to his servants for the reparation of his realms. And God is the director, who is a great incomprehensible might, and the most high.[52]

Statements of this kind, which are commonplaces of the genre, make it easy to understand the network of forces that operate magical images as existing for human use within the Christian dispensation. This epistemological framing in no way guarantees that works of image magic are free from demonic taint, but it does distinguish them from the category of *nigromancia* in the explicit or hard sense.

In John's prayer for *nigromancia*, the attributes of this branch of knowledge, while rather general, suggest the traditional context of intentional demon conjuring, with its sacrifices and suffumigations. *Geonegia* is clearly distinguished from this: it has at least partly recognizable textual content. The fact that John includes prayers for both *nigromancia* and *geonegia* in the Old Compilation of Figures suggests that both branches of knowledge are part of the divine archetype of knowledge (for how can any knowledge available to us not preexist in God?), but that the categories are discrete. The category called *geonegia* encompasses some obvious works of magical images as well as a work on divine names that traveled with the *Raziel* corpus (though John does not remove the ban on performance, and here as elsewhere among exceptive arts requests only theoretical knowledge).

These facts by themselves would not be sufficient to suggest that John was actually drawing on image magic, or works in the *Raziel* corpus, in his Old Compilation of Figures. However, there are a few other suggestive tidbits of evidence in the extant parts of the Old Compilation *Liber figurarum* that seem to point in this direction as well. There is a group of figures that John describes in detail, including seven figures of Mary (which rode on into the New Compilation in a slightly simplified form) and seven idiosyncratic planetary figures. Here is John's description of his planetary figures:

> In the first, let there be made the head of a cherub with wings. In the second, let the head be womanly, crowned with a gold diadem. In the third, let there be a head of Christ in the fashion of a tonsured master with hood removed. In the fourth, let there be two heads of the glorious Virgin, one old and the other young, joined together back to back. In the fifth, let there be a head of God in the fashion of an old man with a long beard. In the sixth, let there be a head of Christ in the fashion of a king crowned with a gold crown. In the seventh, let there be a head of Christ in the fashion of an armed soldier and crowned with a gold diadem.[53]

The images are unusual, but it is possible to guess at which planets are here represented. The cherub with wings might be Mercury; the two feminine images could correspond to the moon and Venus, perhaps; the tonsured master might be Saturn; the old man with the beard and king with a gold crown could represent Jupiter and the sun, respectively; Christ as an armed soldier might be Mars. (I assume that in the lost quires of figures the images themselves were labeled with the conventional names of the planets, which would have given a more certain identification of which planet each figure was meant to represent.)

These are obviously not traditional images of planetary gods of the sort that might be found, for example, in illustrated astronomical treatises (even these traditional images can be varied by artists to suit the occasion, but they are nevertheless more readily recognizable than John's).[54] Nothing even remotely like this is found in the *ars notoria*. Yet image magic does offer precedents for a diverse array of anthropoid images representing the planets. I do not know of any planetary images Christianized in the way that John's were. However, a list of images attributed to different sources is compiled in *Picatrix*. Here is a set for Mercury:

> The form of Mercury in the opinion of wise Beylus is the form of a bearded youth holding a spear in his hand.

> The form of Mercury in the opinion of wise Hermes is the form of a man having a chicken on his head, standing upon a throne; and the feet are like an eagle's feet; and he is holding a flame in the palm of his left hand. And under the feet there are signs which are described below. And this is its form.
>
> The form of Mercury in the opinion of Picatrix is the form of a man standing and having wings extended on his right side and on the left holding a small chicken; and in his right hand a spear, but in the left a round shell.
>
> The form of Mercury in the opinion of other wise men is the form of crowned baron, riding on a peacock, having a reed pen in his right hand, in his left, a chart; and his clothes are of all colors mixed. And this is its form.[55]

The planetary images described here have a similar cartoonlike quirkiness that resists resolution into anything like a clear assemblage of planetary characteristics. There are scraps of traditional iconography in them that may be associated with Mercury or Hermes (the pen and writing vehicle, the peacock, perhaps the "wings"), but these are intermixed with other elements that have no clear occasion in the mythology (the small chickens, thrones, shells, the eagle's feet, and so on). While these descriptions offer no direct precedent for John's, they do give a good idea of the range of variation in representations of the planets that was possible in the tradition of image magic. There might also be further variations in the way specific figures are executed from such descriptions, since in some cases the description offers options: the image in the opinion of Picatrix suggests that the figure should be holding on the left both a small chicken and a round shell, so an illustrator would need to make a decision about which of these objects to include, or whether to work in both.[56] While this does not offer a direct visual model for John's work, it does give a context for positioning John's figures of the planets in relation to a tradition in which variable images of the human form could be creatively combined with suggestive scraps of iconography to create new anthropoid representations of the planets and their powers.

One thing about John's representations that distinguishes them from any of the precedents supplied through *Picatrix* is that they are so clearly meant to be Christian. They cut monkish figures where they are not explicitly mapped onto aspects of Mary, Christ, or God the Father. They are, in this sense, quite legible, despite their quirkiness and lack of labeling, and they carry forward the penitential and sacramental themes and qualities embodied, unmistakably if idiosyncratically, in John's work. If we look at John's figures not as *containing* necromantic figures, but perhaps as *adapting and developing* the visual lexicon of image magic, we may get our best insight both into John's process and into the reaction of the Barking Dogs. In terms of John's process, what we see here is consistent with what we see in his adaptation of the *ars notoria*: it is original, adopting parts of the structure and developing them in novel ways while rejecting others, resulting in a work that is very recognizable as Christian, yet with other influences glimmering through the folds of its newly woven drapery.

In interpreting John's relation to his potential sources in magic other than the *ars notoria*, the scholar must tread carefully around the absence of the figures themselves. There are a few other elements in the extant portions of the Book of Figures that must at least be noticed here, though again it is impossible to supply definitive information about John's sources. One design element that clearly pertained to all the figures in the book is the Tetragrammaton, for which operators were instructed to write one Hebrew letter in each corner of the figures. To enable this, the Old Compilation of Figures includes an example of the divine name in Hebrew.[57] The divine name is also important in the first figure already discussed in chapter 4, which John subsequently cancels, instructing the reader to imagine the simple form of a ring instead.[58]

Instances of Hebrew are sufficiently infrequent in medieval Latin writing that its presence here in a Christian text deserves notice. Magic figures with Hebrew become more common in Christian texts later, but for the early fourteenth century there are not many obvious precedents. There is no Hebrew writing in the *ars notoria*, either in its text or *notae*, despite its general air of Jewish filiation. The *Summa sacre magice*, a Christian compendium of magical works by Berengar Ganell, composed probably in the region of Catalunya some time in the 1340s, is too late to have been a model for John's work, but it offers interesting parallels in its general preoccupation with alphabets and its use of Hebrew in various locations, including many permutations of the divine name.[59] It does not, however, contain any analogue for the layout of the Tetragrammaton in the four corners of the figures that John prescribes; for this, the only parallel I have found is in the manuscript of the *Liber Razielis* in Rome, Vatican Library, Reg. lat. 1300. This figure comes at the end of the sixth book, the *Liber Samayn*, a portion of the book comprising seven prayers, each of which is labeled as having a figure going with it, but only the first figure is actually executed in the book (see fig. 5).

The writing around the square figure runs: "God of i.s.r.a.e.l / God of all ages / God cause of causes nature of natures / God without beginning without end." Beside it, the beginning of the chapter reads: "Chapter 25 on the holy name

... peccarit debet notare nomen temporis in quo fuit. et nomina suorum maiorum et suorum angelorum. Et nomen mensis in suo tempore. Et nomina angelorum mensis. Et nomen diei in suo tempore. et nomina suorum angelorum. Et nomen signi in quo est sol. de die et luna de nocte. secundum suum tempus. Et nomina suorum angelorum. Et nomen solis de die et lune de nocte in suo tempore. et nomina suorum angelorum. Et nomen celi in suo tempore. Et nomen terre in suo tempore. Et si de igne operatus fuerit. nota nomen solis. in suo tempore. Et nomina suorum angelorum. Et nomen etiam primi mundi in suo tempore et nomina suorum angelorum. Et magnum nomen et septem nomina xxxj. diabus et perficies. Et ista sunt que non potest excusare in omnibus que feceris. Et verum est quod supradicta dixi. Et perficies in omnibus Capitulis. Et de scto nomine semper scias quod scilicet

Istud est magnum nomen debet notari 2 diei semiforas. explanatum quod debet notari in omni magna causa quam feceris unde et scribe in loco secreto Versus quatuor partes mundi incipiendo ad orientem et deinde ad occidentem sep^{te}...

semyforas and how it should be named and said. This is the great explicit name semiforas which ought to be named in every great matter that you undertake, of a clean and holy kind, in a secret place, facing the four directions starting in the east."[60] The chapter contains long lists of angelic hosts by name, similar at first glance to the unknown words in the *ars notoria*, except that the angel names in the *Liber Samayn* have recognizable Hebrew morphologies and the structure encapsulating them is organized according to the twelve altitudes and the seven heavens. While John is explicit that neither the operation nor the visionary results of the prayers in his *Liber florum* need to be kept secret, his book shares with the *Liber Samayn* the lofty religious tone and reverence around the divine name.

Two more oddities from the Old Compilation of Figures deserve mention before we move on. In the list of letterings given for the figures, there is a lettering for figures of seven angels (here followed in each case by the operator's name, Geoffrey): (1) Michael Galfridi, (2) Secreciel Galfridi, (3) Gabriel Galfridi, (4) Raphael Galfridi, (5) Sabbatiel Galfridi, (6) Pamphiosel Galfridi, (7) Vriel Galfridi.[61] A list of seven angels is common in the magical literature, often linked with the seven planets or seven days of the week; however, the standard list differs from John's. Instead of Secreciel, Sabbatiel, Pamphiosel, and Vriel, it typically features the names Casziel, Satquiel, Samael, and Anael. This standard cluster of seven angels is inscribed, for example, on the seal of God in the *Sworn Book of Honorius*, in the manuscript transcribed in Kieckhefer's *Forbidden Rites*, in the *Liber Razielis*, and in other lists elsewhere.[62] I do not know where the names in John's list derive from, but what is conspicuous about the anomalous names is that they appear to involve a conscious Hebraicization; that is, they all end in "-el" (a widely known word for God and angel name suffix, to be sure). But "Secretiel" appears to add the Hebrew suffix "-el" to a Latin prefix, "secret-." It is not necessary to lean too hard on this one example, because there is another list of letterings, slightly further on, for which this is clearly the operating procedure:

Litera figure intellectus:
Intellectuel Maria prudencie Galfridi.
Memorie:
Memoriel Maria continencie Galfridi.
Eloquencie:
Eloquenciel Facundiel Maria et iusticie Galfridi.
Perseuerancie stabilis:
Perseueranciel Stabilitatiel Maria et fortitudinis Galfridi.

Here, evidently, John sought to create names of angels governing intellect, memory, eloquence, perseverance, and stability, by adding "-el" to the ends of the Latin words. This process is not found in the *ars notoria* and is not used by John in the prayers, though he does generate long lists of angels by associating specific ranks of angels with attributes generally given to them in the angelological literature.

While it is not possible in the present state of our knowledge to identify John's sources in the Old Compilation of Figures more closely, it is certainly demonstrable that his ideas derive from a different set of magical influences than the *ars notoria*. It seems reasonably clear that lurking in the background here are translations of Hebrew and Arabic texts that might, for good or bad reasons, have been classified under the rubric of *nigromancia* in John's day— works with an astrological component that prominently made use of figures and images, as do both the *Liber Razielis* in its Latin forms and image magic works like the Ptolemaic *De imaginibus*. The presence of planetary and other astrological figures in John's Old Compilation of Figures, as well as the iteration of planet names in the prayers, the links to astrology suggested by the Barking Dogs, and the inclusion of image magic texts as well as the *Liber Semhemforas* in the exceptive category of *geonegia*, all conspire to suggest as much. If John was attempting to reestablish some principles for a more purely and clearly nondemonic form of *nigromancia*, such a goal would be consistent with his enterprise elsewhere; the evidence I have pieced together here suggests that the categories of John's understanding, especially insofar as they are informed by the totalizing knowledge project of the *ars notoria*, would have encouraged this.

I began this chapter with John's visionary confession to owning a set of *libri nigromantici*, about which he felt profound compunction, yet which he could not bring himself to destroy. It is clear that the knowledge categories within the "exceptive" arts would have been extremely difficult to eradicate from any ritual work aiming to reflect the integration of the self, the world, and the divine as a single system. Throughout the *Liber florum*, we see John struggling with different ways of making all his knowledge and self-knowledge consistent with what he knew from experience about the world and the divine. The Old Compilation *Liber figurarum* must be seen—as John encourages us to see it—as a part of this attempt. The burning question, then, and the theme of the next chapter, is how John held together his sense of a sacred integration of all knowledge when the Dogs began to bark.

6

VISIONARY EXEGESIS AND PROPHECY:
MILK AND MEAT

It is clear that there could be various ways of interpreting the appearance and use of John's figures in the Old Compilation, both for medieval viewers and for us. If *nigromancia* in the sense of "demon conjuring" was illicit by most standards,[1] nevertheless there might be considerable variation as to where the line between "licit" and "potentially licit" was drawn in the case of individual texts and practices. We could thus grasp John's figures benignly as an interesting (perhaps novel, but still not unorthodox) attempt to provide a devotional enhancement of the prayers; this was likely the view of users of the book in John's immediate community (like his sister Bridget and his Cistercian friend John of Fontainejean). Or we could see the figures in a more complicated light as a straying into a gray area—a perhaps well-intentioned but still mistaken concession to a suspect form of idolatry. (I suspect this is how the Barking Dogs saw them.[2]) We could even see in the whole text a willful embrace of the principles of condemned magic thinly veiled under a poorly contrived and largely unconvincing cover of devotion; it is this latter reading that seems to be the view of the writer of the account of the burning in the *Grandes Chroniques de France*, our main source for the New Compilation text's condemnation less than a decade later. While all of these were possible stances that medieval readers might take toward the text, none of them quite accurately sums up the profound *integration* of magical and other forms of knowledge with theology, prayer, and devotion to the Virgin, as this becomes articulated in John's own text.

In this chapter I want to focus on how this integration is achieved, both before and after the Barking Dogs broke the *Liber florum* in two by failing to concede the orthodoxy of the figures. As I have been suggesting throughout this book, the forms of magic with which John shows some familiarity, including not only the *ars notoria* but also texts in the image magic tradition and the various works that were compiled in the *Liber Razielis*, understood their own processes in ways that either derived from, or were easily mapped on to, the sacramental world of the Christian dispensation. Their rituals were undergirded with the same basic Platonic model of cognition as a cleansing of the bodily stain, which was also a fundamental idea in John's theological sources and in the curricular models provided by the didascalic literature. Wherever this Greek philosophical idea meets with the Bible, we find it hooked first to quotations from the books of Wisdom, second to the topos of the loss of knowledge as the loss of paradise. The *ars notoria* particularly, but also the works traveling under the banner of the *Liber Razielis*, encouraged the understanding of the ritual cleansing both texts prescribe as enabling a return to a pristine state in which the lost inheritance of Adamic knowledge could be recovered. This return was not merely possible; it was divinely desirable, an original part of the cosmic plan. Thus, John's confident modeling of his own Book of Figures as a working piece of the Christian dispensation had some clear analogues in the magical literature he was drawing on, even if we find nothing in them that is exactly like the figures themselves. John's own writings pull the magical ideas ever closer to their theological underpinnings, elaborating and integrating them exegetically with more biblical locations, filtering these through biblical and liturgical commentaries he knew equally well.

John's prologue to the Old Compilation of Figures is distinguished by its confident use of traditional topoi drawn from a standard exegesis of the Song of Songs and a catena of quotations from the biblical books on Wisdom. The Book of Figures opens:

> For Moses says that some things are not just holy, but indeed Holy of Holies, and others are not just Sabbath, but Sabbath of Sabbaths. Thus we say that some things are not just "knowing" but "Knowing of Knowings." And just as he is blessed who enters into the holy, and more blessed he who enters into the Holy of Holies; and blessed he who celebrates the Sabbath, and more blessed he who celebrates the Sabbath of Sabbaths; in the same way blessed is he who enters into knowing and wisdom, but much more blessed he who enters into the Knowing of Knowings and Wisdom of Wisdoms, because all good things come along with Knowing and Wisdom, and immeasurable honor through their hands. For they are better than commerce in gold and silver, and I have said riches are nothing in comparison to them; through them kings reign and just lawgivers make judgments; for they love those who love them, and those who keep watch for them early discover them, and those who discover them will discover life and drink salvation from the Lord. Blessed therefore is the

man who enters upon Knowing and Wisdom, and whose heart is vigilant for them, because Knowing is the cognition of everything whose description is in the soul. It is the apex of nobility in the present and cause of eternal felicity in the future. Wisdom is the exhalation of the power of God, and the emanation of a kind of pristine clarity from the omnipotent God, and therefore incurs no iniquity, for it is the brightness of eternal light and spotless mirror of the majesty of God and image of his goodness.[3]

The opening sentences of this paragraph are based closely on Jerome's Latin version of Origen's first homily on the Song of Songs, concerning the title: "In the same way we learn from Moses that certain things are not just holy, but Holy of Holies; and others are not just Sabbath, but Sabbath of Sabbaths; so now in Solomon's writing we are taught that some songs are not just songs, but also Songs of Songs."[4] The passage quoted here is part of all standard interpretations of the title of the Song of Songs, and parts of Origen's homily are incorporated into the *Glossa ordinaria*.[5] Following this in John's text is a catena of extracts from other staples of the biblical Wisdom literature (including extracts from Proverbs and other passages from the Song of Songs). The appeal to Knowing as "cognition of everything whose description is in the soul" ultimately derives from book 1 of Al-Ghazali's *Metaphysica*, though it appears in many forms in thirteenth-century didascalica, where John most likely knew it.[6] John ends with the *speculum sine macula* passage from Wisdom 7:25–26, which he also drew into prayer *1, "O Rex regum." If John's figures have an unusual aspect as devotional forms, nevertheless the principles on which his Book of Figures is founded are conscientiously traditional echoes of the Wisdom literature.

It is clear, too, that from John's viewpoint the whole *Liber florum*, including its figures, fit into a traditional understanding of liturgical practice. In the Old Book of Figures, John elaborates an exegesis that contextualizes the figures against the normal liturgy of the mass, clarifying the significance of the crosses:

> Also there may be found in this work a trace and mystery of the holy and ineffable Trinity. We have set out that praying in this art is threefold: we pray in the Word first, we pray in the Figure and the Word second, and in the Visualization, Figure and Word third. And these three are not three prayers but one perfect Prayer. In itself, Prayer comes from no one. Figure proceeds from Prayer, and Visualization from both. Through Prayer we are conjoined to the Father, through Figure to the Son, and through Visualization to the Holy Spirit....

But someone might say that this is a new fashion of praying, and that it is not sanctioned by the church; but it would be false to say this because the church prays in a threefold manner in the mass: first with the prayers we call collects and in the beginning or introit of the mass; second ... with prayers and figures, and this is in the secrets and in the beginning of the Canon (since this cannot be done without the figure of the cross); and third ... with mental visualizations, prayers, and figures, and this in the first and last commemoration (which is done only with a visualization in the mind ...). And yet these are not three masses, but one mass. So also here.

And note that in any figure in this art, anything that is there beyond the sign of the cross (whether round, square, triangular, or more or less so, or something else) is to be understood as circumstantial to the figure and not as the figure itself. Only the sign of the cross (one or more) is understood as the figure. ... And if you find some figure in which the sign of the cross is not expressed ... it is nevertheless always to be mystically understood. ... It is hidden in them in order to demonstrate that, in that which pertains to the efficacious property of those figures (the sign of the cross), it is not spiritually possible for it to be enclosed in the boundaries of human sense and understanding.[7]

John's thinking in the prose portions of the Old Compilation of Figures, here as elsewhere, is informed by the discipline of traditional liturgical exegesis, though its diverse sources travel outside the normal ambit of sources used, for example, in Durand's work. In fact, among other things, the pattern here shows a structural debt to a passage in the *ars notoria*: "Again it should be known that in this marvelous art three things are inspected, namely note, figure and prayer. It is described in the art itself what a note is. Figure is a certain sacramental and ineffable prayer that cannot be expounded by human reason. Prayer, moreover, is a pious beseeching in the voice of the one praying, not striving, but overflowing in soft reading."[8] In John's version, the cross roughly corresponds to a "figure" here, but his wording owes a debt to traditional exegesis, too. There is a traditional explanation for why the Tetragrammaton is called the "ineffable name," passed on through Isidore in his discussion of God's names: "The ninth name, 'Tetragrammaton,' is the set of four letters that is applied to God properly among the Hebrews. ... It is called "ineffable," moreover, not because it cannot be spoken, but because it cannot in any way be enclosed in the bounds of human sense and understanding, and so, because concerning it nothing worthy can be said, it is called 'ineffable.'"[9] John's implicit linking of the cross and divine name here and elsewhere (most importantly in the figure that originally accompanied the Tetragrammaton prayer) is not original either. In the *Glossa ordinaria* on Exodus 28:36–38, a gloss attributed to Bede suggests that the four-letter name written on the gold plate on the forehead of the high priest is equivalent to the four points of the cross traced on the forehead at baptism.[10] This also may be a source for the gloss on the four letters that is interwoven with John's Tetragrammaton prayer itself: "The ineffable name of the lord consists in four letters, namely *he,* which means 'that,' *ioth,* which is 'beginning,' *heth* which is 'passion,' and *vau* which is 'of life.' Which all together means 'this, the beginning of life by the passion,' because Christ was the beginning of the life lost in Adam, which he repaired by his passion."[11] Here as elsewhere in John's book, he can be seen pulling the divine name and its Christian commentaries together with an idea of the passion signified by the cross and other signs and instruments of the passion, specifically the nails, to be further discussed shortly.

It may be noted that in this passage, and others like it in the Old Compilation, John never suggests that the figures have either a special affiliation with, nor a special distance from, necromantic images. This is very much unlike the relation that is always on view between the earlier Book of Prayers and the *ars notoria*, in which John positions *Liber florum* against the *ars notoria* at almost every turn: it is a cure, an antidote, a superior alternative, a sort of inoculation precisely targeting the *ars notoria*. No such preoccupation with necromancy is in evidence in the Book of Figures in either version, and what John does say about necromancy overall is much more muted. Despite what seems to have been the extravagance of their complex design, despite even the Virgin's failure to license the figures as she had the prayers, John expresses no real doubt about his Book of Figures at this stage of his writing, no sense that it has affiliation with necromancy either visually or substantially. This is about four years before the Barking Dogs' attack.

In 1315, when the figures came under fire, there was evidently another issue drawing the attention of critical authorities as well: John's visions. His manner of inducing them, his reception of their meaning, and the fact that they actually guided his actions raised many questions about discernment of spirits. The evidence for this is found in a triptych of chapters in the New Compilation of Figures, wherein John offers grounds for defending his work against naysayers and critics of his book.[12] It is clear that the main reason for the inclusion of these chapters was the scandal brought on by the attack of the Barking Dogs, though these chapters seem to be preemptively directed at future carping as well; they contain a general array of ammunition "against the mordant attacks of Barkers and against poisonous tongues."[13] Two out of the three chapters concern the legitimacy of dreams as a vehicle for prophecy. The gist of both chapters is that prophecy through dreams is attested in numerous locations in scripture; that the gloss at the beginning of the Psalms makes clear that dreams are one manner by which God speaks to his prophets; and that it is possible to know that dreams are conveying true information both by the initial disposition of the sleeper (if waking hours are spent in devotional activities contemplating celestial things, the dreams are unlikely to be caused by sinful thoughts) and by the effects of the dreams (if they encourage virtuous thoughts and habits, they are unlikely to come from a malevolent source).[14] John argues finally that "the whole benefit of this science consists in dreams: therefore it is permissible, and those following it are disciples of truth, as is clear from the authority of the holy canons."[15] In effect this constitutes a defense of John's own work as prophecy. As will be shown further below, the idea that John's visions contain prophecy is a continuous and sustained theme here, just as it was in the Old Compilation of Figures.

These two chapters defending dream incubation set up an important third chapter, "Concerning the Attack on This Science," in which John describes four related charges brought against his work, all based in Gratian, all conspiring to suggest that his dreams are delusions or demonic contrivances. It appears that he is quoting here from a written document, since his argument preserves recognizable quotations from Gratian, with chapter and verse citations. The chapter begins, "This science is attacked by means of the sacred canons which are held in the twenty-sixth *Causa*, third and fourth questions."[16] In the concluding passages of this chapter, John turns each passage from Gratian around to show how it can be used to defend the *Liber florum* instead. This chapter offers more clarity on the issues behind the critique, since the allegation that the appearance of the figures evokes *nigromancia* in fact makes no explicit *theological* point. John responds to this emotionally, as to a slander. By contrast, to the charges from canon law, itemized below, he responds as an expert in canon law. I will illuminate the four charges first, in the order that John lays them out, and then give John's response to each.

The first charge against the *Liber florum*, from *Decretum* C. 26 q. 2–3 c. 2, draws on a passage derived from Augustine[17] to the effect that "demons foretell and predict certain future or present things that are going to be done or going to happen to men, and they are capable of intermingling themselves with human thoughts through visual illusions confected by the imagination [*imaginaria visa*]." The charge against John's work more precisely is that his book "teaches about and concerns certain future or present things that are going to be done or going to happen in marvelous and invisible ways, through visual illusions."[18] In a sense this boils down to an accusation that John's book is either not prophetic, or dangerously so; John's book teaches operators to do what amounts to divination by dreams. The apparitions of the Virgin could equally well be demonic illusions brought about by manipulations of the imagination.

The second charge, drawn from the same place in Gratian and another well-known Augustinian locus,[19] has to do with idolatry and superstition, worshiping of creature as Creator, and in particular the vanity of "pacts of significations agreed upon and confederated with demons, as are the volumes of magic arts." The charge against John's work is that "it seems that it was taught in this science rather to adore the creature, that is the virgin Mary, than God, or as God," and that the volume contains certain "pacts of significations, both agreed upon and confederated, for consultation."[20] The charge that John's devotion to the Virgin is idolatrous may be only to say that his prophetic capacity is not demonstrably grounded in intellectual (imageless) vision, not that God never acted through Mary. It should be clear that the concern with "demonic pact" in this regard is a concern with what Thomas Aquinas would have labeled "tacit pact,"[21] not the explicit pact of Theophilus earlier or Faustus later. John's error is not of summoning malign spirits on purpose, but rather of trusting the apparitions of the Virgin too readily, reading his dreams *as if they signified prophetic things*, and acting on them, rather than cautiously remaining agnostic about their news. The next passage supports this reading.

The third charge, deriving from *Decretum* D. 68 c. 2 and D. 4 c. 110, *De consecratione*, turns on the general idea that where there is doubt, it is safer to interpret things negatively. The charge against John rests in the supposition that, since the devil can transform himself into an angel of light, "there is doubt whether it is the Virgin herself, or the devil. . . . And because these things are doubtful we ought to interpret them negatively because it is safer; in this case, we ought to say the visions of this science are from a devil, not from the virgin Mary."[22] John's error here is seen as an error of discretion.

Finally, and most interestingly, the last charge against the *Liber florum* actually rests on something John reported the Virgin saying to him. In a vision on the eighth ides of September, John writes that the Virgin spoke to him, saying, "'You are the receptacle of the Holy Spirit.' And immediately, without stopping, indignantly moving her head, mouth, nostrils and eyes, she added with a grimace: 'And you are the phantasm of all the others.'" The charge rests on this exegesis of the vision by John's opponents. He reports their words as follows: "It is as if she meant to say: 'Because you are a Christian monk and a priest, in this sense you have been born a fit receptacle for the Holy Spirit. But because you write and teach others the phantasms of the dreams of this science, in this you are made the phantasm of all others.' Therefore this science is the product of a fantasy. From these authoritative passages and things like them this science is impugned."[23] The interesting aspect of this last accusation is not merely that it rests on an exegesis of John's account of his own vision, but also that, in doing so, it also seems to give some credence to the visionary content itself. Perhaps this was only to ensure there was some leeway for John to back away with dignity, but whatever their reasons, John by no means misses their inconsistency, and he presses it home. In his defense against this point, he writes,

> To the fourth charge, it is answered: the interpretation made of the words of the vision in this passage cannot stand, because the manner of this vision was just like all the others. And so it follows that the entire vision must be a fantasy, just like all the others; and thus its words would not be trustworthy, and it would not stand, just as the others do not stand, which is not tenable. And therefore the aforesaid interpretation cannot stand, and it does not constitute a hindrance [to the moral value of the book].

In defense, he offers his own interpretation of Mary's words:

> But in fact the passage should be interpreted as a whole: "Because you composed this science, and had many graces of revelations, therefore the fact will also be clear, and is clear to all among the contemplatives and those truly loving God, that you are the receptacle of the Holy Spirit. But also you have become the fantasy of all the others, those not truly loving God, and not truly contemplatives, into whose hands it will sometimes come" (as is plain through the words of the visions subtly understood) "because such persons do not reckon this science as true, but as a fantasy." And she spoke of the "others" [aliorum] for the reason that they were estranged [alieni] from the grace of the Holy Spirit.[24]

The key point for John has to do with the fact that his liturgy is offered as a mode of practice for contemplatives, meaning for him that it is seen as an extension of monastic practice, designed for sublimation of the soul in its earthly crucible. The secular cleric cannot know the rewards of those who engage in a life of contemplation; the *Liber florum* is one mode of access to that life.

Against the first three charges—that he has been deluded by demons, that by incubating dreams of the Virgin he has actually been forming "pacts" of significations agreed upon with demons, and that it is safer to interpret doubtful visions negatively—John's apology similarly makes the liturgies of his *Liber florum* an extension of his monastic training. He suggests that those the demons habitually deceive are those who do not hold God in their hearts (unlike the operators of his art or science, who think pure thoughts and are occupied with heavenly things). His defense against the second charge, that he has engaged "pacts" with demons, is particularly interesting, because it suggests that there *is* a sort of pact in operation, but it is rather a pact covenanted with God. In describing demonic pact, the Augustinian passage on which Gratian's case rests here uses the words "pacta foederata"; "foedus" is the cognate Vulgate term, usually translated as "covenant" in English. John makes the case that what they see in his work is not the signification of demonic pact but rather of divine covenant:

> To the second argument it is answered thus: the chapter adduced as evidence here is understood to concern teachings by human beings about making idols and things to be worshiped and things in that category, because that is something merely superstitious and vain. But here [in my book] there are teachings concerning the worship of God and the glorious Virgin, and things in that category. "Because there is no comparison between Christ and Belial" [2 Cor. 6:15], there is no problem with this "pact," since these are permitted in Genesis, where it reads: "I will remember my covenant that I have made with you" [Gen. 9:15; Lev. 26:42], by which authority it is shown that there is a "pact covenanted" [pacta federata] between God and humanity.[25]

By saying this, John suggests that his book of prayers is continuous with the sacraments, working as one of many agents of grace in the dispensation to pull human beings through the earthly life toward the divine one. In this location, he does not imply that a covenant has been made with him personally and specifically, except insofar as he is a Christian aiming at salvation. However, he is also aware that in Old Testament references, the covenant operates through specific people: Abraham, Isaac, and Jacob (Lev. 26:42), Noah (Gen. 6:18), and Moses (Exod. 34:27). The prophets also may be agents of covenant, their prophecies being its expression (see Isa. 59:21). The assumption that runs beneath John's apologia in these chapters is that in becoming one of those persons more actively involved in furthering the work of the dispensation (as are monks, friars, and contemplatives), he becomes one of those people to whom God is more likely to speak. In this way he shares with other contemplatives an inheritance from the Old Testament prophets. This is a point that becomes still more visible in his response to the next charge.

Here it is suggested that it is safer to read ambiguous or doubtful visions negatively, but John has already stated that the visions he reports are not really in doubt. He draws evidence for this both from their context (he is a religious and a contemplative) and their effects (they have given him power over his sinful habits and changed his life for the better). John's theodicy is essentially optimistic; ultimately his defense rests, as Nicholas Watson has put it, on a principle of *trust*.[26] He trusts that God will honor the sacraments, and he trusts that, while demons do have work in the world that is permitted by God, they do not have the upper hand. As to the third point, then,

> it is answered: although the devil can transform himself into an angel of light . . . this should be understood as meaning once, or twice, or three times, or several more times, but not as *always*—except among those perverse people that are spoken about in the first response. Because from this, one very unsuitable and erroneous thing would follow, namely that all the things that were demonstrated, seen and done for our predecessors [i.e., the biblical prophets] by the grace of the Holy Spirit of dreams would have been revealed at the suggestion of the devil. Which would not merely be absurd to believe, but also erroneous. And it is not to be believed that God would be so unjust that he would *always* dismiss the people who reflect on him perfectly . . . even if he might sometimes permit this, twice, or three times, or several more, not to destroy them but to test their faith.[27]

The principle of trusting the work of God's dispensation as it unfolds, despite the interventions of evil, is clear in this passage. The idea that he is in the lineage of the prophets because of his contemplative life is also fairly transparent.[28] John's main point is that—as in Romans 8:28, a verse he quotes in the Book of Visions—"for those loving God, all things work together for good, for those who are called to be holy, according to His purpose."[29] John's vocation as a monk makes this verse apply more or less explicitly to him; he is witness to a process in which things are working out as they must, for a good end that is always humanly known only in part, but is also always in the process of being revealed.

And he is aware, too, that he is part of that process of revelation as the writer of a delivered text—and that he is not a static cog in the machinery, but rather a dynamic agent, a person capable of error as well as self-knowledge. Thus, proper recognition of God's representations really *matters*. As we saw in chapter 3, in the analysis of vision 9, the recognition of God's apparition in mimicry of the flawed self encouraged the corrective mode of praxis, humiliation, and instruction demonstrated by Christ in John's vision. The vision was a divine lesson, and as such a revelation of God; at the same time it was a revelation of John's self as seen by God. In this mutual recognition, John's eye becomes God's eye. We may imagine that God is looking critically at his own image in the mirror of his creation, both seeing the same thing at once. And so the whole dispensation inches toward its fulfillment.

Likewise, in the Book of Figures, the revelatory process of the dispensation is imitated by, and integrated with, the process of self-revelation and self-shaping that comes about through penance. This is true both universally and personally. The small moments of contrition and penance in John's visions are moving parts of the divine self-revelation that occurs as the dispensation unfolds, but the *Liber florum* itself is part of the unfolding, and every fracture of John's self-understanding, every movement of his mind to contrition, becomes immediately a new window onto the divine that must be marked onto his book as it is marked on his conscience. If his eye becomes God's eye through the visions of himself in error, his book becomes God's book as he acts out both the error and its penance in writing and drawing, in inscription.

In the New Compilation Book of Figures, the fraction and refraction of self becomes a kind of ongoing divine display that is signified in the deliberate disarrangement of the three chapters concerning the defense of the work just discussed. This disarrangement is cast as penitential; it is the sober marking of an error made when he moved his figures too hastily to the end of the book, not waiting for the divine directive to do so, although such a directive had been declared forthcoming by the archangel Michael. John introduces this topic early on in the first part of his New Compilation of Figures, right after a description of the forms they were meant to take: "In fact," he says, "we put the figures here at first, just as they were devised above.[30] But afterward, for the reason stated below, we took and transferred them." The statement is strengthened by a gloss: "Here in this paragraph the figures of this book were first placed, but they were moved to the third part of the book for a reason; and here begins our florid error."[31]

In chapter 4, John explains his error concerning the figures:

> *The reason for moving the figures from this place to another.*
> Put in a vision, I asked the glorious Virgin if it would please her for me to compile anew the instructions and old figures of this book on account of the mordant attacks of the Barking Dogs, and for the advantage of my many successors. Responding to me through the archangel Michael, she said: "do not move or change them yet; we will bless you when the time comes." Awakening from this vision I did not await the promised time, but began to compile the figures and instructions for this science anew, devising the figures as they are devised above, wishing and believing that

afterwards they would be confirmed by the glorious Virgin, just as I had done before in the Old Compilation. . . . But I did not await the time; and because I did not await the time I fell into error—only as to the forms of the figures, as appears below,[32] not as to the instructions. And wishing to correct my error in a way that might be an example for all my successors, so that they might fear to do what was prohibited in this science, and act according to its teaching, we determined and decided that the manner of forming the figures dictated by us above before the stated time perpetually remain in the place where we had instructed them to be made and placed.

The following chapter, which is about the defense of this science, and which was supposed to be situated in the third part of this book, as will be seen there, I write in my own hand as a sign of compunction.[33]

The "following chapter" is the one entitled "Qualiter ista sciencia debeat defendi," or "How this science should be defended," which is chapter 2 of the apologetic triptych. In it, against the caution from Gratian that wicked thoughts about worldly things in the mind of the waking person can give rise to delusive dreams,[34] he asserts that the contrary is true for those who spend their waking hours occupied with pure thoughts and contemplation of celestial things, as the followers of his art necessarily must. John additionally notes that all his dreams have had a good effect on him personally, increasing his practice of virtue rather than diminishing it. After transcribing this chapter, John writes, "in the place where the error was previously contained, let a place of truth succeed."[35] Here, clearly, the "error previously contained" was the premature sketch of the figures, done without the divine directive; the "truth" that replaces it is the chapter outlining the reasons for John's continued faith in his visionary capacity. He goes on to make a further interpretation and a suggestion to other operators of his text:

> And this error of ours was not permitted by God and the glorious Virgin without cause, but rather so that the future good of the truth might shine more brightly, since according to what is said about the first psalm: "It is not possible to show the excellence of something better than by showing the baseness of its contrary." And so it is concluded that our error has made and brought forth the flower of the truth of excellence. And from that aforementioned place where it begins, right up to the present place, whoever wishes it as a sign of the truth may have depicted images with flowers and leaves on the pages of this book.[36]

John here imagines the designs of flowers and leaves as a *signum punicionis* potentially shared by the whole community of followers—known and unknown, down through the ages—who will succeed him in his ritual and textual practice. Such shared marks of the chastisement of error may be seen in other contexts in the literature of the fourteenth century, perhaps the most famous instance occurring at the end of the poem *Gawain and the Green Knight*, when other knights in Arthur's court are said to adopt the wearing of green sashes in imitation of Gawain's green sash, the penitential token of his error at Bertilak's castle. It is different for John, of course, in the sense that, unlike Gawain, he is making a kind of pastoral use of his own error, using it to teach operators the importance of sustained and respectful attention to the content of their own dreams at a point where they are still engaged in the ritual copying of the book. Extant manuscripts show that few operators in fact added these decorations to their copies,[37] though it is clear that John's own copy—the primal exemplar—was so decorated. In the third and last part of the New Compilation of Figures, in the place where the chapter on the defense of his Art once stood, he refers to the flowers and leaves again: "there should be written and situated after these things the chapter which concerns the defense of this science. But we have placed it surrounded by flowers and leaves in the first part of this book, and for the reason given there, that is, as a sign of the chastisement of our error and of the excellence of the truth."[38] Yet more is marked than just "truth," for a part of John's penance is to leave the erroneous *descriptions* of the figures in place in perpetuity. Specifically, the descriptions in NC III.i.2 contain a cancelled directive to put one of the four Hebrew letters of the divine name in each corner of each figure, and to put the names of all designated operators in a circle around the image of the Virgin. To prevent subsequent copyists from actually following the instructions, and so wasting work, John added corrective glosses, perhaps originally in the margins or else on an extra leaf, which were adopted into the body of the book by later operators. The decisions about static text and displaced text do make for confusing reading in this part of the book.[39]

Even so, these penitential moves demonstrate that John's contrition connects to his loss of faith in the divine guidance he was receiving; it is about his failure to attend to the prophetic words of his vision, not about the figures themselves. More specifically, it is not about a shameful experience of drawing on texts that he knew could be classed as *nigromancia* when he put the figures together. I do not mean to suggest that he did not draw on texts that might have been classifiable in this tradition, though as I suggested in chapter 5, there was enough breadth and ambiguity around *nigromancia* in practice to leave some wiggle room in this area. The extant figures seem to be a unique hybrid of Christian devotional meditations and images with a visual lexicon of shapes and symbols from image magic and the theurgic tradition of the *ars notoria*. But what comes out most clearly in the New Compilation of Figures is that, from John's point of view, the entire *Liber florum*, including the figures, is an outflowing of the spirit of monastic reading and prayer into a new discourse of contemplation that extends to prophecy.

John does anticipate other questions about the cancellation of the Old Book of Figures. Near the end of the book, in the antepenultimate chapter of the New Compilation Book of Figures, John writes:

> Someone might ask why the [New] Compilation of Figures made and published by us was not worth confirming or could not be confirmed at the beginning as was the Old. I answer that the Old was confirmed, and this one was going to be revealed; and so it would have been superfluous if anything else came between them which likewise would have had to be revoked. And the mystery signified by the Old would have ceased, from which this one was later going to be revealed.
>
> Why did God permit us to compose it even though he knew it was of no moment and another had to be revealed? I answer: this was so that its truth might shine all the more brightly....
>
> Also, note that this New Compilation was prefigured because in the substance of a certain vision from the beginning of the Old Compilation there were things that were going to come to pass, but we did not understand them until this New Compilation was complete. In that vision we asked if we would be composing the book to the end, and the blessed virgin Mary, smiling, answered "No."[40] And she spoke the truth in the literal sense, although we interpreted the said vision in a different way in the Old Compilation (although still well). For it is clear that we are not finishing this book, but God himself and the blessed virgin Mary.[41]

Here, John casts the new Book of Figures as a divinely revealed text, its revelation something loftier than the "confirmation" that declared the old figures fit to be used. It should be remembered that the Old Compilation Book of Figures had to be "confirmed" only because the Virgin had denied the license for it that he initially sought. Indeed, the vision John recapitulates above (in which Mary smilingly says "no") focuses on the moment of that denial, now exposed as the signification of the future revelation of the book's real ending. The idea that the Old Compilation contains a "mystery" from which the New is destined to be revealed keeps the Old Compilation meaningful, even though its ritual instructions have been superseded; it also concretizes the claims to prophecy intimated earlier, by mapping the book onto a scriptural pattern. John understands that the New Compilation is the key that unlocks the Old, so that its truth can shine more brightly. The book begun by him contains the prophecy that it will be fulfilled by God.

The moment of fraction in the *Liber florum* thus becomes analogous to the turning point of the entire dispensation in the incarnation and passion of Christ, for the Bible is also a book broken in two, broken between the Old and New Testaments, along the line scored by the dispensation of grace in the body of Christ himself. John is quite explicit about this analogy. He describes the translation of the law and the priesthood as analogous to the translation of the Figures and the Particular Experiments in the New Compilation;[42] he speaks of the Old Compilation as prefiguring the New, just as the Old Testament prefigures the New;[43] and more pointedly still, he refers to his own instruction to inscribe the four letters of the Tetragrammaton in Hebrew in the four corners of each figure as being superseded by a new instruction, which he gets directly in a vision from God the Father, to replace these letters of the divine name with the four nails of the crucifixion. His exegesis of this action makes explicit that he sees himself as transcending a form of Judaizing that might be perceived in the Old Compilation, a theme I have discussed elsewhere.[44] The nails decreed as part of the figures here are also a metonymy of the subjective and embodied brokenness through which divine fulfillment operates; they are to be impressed on the images of John's book, just as they were on Christ's flesh.

But just as past knowledge cannot simply be excised from the self without distorting or destroying present knowledge, so also every part of the book is necessary to the whole process of the dispensation that occurs in and through it. Just as John casts as revelatory the discovery of his own error in his penitential visions, so also these distortions in the book's body reflect John's knowledge at the moment of his correction. John goes on to delimit the sacral aspect of the Old Compilation of Figures as pertinent to a spiritual childhood that has given way to maturity, using a familiar Pauline trope:

> Whence the blessed Virgin gave us milk to drink in the beginning of this knowledge, as the milk of spiritual grace is duly signified by her holy breast which she placed in my mouth, breast-feeding me, showing me to be still a youth. And so it was permitted me to gird myself in this knowledge and to stroll through it wheresoever I wished, playing ball at will with a boy, our lord Jesus Christ, making and discovering whatever kind of figures I wanted, and the instructions for uttering them. And all things for me as though for a boy, in case I should have wept the tears of loss or renunciation for this holy knowledge, were confirmed by the same lord

Jesus Christ and by the same blessed Virgin, as these things all are gathered from the Old Compilation.

But because I then grew and matured in knowledge, the Virgin no longer gave me milk but rather solid food as nourishment, in such a way that I cannot gird myself any longer, but it is necessary to stretch forth the arms of virtue and another shall gird me: that is, the Virgin herself, leading me whither I do not choose (and yet it is pleasing); handing on and revealing to me the figures and their revisions, since not according to my will but that of God and the Virgin herself it was necessary for them to be made and also confirmed. And so from all these things it is clear that this science was designated in prophetic visions, announced as if by miracles, and by figures and enigmas foretold.[45]

Here then is the fulfillment of the prophecy already begun in the visions of the Old Compilation. These paragraphs weave together quotations from several biblical loci with several of the Old Compilation visions, newly understood. When John suggests that the Virgin gave him milk to drink "in the beginning of this science," he is referring to the sequence of visions "briefly listed," near the end of the Old Book of Figures:

> After I, John, recovered my visions, I saw these visions. . . . I saw myself lying and sleeping on the breast of the virgin Mary, and she put her breast in my mouth, and I suckled and slept. . . . Also, I saw myself playing ball with Christ as a boy. And I saw that our lord Jesus Christ kissed me on the mouth, and on the morning after that I entered into the office of preaching. Also, I saw that the crucified one was above my cup and drops of blood from his feet ran into my cup. Also, I saw that I was climbing the cross where the crucified one was, and the blood from his feet flowed over my head.[46]

A kind of self-portrait with the holy family, these itemized visions detail John's keeping company with the infant Christ, sleeping on Mary's breast, drinking her milk, and playing with the boy Jesus; he sees himself at the passion catching his blood in a cup and climbing on the cross. I commented in chapter 4 on another image of milk in the Old Compilation of Figures that brings together, in a set of linked juxtapositions, the idea that his own book is a spiritual food deriving directly from Mary, flowing forth "from the emanation of the milk of spiritual grace and the holy mercy of her nipple with which Christ was nourished and I was spiritually nourished and comforted. In the strength of this spiritual food, I journeyed all the way to the mount of God, Horeb, and thence I drank what I have written and am about to write, the sacred flowing words of this book."[47] Here, the "milk of grace" begins as the Virgin's milk that sustained the holy flesh of the infant Christ, and simultaneously (because John casts himself as almost a sibling of Christ here, a foster child of Mary) as the milk that sustains John's own visionary body. Metonymically, the Virgin's milk is the flesh of Christ that is shared by John (as in practice by all Christians) in the body of the Church. It has a liturgical equivalent in the Eucharist. By the end of the paragraph, however, in a rapid double metalepsis, this milk becomes, first, the angelic food that enables prophecy for Elijah, and immediately after this, the *Liber florum* itself. The milk thus represents the deep source of the prophetic function he ascribes mystically to his own book.

This was how he saw things already at the end of the Old Compilation. Within the framework of the New, these visionary figures in the Old Compilation remain prophetic, but the whole is seen as the letter of a prophecy only now revealed in its full intent; the milk has hidden a deeper parable. In his rereading of these visionary episodes in the New Compilation, John emphasizes, as we have just seen, another idea of spiritual childhood in the opposition of milk and meat.[48] The "tears of loss" seem a sufficient acknowledgment that his own will went against the divine will in the matter of the figures, yet his discovery of "whatever sorts of figures he wanted" took place in a space enclosed and protected by the holy family, with the boy Christ at his side, both under the watchful eyes of Mary. Thus the acknowledgment of his own willfulness does not sacrifice the sense of prophecy originally figured by the milk, but rather extends it, depicting his "childhood" in the discovery of the figures as a time of lost joy.

Two biblical loci are tied together here. One is an image of milk and solid food taken from Paul's first letter to Corinthians 3:1–2: "And I, brethren, could not speak to you as unto spiritual, but as unto carnal. As unto little ones in Christ. I gave you milk to drink, not meat: for you were not capable as yet." The traditional readings of this passage offered in the *Glossa ordinaria* relate "solid food" in various ways to the spiritual sense—a level of reading that comes wrapped in the literal sense (the "letter"), but is unavailable except to spiritual maturity, that is, to the wisdom of adulthood, but simultaneously, to Christendom. A gloss (drawn from Augustine) explains that the burden of understanding the spiritual sense of scripture is upon the individual:

> For just as the cross of Christ is foolishness to some, a scandal to others, but to the called is the power of God, so the same thing is milk to some, solid food to others, according as their capacity takes more or less. . . .

They hear the same things at once, spiritual and carnal, each according to their own measure, and it is not necessary that any secrets fit to be spoken to the perfect should be hidden from little children. So the Apostle said, "I could not speak to you as spiritual," which is to say, "You could not understand what I was saying as spiritual."[49]

John's link to this passage shows that he understands his earlier grasp of the Virgin's words to have been (not to put too fine a point on it) wrong, or at least pertaining to a childish rather than mature sense of the prophetic import of the Virgin's words.

There is another scriptural quotation on which this passage depends, that is, the words of Christ to Peter in John 21:18: "I say to thee, when thou wast younger, thou didst gird thyself and didst walk where thou wouldst. But when thou shalt be old, thou shalt stretch forth thy hands, and another shall gird thee and lead thee whither thou wouldst not." With this passage it was understood that Jesus predicted the martyrdom of Peter by crucifixion. As the gloss, dependent on Augustine, makes clear, although no one wants to die, the glory of martyrdom depends on its troublesome nature:

> "Stretch forth your hands" means "you will be crucified"; and he adds how this will happen: "And another will gird you, and lead where you do not wish to go," because he was led unwillingly to that trouble, unwillingly he came to it, but willingly he conquered it, and left behind the disposition of weakness on account of which no-one wishes to die, which is natural inasmuch as old age was not about to take him away from Peter. Whence also the Lord: "let this cup pass from me." But no matter how great is the trouble of death, the power of love may conquer it; if there were no small trouble of death, the glory of martyrs would not be so great.[50]

Is martyrdom an extreme metaphor here? After all, what has John actually given up? A plethora of figures that it appears operators found too difficult to work with anyway. The metaphor may seem exaggerated, inasmuch as unlike Peter, or Christ, John is not actually being taken away to an ugly death. It is not his body that is broken, but only, so to speak, the book's body. But this body, as we have seen, has developed in parallel with John's self; as much as his body it is a part of him, and as much as his body also it is a part of the dispensation. Along with the "tears of loss or renunciation" that might have been if the Virgin did not allow John the pleasure of play in the book's creation, these metaphors must be taken to reflect a depth of feeling about the project as John was giving it up.

There is certainly a part of him that wished the Old Book of Figures could have lived another kind of life. A strong belief in his own original sense of the figures persists. The general tenor of John's commentary on his work makes clear that all along, in both Old and New Compilations, John has been intimately concerned with the operator's prayerful attitude in the handling of the figures and generally with a Christian orthopraxis. In the Old Compilation, as we have seen, he wrote of the prayers, figures, and visualizations in terms of spiritual or allegorical understanding. The entire work figures the Trinity, and the practice of praying in this threefold manner induces faith, hope, and charity; the three types of prayer further represent three phases of the sacramental action, the operator's devotion, and the divine confirmation and execution of the salvific action; the three actions of prayer represent humility, stability, and sanctity. The most important and most powerful sign in the figures is the cross.

The cross is an interesting sign to focus on here because it transcends the Old Compilation and is one of the signs particularly directed to appear in the figures of the New. In the Old Compilation, John elaborates the idea that a cross is the most potent part of every figure in his book—it is that which constitutes the efficacy of the figure in the transmittal of knowledge, and it is so important that it is actually understood to be there even when it is not there. It is hidden in his figures, he writes, "in order to demonstrate that, in that which pertains to the efficacious property of those figures (the sign of the cross) it is not spiritually possible for it to be enclosed in the boundaries of human sense and understanding."[51] As we have seen, this gloss pulls the cross into alignment with the ineffable name of God represented by the Tetragrammaton, the invisibility of the cross here becoming an analog for the unspeakability of the divine name. Unlike the Shem ha-Meforash, the cross is not a letter, nor composed of letters, but its shape unites the four letters of the divine name in the Tetragrammaton figure (and presumably in all of John's figures, which all contain the Hebrew letters of the divine name in the corners, and the cross either hidden or visible). The cross is a sign, but not a word or letter, and a seemingly infinite variety of meanings can be read out of it. At the same time, what is encapsulated in it is not actually susceptible of restriction in the bounds of human sense—a fact that John represents by sometimes not including it.

None of this is consistent with the generally apotropaic features of the cross used in traditional necromantic figures; all of it is very consistent with the way the compressed signification of devotional images operates. Even though their representational elements may be somewhat original, John's figures are designed to bring together the instruments of human redemption in various configurations, all entwined with soteriological desire: they mingle the divine and human, the property of the figure, the cross, Mary, the Son, and the names of God, sometimes represented by the use of acronyms, or Greek or Hebrew letters. Their configurations may stretch the limits of the speakable, but nevertheless, as I also showed in chapter 4, they *have* a sense to which the operator becomes alert in putting them together.

There are only eight figures in the New Compilation—seven figures of the Virgin, and one apocalyptic Christ. John explains how everything that he intended can actually be signified by, takes its sense and existence from, the image of the Virgin and child, which he repeats in each of the seven images, accompanied by the words "Alma Maria," a set of crosses, and seven different birds and plants. Among the most beautiful images actually found executed in manuscript may be those of the manuscript in the Salzburg University Library, M I 24. A single image (see fig. 6) shows their most important features.

We no longer see the four letters of the divine name, which have been supplanted, as God directed in John's vision, with the nails of the passion in the four corners of the image. Other symbolism is carefully restrained: atop the cypress (a fragrant wood mentioned in the Song of Songs, and one of the trees Wisdom associates to herself in Ecclus. 24:17), a pelican feeds its young with its own blood. All the superfluous designs of the figures in the Old Compilation are boiled down to the centrally placed icon of the Virgin and child, their eyes lovingly engaged.[52] Gone are the complex figures, inscrutable letterings, and interwoven names.

Though they were to be prohibited, and eventually lost, it is patent from many things that John says in the New Compilation that the Old Book of Figures remained deeply important to him. Its dropping away does not appear to have been a part of John's intention but a result of the fact that operators did not copy parts of the book they did not mean to use. In general, the scribes and operators of the New Compilation, in the primary form in which it has come down to us, are innocent of knowledge of the Old Compilation or the real spiritual terms of its mystery. The Bodleian manuscript of the Old Compilation puts us in a privileged position, in this one way, to know a bit more than the fifteenth-century operators of this work, though in many other ways, of course, we know far less.

One thing that we are privileged to catch a glimpse of is that John's original figures were much more complex than their association with "necromancy," at the opening of the New Compilation of Figures, suggests. In the same way that knowledge of the Old Compilation constitutes a privilege of our time (by which I mean specifically the more global access to data on the World Wide Web that allowed me both to locate the Bodleian manuscript and connect it to the other manuscripts I knew), so also is it a privilege of our time to glimpse how very complex a thing John's penance is. The idea that John created the figures during

Fig. 6 Universitätsbibliothek Salzburg, M I 24, fol. 79r.

his spiritual childhood as a creature of flesh is transmuted from its normal set of theological and metahistorical meanings by the notion that he was allowed to do this as a form of "play" in company with the child Jesus.

Mary's children here—John and Jesus—may both be figures of Jewish flesh in this particular picture, but they are also, by a clear turn of these conventional topoi, innocent. The image of John and Jesus playing together under Mary's maternal protection is also, like the *thema* vision that began the book, a figure of John's theodicy of trust. For John, exegesis of the figures in the Old Compilation was part and parcel of the visionary, prophetic, or divinatory knowledge that they catalyzed when they were used. The new but equally exegetical understanding of their displacement by the New Compilation figures is part of one and the same knowledge module. John's book can be seen on one level as a reflection of the Christian theurgy that lies at the heart of both Christian liturgy and biblical exegesis. On another level, and equally strongly, it reflects his own sense of coming into a mature personhood with adult knowledge.

The trick is that the integrity of knowledge has to rely on an account of process that takes in the past sense of truth as well as the present one. The picture of the past and present has to be a whole, or the living person cannot be whole. The sacramental sense of the work, its unity through the idea of prophecy, is also the unity of John's personhood at the moment of the book's perfection.

CONCLUSION:
FUTURE HISTORY

[A game of chess:]

Then, if the game were drawing near to the close, Papa would throw himself back in his chair with an exclamation of bewilderment, for she was always right. He never won now. He would try. I could see him consciously reviving his fires, commanding his mind to be acute and powerful, and prophetic about little things as it had been before; but Rosamund, firm behind the veil of trance, would establish the fact of her game, and it would be other than the game he tried to enforce....

I could not understand it at all. What they had been playing was stranger than a game, for here was Papa thinking out each move, obviously often choosing between two or three alternatives and altering his mind at the last minute, yet here was Rosamund, not using her reason at all, simply knowing what moves succeeded each other in a game that existed somewhere in full completion, even before they had sat down to play it. How could there be one game which Papa made up as he went along, and another which existed before it began, and how could they both be the same game?

—Rebecca West, *The Fountain Overflows*

[T]he obstacles to comprehension, perhaps especially when social things are in question, have less, as Wittgenstein observed, to do with the understanding than with the will. I am often surprised at the time it has taken me—and this is probably not over—really to understand some of the things I had been saying for a long time with the sense of knowing exactly what I was saying. And if I reword the same themes and return several times to the same objects and the same analyses, it is always, I think, in a spiralling movement which makes it possible to attain each time a higher level of explicitness and comprehension and to discover unnoticed relationships and hidden properties.

—Pierre Bourdieu, *Pascalian Meditations*

CONCLUSION 155

Of course no book is perfect. However, the *Liber florum* looks better to me all the time; at least, it seems less of a haphazard jumble as it weathers the process of becoming legible within and without. Retrospectively, my own process of figuring the text out sometimes seems more haphazard, to have in it more of chance and felicitous coincidence, depending as it does on a sequence of unplanned and unplannable events taking place on two continents: manuscript handlists floating under my hand; a chance meeting with a knowledgeable librarian or colleague at a conference; an email from an acquaintance far away who unexpectedly knew something we did not; backward glances suddenly revealing everything as different from what I had thought; none of this possible to quite systematize (except for the backward glances, which become habit, like checking your blind spot when changing lanes), but also none of it quite random, of course, because even though I was not always looking for manuscripts, I was never exactly *not* looking for manuscripts either. I had a stash of unsolved John of Morigny puzzles with me all the time, like a knitting bag, or like a gland filled with spider silk, always being spun out in sticky threads to catch the little flecks of data moving through the inner and outer air.

For me and for Nicholas, the ongoing resolution of textual problems and cruces was an engagement partly at the micro level of the letters, words, and grammar, and partly at the macro level of manuscript transmission, the changing shape of the text as it moved from hand to hand. The solution to a particular crux, when it happened, was always accompanied by a sense of the inevitability of that particular solution: one had no previous knowledge of it, and yet one *recognized* it, as the data surrounding the crux righted itself, reorganized itself in ways that tended to make other things around it clearer too. Sometimes a solution came in the form of a new fact (a newly found source, or another, better manuscript reading), but sometimes it also came with the little shock I have described before, of seeing that something one had seen as *factual* all along was not actually a fact at all. It came in the crumbling of an assumption, which, once it had fallen, made everything around the puzzle change form. Sometimes these local discoveries caused the shape of our edition to change as well, with a new reading, a recognition of a repeated motif, having a ripple effect on the structural layers and referencing system.

I have conversed with many people in the course of working this out, sharing unpublished work freely with those who asked to see it, and many others have shared things too, but of course Nicholas was always my closest partner, especially in the last two years, in the final phases of constructing our Latin edition of the *Liber florum*. The puzzles became more acute as we had to decide on the shape our information would take, especially as we began to work through charts and tables as a way of organizing both what we knew and (at least as crucially) what we did not know. I would array bits and pieces of the puzzle before him, as he would for me. Sometimes one person got the answer, and sometimes the other. He saw completely different things than I did, settled on quite different things as problematic, and never spotted the puzzles I saw as acute—though once we had brought them into the light, sometimes he solved my puzzles, and sometimes I solved his; or sometimes neither did; or sometimes we checked each other's wrong ideas and false solutions. The hope for a resolution sometimes gets ahead of itself.

It felt and continues to feel as if we had two different halves of a single understanding. Bits of the work that seemed absolutely clear to one of us, rooted in memory, always recoverable, were oddly elusive to the other. We had to remind each other of things again and again, things that at any given moment seemed to be "known" by one of us, but not the other. How can knowing be so difficult to hold onto? Even when facts are clear, certain, irrefragable, they get dropped as the mind picks up other scent trails. It is partly that it takes a much bigger network to anchor it than any single person could ever contain. At the same time, without the work of a single person—just one person—sometimes a big piece of the fabric of knowledge would fall away. When there are two people holding what seems to be two halves of a single knowledge, so aware of how much less you would know if the other person were not there, working closely to anchor the text of a still unpublished sprawling fourteenth-century work in a Latin edition, one's sense of the fragility of one's own knowledge becomes acute—the precious information contained in each word of every manuscript is at the mercy of fire and water, of faulty technology, of our inability to communicate with each other, our own emotions, our errors of will, our own aging, diminishing eyesight and unreliable memories. One needs to share it to make it more reliable and stable. And yet it builds faster than it can be shared or anchored. Every search, every hour of distraction with another database or manuscript index, every conversation with a stranger, every article rushed too quickly into print—so much bread cast upon the waters.

As an understanding of John's work slowly came together for me, as the work assembled itself in my head, I was increasingly struck by the brilliance of John's closing moves. I have returned to the New Compilation of Figures again and again to work out what the book's disarrangements, its bits and pieces of penitential signatures, actually mean. This was partly, of course, a matter of working out what the words of the text actually said, the echoes of biblical quotation which did not come through until the orthography of certain words became clear, puzzles that could only be figured out when the Bodleian manuscript came into our hands, others resolved through our (again chance) discovery of a quirky and unique manuscript in Bologna. Initially the Book of Figures was almost entirely obscure; now I can see how John maps the entire experience of writing the *Liber florum* so deftly onto God's dispensation that it seems the book, or the understanding it represents, could never have been complete without the Barking Dogs' critique, which broke it in two—a point of fracture John could hardly have foreseen. The Old Compilation makes it clear that John's visions were supported within his monastic community at Morigny, or he would not have been asked to share them, to preach about them in chapter. Mary was sometimes ambivalent about the figures, to be sure, and John admits her concession to his desire, her allowing the figures in order to forestall his "tears of loss or renunciation." But even so, it is clear from the record left by the text's own disarrangements that John had no preexisting plans to address the situation of such a critique. He was entirely winging it in response to earthly events, divine directives, and his own interpretations (right and wrong) of those directives. His messages from the Virgin always yield meanings that cut sharply in both past and present: they tell him how to act in the moment of their delivery and prophesy how the failure of those actions will be divinely rectified. How could the past map so perfectly onto a future unknown at the time? How could the arc of the book seem at the same time so unpredictable and so *inevitable*? (How could there be *two games*? Or perhaps more pointedly for my purpose here, how can any literary autobiography seem to allow us a glimpse of one game as it looks simultaneously *in aeterno* and *in saeculo*?)

John stitches the sequence of events into the scheme of the dispensation with such felicity, in part, perhaps, because he was aware all along of being himself a book *written within and written without*. He had the expectation and conditioning that allowed him to see himself as written into the dispensation, and the dispensation as written into himself; so also his own book had to be written within, and so also the form of the ring, which seals the operator's relation to Mary, as he makes explicit in the last part of the Book of Figures. The form of the ring "ought to be sculpted on the metal of the heart and worn on the finger of conscience, just as the book also ought to be inscribed on the parchment of the heart and read in the lettering of the conscience—though it has to be written out by hand as well, as is shown in the penultimate chapter of this book."[1] If the writing within is important, the writing without cannot be neglected; neither can be valorized at the expense of the other, since meaning is dependent on relation. If John's theological training encouraged him to see his life thus as *written within and written without*, his book is nevertheless unique, the sort of felicitous engagement with this exegetical patterning of which only John of Morigny could have been capable.

It is not that no other authors see themselves this way. Augustine's *Confessions*, already mentioned as the ultimate model for all medieval autobiographies, is also written (so to speak) against the dispensation, borrowing from the Bible throughout, adumbrating a cosmic pattern. Yet John's book nevertheless does it uniquely. I too am aware of how the writing within and without mirror each other, seeing the hinge within me more clearly than ever now from my engagement with this representation of John's model. Yet the model felt familiar because I write poetry, too. The ending of any poetic work must feel simultaneously unpredictable (if you can see it coming, the poem fails), but it must also hold, and hold in place each line of the entirety of the work. God knows how we do this, but for anyone who has written poetry seriously, there is a hand-knowledge that grasps this principle. It is a magician's trick, too, to rip or break something and then render it whole again in front of an audience (all the more wondrous to the man in the audience if the object first belonged to him).

Let us look again, more closely, at one array of broken pieces, the prayer that ends John's work in the New Compilation version, a prayer that he calls the "first prayer," which he directs operators to place both at the end of the book and at its beginning, and which does appear at the beginning in some manuscripts. This return to a prayer already discussed in two previous chapters allows us to circle our theme in a sort of spiraling motion:

> Ioth: God of intellect and understanding;
>   (Jesus Christ, beginning of life)
> He: God of perfect retentiveness and memory;
>   (You who through the yoke of the cross)
> Vau: God of reason and eloquence;
>   (You who through the death of the Passion)
> Heth: God of stability, perfection and perseverance, fount of all wisdom, knowledge, and prudence;
>   (Became the life of all)
> Begin now, set, perfect, fashion, fulfill in me, you who are as I have spoken above. Amen.[2]

In this prayer we have two interlacing ideas. The odd lines associate the letters of the divine name with the faculties of mind and verbal fluency: intellect, understanding, retentiveness and memory, reason, eloquence, stability, perseverance. These associations of the letters with the faculties seem to be peculiar to John; there is no precedent for them in the *ars notoria*, at least. The even lines (those in parentheses) take off from the traditional Christian gloss on the letters of the Tetragrammaton discussed in the last chapter. But while John's prayer recalls traditional sources, it is elaborated in a way that I have not seen in forms of this gloss elsewhere, which usually do not exceed one word for each letter of the name.[3]

John's elaborated version of the gloss emphasizes the passion as a work of transformative suffering: the "beginning of life" becomes the "life of all" in concrete terms through the yoke of the cross ("patibulum" or crossbar, also gibbet) and through the death of the passion ("obitus passionis," transit or death by suffering). Christ's passion, the external and historical core of the entire dispensation, models the internal and personal transformation sought by the operator for the faculties at the core of human knowing, the mental powers by which things are known and expressed. If Christ models a divine and human penance that moved the entire cosmos in the direction it needed to go, each Christian can choose to collaborate with that movement, or not. The prayer ends in a petition by the operator, who asks God to begin, fashion, and fulfill in him the process by which, imitating Christ, he hopes to be transformed into an agent of the dispensation himself. This transformation occurs through the figure of the cross, the "signaculum" (little sign, seal, signet) impressed upon the ring and the figures which marks them both literally and ineffably, a miniature of the process of God's creative energy. This prayer, braiding at least three strands of thought together, makes a circle of the *Liber florum*, uniting Old and New Compilations, Jewish and Christian signs and testaments, human flesh and divine works, into a single thing, a single activity, simultaneously intra-human and intra-divine.

Thus John's first prayer and the figure that goes with it should be fully comprehensible by traditional Christian theology: it is transparent to theory. Magic has always been difficult, opaque to theory at least half the time, divided and divisive in its theoretical and theological implications. (Is it a transgressive pursuit or a gift of God? An ineluctably compromised, demonically engaged activity or a direct divine extension of the power of words? A branch of knowledge or a branch of non-knowledge—i.e., a false and illusory representation that *feels like knowledge* but is not?) It may help to see how its dividedness reflects the way the experience of knowledge is in any case; the fact that magic can appear as itself equally on both sides of the true/false split is representative. The difficulty is to maintain a view of it on both sides at once, but this is not really harder than learning to check your blind spot while driving. (It is futile to complain that you cannot actually see the road in front of you while looking backwards, since this does not actually turn out to be as dangerous as not checking the blind spot would be.)

One of the arguments urged throughout this book is that the magical traditions on which John drew shared in and capitalized on many aspects of the theology of the sacraments at a very basic level. The knowledge magic texts particularly drew on the same idea of Wisdom, shared through the same biblical loci, as did traditional theology. The *ars notoria* itself, despite its Jewish "look," draws on Christian sources almost exclusively, much of the language of its Latin prayers indebted to Christian litanies, prayers, and offices. Even John's "necromantic" texts—even where they originated in a non-Christian environment, as did some texts concerning astrological images and some of the works compiled in the *Liber Razielis*—were strongly informed by the same strands of Neoplatonic thinking that permeated the didascalic literature and sacramental theology. The affinities pointed out here might as well be regarded as real. They were certainly being consciously attended to; that is, the composers of magic texts are playing the language game that is also engaged by theologians. I do not suggest whether they do it well or badly, merely that it is deliberative.

Thus, even as authors like William of Auvergne, Thomas Aquinas, and the Magister Speculi sought to separate out magical texts and genres according to relative degrees of sinfulness, to regulate their use, to rule out or ban certain elements, and to cautiously allow certain others, they also modeled through their writing a process of making decisions about those texts. The very fact that condemnations proceed from a familiarity with the texts makes it evident how available and accessible such books were to late medieval literati. John himself gets at the *ars notoria* in the schools (*studia*). It is difficult for any generalization made about the situation of illicit magic texts in the Middle Ages to do justice to the kinds of intellectual engagement that this witnesses, an engagement that went even into the process of a work's condemnation. Otherwise put, condemnation is a facet of a knowledge process, simultaneously public and private, inner and outer. John's ultimate condemnation of the notory art and necromancy is rather typical than unusual in this regard; as an intellectual, he condemns errors only a member of the intellectual elite could make. To see condemnation as a unilateral and static form of institutional repression of visionary or devotional praxis is probably always wrong, but it is particularly wrong here, where the practitioner and the theologian are actually involved in the same language game.

Wittgenstein points out that a word (in a language game) is like a piece in chess:

> When one shows someone the king in chess and says: "This is the king," one does not thereby explain to him the use of this piece—unless he already knows the rules of the game except for this last point: the shape of the king. One could imagine his having learnt the rules of the game

without ever having been shown an actual piece. The shape of the chess piece corresponds here to the sound or shape of a word....

We may say: it only makes sense for someone to ask what something is called if he already knows how to make use of the name.[4]

Within the parameters of this analogy, it is possible to work outwards from specific moves to achieve a "perspicuous"[5] representation of a moment in a game. For example, if my king is knocked over by a person who says "checkmate," one could reasonably infer that the person who did this was playing the same game. This does not necessarily mean that he is winning the game, although it might. He could be playing it well or badly; he might not see a move visible to me; I might move to the side, or even capture his queen with a piece he had forgotten or was not seeing at the time. There are multiple outcomes, but nevertheless, his move could not easily be construed as something coming from outside the game. (It would be quite different if the wind knocked the piece over, or the dog's tail.) Without hearing more than the word "checkmate," it would be a mistake to assume that my opponent had won this round, and a worse mistake to assume that he "always won." But this is essentially what is done by anyone who makes an endgame of the condemnation of John's work in 1323.

The condemnation of magic is obviously within the scope of the language game that John himself is playing. The moves against magic are not limited to his opponents; he himself condemns both the *ars notoria* and necromancy. It is possible to look at John's condemnation and reworking of the *ars notoria* as part of a theological tradition of engagement with these texts, one that is fully consistent with the enterprise of other theologians, even though it has different results—results that seem to be at least as much a product of his monastic training and his interest in liturgical composition as they are of his reading in magic. It might be remarked that they are consistent as well with Agrippa's moves in the sixteenth century, both in the *De occulta philosophia* and the *De vanitate*, since Agrippa also uses a sacramental model to elevate heavenly knowledge and denigrate earthly knowledge (both types having magic in them). The game has changed a little bit, but not that much.

By the first quarter of the fourteenth century, the relatively simple distinctions that, in the twelfth century, enabled Hugh of St. Victor to rule all magic arts out of the order of knowledge completely are scarcely possible given the proliferation of new magical and esoteric writings, both foreign and domestic, and the kinds of embeddedness such texts showed in cultural contexts, Islamic and Jewish, that fostered the new learning through the thirteenth century. Of course this does not mean that condemnations of such texts ceased; in fact, the opposite is the case. (In general, condemnations of magic texts will proliferate in a ratio proportional to the proliferation of the texts themselves.) But they were complicated by the array of texts on the ground, many of them suggesting that magic, or its particular branches, might not only be a part of the order of knowledge, but up somewhere rather near its pinnacle. These suggestions about magical knowledge operated in tandem with the increased importance of curricular knowledge in general, the importance granted even the liberal arts for reformation of the soul that was evident in late medieval didascalic texts (including but not limited to Hugh of St. Victor's), and the links between *scientia* and theology apparent in more meditative works like Bonaventure's *Itinerarium mentis in Deum*. In the intellectual world of the later Middle Ages, there was really no branch of formal knowledge that could simply be dismissed as unimportant or worthless. This made the condemnation of magical knowledge a complex engagement indeed for a person vested, as John was, in the head- and hand-knowledge of theology and liturgical composition. John is, in this sense, one among many late medieval scholars who worked to make decisions about what categories and techniques of knowledge deserved to be formalized, to become licit and admissible parts of Christian curricula, for what reasons, and in what ways.

If John's work neither constituted, nor was the object of, an effective, unilateral and static repression of magical knowledge, at the same time the tendency to see condemnations of magic as unilateral and static repressions—permanent, or perhaps somehow eternal, in their effect—is a persistent form of institutional blindness. I would characterize it as the blindness that seeks to schematize single knowledge-moments (such as the checkmate) without attaining a perspicuous vantage of a larger section of the game board, or indeed without tracking the processual and consensual nature of the game in the first place.

Arguments for eschewing "magic" as a category label from scholarly or philosophical use have been laid out by many people for many reasons, all of them, even the most intelligent, tending to adopt such a unilateral and schematic view. In Jonathan Z. Smith's landmark essay "Trading Places," for example, Smith develops the idea that magic marks a "shadow reality known only by looking at the reflection of its opposite ('religion,' 'science') in a distorting fun-house mirror."[6] Elsewhere, scholars of religion have argued that what magic shadows by its opposition more than any other thing is the modern itself, and in many recent writings "magic" is treated as—even becoming a shorthand for—a particular haunting of the modern.[7]

For historians, however (especially historians studying western Europe in that vexed and uncertain space before the "modern" is understood to have started), magic is harder to see as a mere shadow or haunting. I might observe that the very ability to couch the problem in terms of words like "haunting" and "shadow reality" marks a knowledge engagement of a particular kind. Put another way, you cannot use the word "magic" without making a play. If you use it prescriptively to ban it from the game constituted in scholarship, you will be making a quite strong play indeed. In "Remarks on Frazer's *Golden Bough*," his exploration of his own irritation at Sir James Frazer's view of primitive religion, Wittgenstein writes, "Indeed, if Frazer's explanations did not in the final analysis appeal to a tendency in ourselves, they would not really be explanations." A little later, he remarks,

> I should like to say: nothing shows our kinship to those savages better than the fact that Frazer has on hand a word as familiar to himself and to us as "ghost" or "shade" in order to describe the views of these people.
>
> (That is certainly something different than were he to describe, for example, the savages as imagining that their heads will fall off when they have killed an enemy. Here our description would contain nothing superstitious or magical in itself.)
>
> Indeed, this peculiarity relates not only to the expressions "ghost" and "shade," and much too little is made of the fact that we count the words "soul" and "spirit" as part of our educated vocabulary. Compared with this, the fact that we do not believe that our soul eats and drinks is a trifling matter.
>
> An entire mythology is stored within our language.[8]

The point here is that the word "ghost," like the king in chess, or the word "checkmate," is attached to a body of rules about its usage. The knowledge of ghosts is not predicated on a notion that ghosts are "true" or "false." The fact that there are "true" and "false" options for the word means that the word "ghost" imports into a perspicuous view of that moment in the game the mythology that includes the possibility of belief (but not the belief itself). This is not true only for Frazer, and it is not true only of ghosts. One of the ramifications of my argument in this book is that the medieval problem of magic is actually not something that can be let go of in trying to understand the modern one; indeed, it is actually a crucial piece of the modern problem. The current view of magic as a modern haunting, almost a modern *invention*, is historically deracinating. It does not give a perspicuous view of the game we are playing in its usage. Otherwise put, the view of magic as a haunting of the modern needs to check its blind spot, the haunted area itself (the shadow reality, i.e., the medieval).

It is not just magic, of course; all knowledge has a shadow side. Mary Douglas, in *How Institutions Think*,[9] does a good job of showing how institutional knowledge is actually constituted in a kind of selective blindness. It is filled with holes; but, as she shows, the holes also make the net. A predetermined selective blindness is necessary, because there would be too much information for efficiency if everyone always made free and rational decisions based on close scrutiny of all available and relevant data. But this selective blindness that is vital for decision making also means that there has to be a certain amount of looseness, of mess, illogical procedure, dead weight, and so on, in any given system. It will not be noticeable as long as the system is working; it may become more obvious in crisis, or it may emerge clearly when you delve into how any institution has operated at an earlier moment in its history. In combing through historical systems, a certain amount of detritus becomes visible, broken links, old information that was taken for granted, that smelled real at the time but turned out later not to be.

To state the fact that we absorb our rules from collectivities and could not operate without them is not in any way to suggest that systems of rule following must reproduce themselves identically in every act of engagement. They obviously do not. In fact, they could not survive if they did. Change is manifest in many ways. If you compare a medieval outline of a university curriculum to a modern one, it is easy to see, first, that the two are related, and second, that they are different—indeed, that some parts of both involve rule systems completely alien to each other. Add to this that any number of significant branches of knowledge have developed and been lopped off in between, and that the sense of entire branches of knowledge has changed, and you get a pretty clear picture of the fluidity of knowledge. Despite the need for a stable selective blindness to enable swift decision making, knowledge systems are open and dynamic because they have to be.

But how do changes happen in conditions where selective blindness is a necessary part of the operating system? It is possible to answer this question in a variety of ways, but a formulation that will probably have some application in most cases is to say that one may experience what Thomas Kuhn—discussing the contingencies of the milieu in which Copernicus's positing of a heliocentric cosmos became a logically inevitable theoretical choice—called a "breakdown of the normal technical puzzle-solving activity."[10] Kuhn points out that this was not the only pressure on Copernicus at the time, but it was one part of what constituted the crisis to which a heliocentric cosmos became the solution. The problems that cause such changes are complex and typically involve several interacting and conflicting language games at once.

My object in this book has been to look closely at some small necessary adjustments in two contiguous knowledge systems. One was John's ritual system for attaining knowledge, which had to change in response to a crisis in John's environment, the critique of the Barking Dogs. The other was a set of selective and fossilized historical blindnesses that created, for me and for the handful of others who interacted with this text, a set of small breakdowns in the technical puzzle-solving activity of normal history. The reason I have taken Wittgenstein as an initial and concluding point of reference for my engagement with John of Morigny, in preference to other available ways of looking at knowledge systems, is that his formulations make the essential fluidity of the system much more visible. He makes it possible to see, as David Bloor puts it, how "meaning is generated in a step-by-step fashion as we go along. It is not progressively revealed by usage. It does not preexist, but is created in response to the sequence of contingencies attending each act of concept application. This is the true significance of the Wittgensteinian slogan that meaning is use. Use is not to be explained by reference to meaning, because use does not come from meaning. Rather, meaning comes from use."[11]

I have tried to show what this means in certain limited and specific ways with regard to John of Morigny and myself. For John, there is a set of rules for exegesis, but the meaning of John's exegesis of his own liturgy derives not only from these rules but from their particular application to his situation. He came up with a novel and yet legitimate play to address a problem that refused to dissolve in the institutionally available solutions. John's solution involves rules that are embedded in the collectivity, but the outcome of his game, the making of meaning in its particular application, is not determined by the rules, even though it is an outcome of a game played by those rules.

I was the more willing to embrace John's theological solution as inevitable and proper, one that worked by the rules, because of the intrinsic difficulty of finding any satisfying way to read what he wrote through the lens of any existing institutional histories. The Paris condemnation of 1323 is part of what allowed the text to be effaced in the historical record, or to be recognized only as a shadow or type of the *ars notoria*, but the manuscript record makes it clear that this condemnation in itself had no effect to speak of on the transmission and use of the text. The question then becomes, What happened here? If the condemnation did not terminate the text in use, why was it then so utterly lost to history?

If we trace not the record of condemnation but the record of transmission, the picture looks a little different. The latest copies of John's work known to us are dated 1519 (in Austria) and 1522 (in England). No later copies either in manuscript or print have yet been found, nor any knowledgeable reference to John's work after this. Thus, while the *Liber florum* was actively transmitted and practiced across Europe for two centuries after the Paris burning, his book apparently loses its audience a few scant years after Luther published his ninety-five *Theses*.

As Frank Klaassen has pointed out, manuscripts of ritual magic, generally speaking, proliferate in increased rather than reduced numbers as we enter the early modern period, so the magicality of the *Liber florum* is probably not the main explanation for the death of this tradition in manuscript.[12] We need to glance gently at these facts, remembering that the *ars notoria* persisted, in both print and manuscript forms, despite the Protestant Reformation, ongoing condemnations, and all else.[13] It is true that John's investment in sacramental theology is deeper and more learned than that of the master of the *ars notoria*, and perhaps it is possible to suggest that among the array of possible reasons for the loss of this text was that it engaged knowledge practices simultaneously too Catholic, too specialized, and too labor intensive to survive the various transformations of modernity. Its rediscovery now, and its rising importance in the research agendas of scholars on both sides of the Atlantic, suggest that the kinds of knowledge it engages may after all become more recognizable in the knowledge ecologies of the new millennium than they were in the centuries immediately following Luther.

Learning happens. It is absurd to think that all the premises of childhood persist forever in us, even though some of them do. However, we lose most of them because we have to. This happens to us with or without our consent. We can choose whether to embrace the process (it does hurt) or whether to fight it tooth and nail, but we actually cannot choose to learn *nothing*. Ultimately it is only through us that institutional knowledge is created and only through us that it changes. It is reproduced more or less felicitously, and it is also changed, precisely through our knowledge engagements, through our learning, through our rereading, and through our large or small recoveries of lost history. We notice more when we are making it our business to notice things, as when we undertake the practice of recording dreams, we remember more and see more in what we remember of our dreams. So too with the books we engage in reading and rereading in a disciplined manner. At the end of *On Rereading*, Patricia Meyer Spacks writes,

> All readers . . . change as a result of their experiences with books. . . . Rereading . . . is a way of paying attention. . . .
>
> Both the stability and change that ground rereading's appeal can seem alternately illusions and facts: so the experience of writing this book

leads me to conclude.... Particularly if a long time has elapsed between readings, the sense of change can feel so persuasive as to override rationality. Emotional rather than factual knowledge grounds the conviction that change has taken place—and, indeed, something has certainly changed in order to generate such a conviction. That "something" is the reader's consciousness. The scope and degree of shift—radical alterations in assessment, radical mutations of perception—can be startling: reminders, if seriously contemplated, that we remain always works in progress.[14]

History, too, is always a work in progress. Over time, institutional knowledge changes as radically as we ourselves do. We get at knowledge (past knowledge for example, but all knowledge relatively new to us) through understanding its practice, which means understanding, through familiarization and use, the language in which it is couched. Some of John's game, particularly his endgame, may be missing for us because so much of the literature on which his understanding depended (particularly, though not exclusively, the magical literature) is yet to be retrieved. Yet much of it is still *susceptible* to historical recovery, *not* ineluctably lost. It is the potential recoverability of this past knowledge—not just its lostness—that makes it all the more important to carefully track our own processes as we write.

The honorable practice of history aims at truth, in the reasonably simple and achievable disciplinary sense of working not to rely on old data that is actually wrong, to use the best and most current editions of primary texts, to look back repeatedly at the evidence, to track it in the notes, to use the actual words of our primary sources where possible, to be careful and suspicious of easy, obvious assumptions, and to track as best we can our own stake in the matter. If we see history as an ethical practice, a way of practicing ethical judgments, then that practice is partly about scholarly reflexivity; it is about being careful with our agenda to minimize errors of will. Beyond this, the ethical practice of history is a process of working out how to be an honest, honorable witness to the traumas of the dead. This is not about perfect objectivity so much as about the etiquette of managing our relations to the communities—living or dead—in which our historical fieldwork takes place. My book tries to honor these protocols in looking at what John went through in the public condemnation of his book, how he wrote, how he responded to events. I have tried to tell a story that is a little more true to John's life and circumstances than the story told by his detractors, and a little more like the story he himself would have wanted told.

In undertaking a history that aims at truth in this particular way, sometimes it is wrong to leave ourselves outside the picture. What I have learned from John, and put forward here as a necessary risk of honorable witnessing, is to bow to the inevitable process of change, willingly to undergo shifts in the boundaries of the self, to allow knowledge its necessary metamorphosis, which means finally allowing yourself to be broken in order to take on the larger shape of that knowledge that exists outside or beyond yourself. The base model is John's; what he sacrifices to further the dispensation is his identity as himself. So, through John's book, I myself have been broken and restored by the knowledge that made me who I am.

Do I know the "real" John of Morigny? The question implies that knowing is a process that can be completed, resulting in a sort of "finished product," the real thing, as though one had a plan for a particular knowledge product that one could market as more or less authentic, like purified water, or single malt scotch. The question is not answerable without changing the grammar. The John of Morigny I know is quite real. I know him moderately well. Knowledge is the interface between ourselves and the world (textual, scriptural, factual, or spiritual); it is the complex of practices that, as we become more skilled, enable better, more delightful, and more sufficient relations with the object of knowledge. It is knowledge that enables one to have a certain kind of conversation with a person who is well known better than one could with someone else less well known. Knowledge at best enables an appropriate response, enhances communicability, and facilitates, in some cases at least, hope and charity.

In this book I have tried to introduce you to the John of Morigny I know. Undoubtedly the knowledge it presents is imperfect, but it is also me (always a work in progress, as Patricia Spacks writes), the fleshly avatar of my reading and rereading of John's book, cast as more bread upon the waters. I look forward to the day when John's *Liber florum* is recognized in textbook histories of the Middle Ages, not as a burned book, not as another avatar of the *ars notoria*, but as a book by John of Morigny, visionary, exegete, storyteller, sinner, and penitent, friend of the Virgin Mary, a man who had faith that God wanted his book to be written so that it could be read. His faith has moved me and I have tried to further it. So the poor have hope, and injustice shuts its mouth.

NOTES

The following abbreviations appear in the notes and selected bibliography.

CCCM	Corpus Christianorum, continuatio medievalis. Turnhout: Brepols, 1966–.
CCSL	Corpus Christianorum, series latina. Turnhout: Brepols, 1953–.
CSEL	Corpus Scriptorum Ecclesiasticorum Latinorum. Vienna: 1866–.
Glossa ordinaria	Biblia latina cum glossa ordinaria: Facsimile Reprint of the Editio Princeps, Adolph Rusch of Strassburg 1480–81. 4 vols. Turnhout: Brepols, 1992.
HMES	Lynn Thorndike. *A History of Magic and Experimental Science*. 8 vols. New York: Columbia University Press, 1923–58.
Liber florum	John of Morigny. *"Liber florum celestis doctrine," or "Book of the Flowers of Heavenly Teaching": The New Compilation, with Independent Portions of the Old Compilation; An Edition and Commentary.* Edited by Claire Fanger and Nicholas Watson. Toronto: Pontifical Institute of Medieval Studies Press, 2015. (OC = Old Compilation; NC = New Compilation.)
PL	*Patrologia Latina*. Edited by Jacques-Paul Migne. 210 volumes. Paris: Imprimerie Catholique, 1844–55. Cited from pld.chadwyck.co.uk.
Véronèse AN	*L' "Ars notoria" au Moyen Age: Introduction et édition critique*. Edited by Julien Véronèse. Florence: Sismel, Edizioni de Galluzo, 2007.

INTRODUCTION

1. Nicholas Watson and I have published a partial edition online: "John of Morigny, Prologue to *Liber Visionum*," *Esoterica* 3 (2001): 108–217 (www.esoteric.msu.edu/VolumeIII/Morigny.html). Prior to that, some of John's prayers appeared unattributed in an edition of Wladislas Warnenczyk's Prayer Book, Ludwik Bernacki and Ryszard Ganszyniec, eds., *Modlitewnik Wladyslawa Warnenczyka w zbiorach Bibljoteki Bibljotanskiej* (Kraków: Anczyc i Spólka, 1928). A full edition is in press as I write: Claire Fanger and Nicholas Watson, eds., *"Liber florum celestis doctrine" or "Book of the Flowers of Heavenly Teaching": The New Compilation, with Independent Portions of the Old Compilation; An Edition and Commentary* (Toronto: Pontifical Institute of Mediaeval Studies Press, 2015).

2. For a more detailed breakdown of the work, see the Structure and Referencing System for the *Liber florum* at the front of this book. This table, in turn, is a much-condensed form of *Liber florum* table 1 (which includes a full breakdown of prayers with incipits) to which readers are referred if they want to see further into the structure of text and edition.

3. I will continue to use the English word "necromancy" to translate medieval Latin *nigromancia*. The word "necromancy" has been in use for a long time in English as a general term for "black magic," and its ordinary sense is closer to medieval Latin *nigromancia* than it is to Greek divination by the dead.

4. The terms of the condemnation are discussed in more detail in part 2 of this book.

5. See Dupèbe's "L'*ars notoria* et la polémique sur la divination et la magie," in *Divination et controverse religieuse en France au XVIe siècle*, Cahiers V.-L. Saulnier 4 (Paris: L'É.N.S. de Jeunes Filles, 1987), 128 n. 22.

6. English translation quoted from Nicholas Watson, "John the Monk's *Book of Visions of the Blessed and Undefiled Virgin Mary, Mother of God*: Two Versions of a Newly Discovered Ritual Magic Text," in *Conjuring Spirits: Texts and Traditions of Medieval Ritual Magic*, ed. Claire Fanger (University Park: Pennsylvania State University Press, 1998), 164. The French is given in Watson's note 5, on pages 181–82, and is drawn from the French edition by Jules Viard, vol. 9 (Paris: Honoré Champion, 1937), 23–24.

7. *Chronique latine de Guillaume de Nangis de 1113 à 1300: Avec les continuations de cette chronique de 1300 à 1368*, ed. H. Géraud, vol. 2 (Paris: Jules Renouard, 1843), 50: "Eodem anno liber quidam cujusdam monachi de Morigniaco juxta Stampas, qui liber habebat beatae Mariae multas depictas imagines, qui etiam cum hoc continebat multa ignota nomina quae, ut firmiter dicebatur, nomina daemonum credebantur, quia delicias et divitias promittebat, quinimo et quidquid homo optaret si librum pro se depingi faceret, et nomen proprium bis in illo inscriberet, et multa alia quae nihil vel error videbantur, merito tamquam superstitiosus Parisius condemnatur." In fact, John does not use any unknown names.

8. Gilles Corrozet, *Les Antiquitez, croniques et singularitez de Paris* (Paris: Nicolas Bonfons, 1581), chap. 16, p. 182: "En ce temps, fut á Paris condemné l'heresie appellee Ars notoria, dont auoit esté inueniteur vn moine de Morigny, pre d'Estampes, le liure duquel fut bruslé." Noted by Thorndike, *HMES*, 3:21.

9. Lea, *A History of the Inquisition of the Middle Ages*, vol. 3 (New York: Macmillan, 1887), 437. As the original account makes clear, it was the book, not John, that was seized. There is no indication that the book burning took place in John's presence, nor, in fact, has evidence of any legal process against John been found. See discussion by Nicholas Watson in *Liber florum* Introduction A, §§100–101, and Fanger Introduction B IV.1.

10. See Thorndike, *HMES*, 4:278–79. There are no modern editions of Jacobus's *Sophologium*, though several early printed editions are available through Google Books. See, for instance, *Sophologium magistri Iacobi magni* (Lyon: de Vingle, 1495). The mention of John occurs with the discussion of the *ars notoria* in the section on magic arts at the end of bk. I; this is on folio xix verso, column 2, in this edition.

11. The first scholarly writings on John of Morigny were published in French by Sylvie Barnay, whose articles remain a primary touchstone for all who work on him. See Barnay, "La mariophanie au regard de Jean de Morigny: Magie ou miracle de la vision mariale?," in *Miracles, prodiges et merveilles au Moyen Age*, by the Société des Historiens Médiévistes de l'Enseignement Supérieur Public (Paris: Publications de la Sorbonne, 1995), 173–90; "Désir de voir et interdits visionnaires ou la 'mariophanie' selon Jean de Morigny (XIVe siècle)," in *Homo Religiosus* (Paris: Fayard, 1997), 519–26; "La mariophanie de Jean de Morigny ou les manipulations de la vision mariale au début du XIVe siècle," *Rivista di storia e letteratura religiosa* 33 (1997): 483–50. Barnay's unpublished Ph.D. dissertation, "Un moment vécu d'éternité: Histoire médiévale des apparitions mariales (IVe–XVe siècle): Lire et traduire le langage visionnaire" (Université de Paris X–Nanterre, 1997), contains work on John based on Turin, Biblioteca Nazionale G. II. 25, but remains difficult to access. John's work is briefly discussed in her book *Le ciel sur la terre: Les apparitions de la Vierge au Moyen Âge* (Paris: Cerf, 1999). In an anglophone environment, the first articles on John of Morigny came out in *Conjuring Spirits: Texts and Traditions of Medieval Ritual Magic*, ed. Claire Fanger (University Park: Pennsylvania State University Press, 1998). Watson and I edited the Book of Visions based on Graz University Library 680, which came out three years later in an online forum; see John of Morigny, "Prologue to *Liber Visionum*."

12. For a more extended account of what the manuscript evidence shows, see *Liber florum*, Introduction B.

13. Copies residing or originating in the libraries of religious houses include Seitenstetten, Benediktinerstift Cod. 273; Klagenfurt, Universitätsbibliothek, Cart. 1 (from the Benedictine monastery of St. Paul's in Carinthia); Klosterneuberg, Augustiner-Chorherrenstift Cod 950; Studienbibliothek Salzburg Cod M I 24 (this book was originally made for the use of monks at the Benedictine community of St. Peter in Salzburg); and another Benedictine production, Vienna, Schottenkloster, MS 140 (61). These are the copies that can most securely be traced to religious houses, but other copies may also have belonged to monks or friars, including Oxford, Bodleian Liturg. 160 (the book is personalized for a "frater Galfridus").

14. John directs that personal names of operators should be written to either side of the image of Mary in the figures (*Liber florum* NC III.iii.23.a). Names were written into the prayers as well, a practice that seems to have been transmitted by the manuscript tradition itself.

15. Copies of this type include the Klagenfurt and Klosterneuberg manuscripts mentioned above, with .N. (for *nomen*) where names go in the prayers.

16. It may seem commonsensical that burning a book would terminate its use, or at least make it considerably more difficult, but in fact this is not a logical assumption. Book burning tends to occur in the face of widespread interest in a text, a situation where multiple copies are likely already to exist. As the public declaration of a stance about a rapidly proliferating text, it cannot hope to eradicate all copies, nor can it reasonably aim to do so. It is at least as likely to call additional attention to the text as to suppress it.

17. There is increasing evidence beyond John's work for a deliberate and thoughtful monastic negotiation of these categories. See the recent work by Sophie Page, *Magic in the Cloister: Pious Motives, Illicit Interests, and Occult Approaches to the Medieval Universe* (University Park: Pennsylvania State University Press, 2013).

18. For more on the connection between Wittgenstein and Bourdieu, see Bourdieu's interesting discussion in *Science of Science and Reflexivity* (Cambridge: Polity, 2004), especially the last chapter, "History and Truth." For a brief but clear exposition of the relation between habitus and language game, see "'Press 1 for English': Practice as the 'Generic Social Thing,'" chapter 2 in Alastair Pennycook's *Language as a Local Practice* (Abingdon: Routledge, 2010). For another lucid exposition of "practice," see James D. Faubion's introduction to *Rethinking the Subject: An Anthology of Contemporary European Social Thought*, ed. James D. Faubion (Boulder, Colo.: Westview Press, 1995).

19. James Faubion's *An Anthropology of Ethics* (Cambridge: Cambridge University Press, 2011) dances with religious models (deriving a functionally Christian vocabulary in part from Max Weber's discussion of charisma) in its attempt to locate a theoretical basis for ethical action.

20. See §2 of the *Philosophical Investigations*.

21. This makes the writing of books a means of autopoiesis, in Faubion's terms, and potentially a conscious manner of creating an ethical subject. Ethics, according to Faubion, does not belong to the domain of social system reproduction, but rather of social system adjustment. See *Anthropology of Ethics*, 104–5.

22. For a more detailed view of the parts and structure of John's *Liber florum*, see the Structure and Referencing System at the front of this book, after the preface.

CHAPTER 1

1. Letter to George and Tom Keats, December 1817, in *The Letters of John Keats: 1814–1818*, ed. Hyder Edward Rollins, vol. 1 (Cambridge: Cambridge University Press, 1958), 193.

2. For "interest," see s.v. in Merriam-Webster sense 4, "a feeling that accompanies or causes special attention to an object or class of objects." But why should a book of prayers be an object of any interest to anyone? Or alternatively, why should it not be? Interest is one's own stake in the matter.

3. *Liber florum* III.iii.32 [c]: "Et ideo in hac sciencia signat perfeccionem et dileccionem, et est signum tocius gracie et virtutis habite et habende. Et per omnia alia signat ut annulus prelatorum." The prelate's ring is a part of episcopal vestments given to the bishop on ordination with a symbolic character elaborated by Durand in his *Rationale*, bk. III, "On the garments and equipment of Priests, Bishops and other Ministers," chap. 14: "The ring is a pledge of the faith with which Christ has married his spouse, Holy Church, that she can say of herself, 'the Lord Jesus Christ has married me with this Ring'; the Church, whose guardians and teachers are the Bishops and Prelates, who wear rings as a sign and testimony of this marriage." See *William Durand on the Clergy and Their Vestments: A New Translation of Books 2–3 of the "Rationale divinorum officiorum,"* trans. Timothy M. Thibodeau (Scranton: University of Scranton Press, 2010), 195. Other Church officials also customarily wore rings, including abbots; for more information, see John Abel Nainfa, *Costume of Prelates of the Catholic Church, According to Roman Etiquette*, rev. ed. (Baltimore: John Murphy, 1926), part III, chap. 2, pp. 138ff.

4. *HMES*, 4:279–83.

5. Google began in January 1996 as a research project by Larry Page and Sergey Brin when they were Ph.D. students at Stanford University, according to Wikipedia; the company was not incorporated until September 1998.

6. We know much more about the *ars notoria* than we did even a decade ago. A number of scholars have made important contributions to this area, but the major groundbreaking work has been done by Julien Véronèse, who documented the manuscript distribution of the text and sorted through its complex and partly legendary history in his 2004 dissertation. His edition of the *Ars notoria*, published in 2007, is the current starting point for scholarly study. It is based on the second volume of his dissertation. A revised version of the invaluable first volume is forthcoming from Honoré Champion, and meanwhile a digital copy of the dissertation text is available at his home page, http://www.univ-orleans.fr/node/653 (as of January 1, 2014), where a list of his other publications, many with direct links, is also available. A good account of the *ars notoria* in English is Véronèse, "Magic, Theurgy, and Spirituality in the Medieval Ritual of the *Ars Notoria*," in *Invoking Angels: Theurgic Ideas and Practices, Thirteenth to Sixteenth Centuries*, ed. Claire Fanger (University Park: Pennsylvania State University Press, 2012), 37–78.

7. *HMES*, 2:281–82.

8. Munich, Bayerische Staatsbibliothek Clm 276, on fol. 48r1.

9. The HMML collects microfilms of manuscripts from monastic libraries and has a particularly large array from Austria, Germany, and Switzerland. The catalogue has since been put online and remains an invaluable search tool: see http://www.hmml.org.

10. *Liber florum* I.i.4: "quadam die, ieiunio facto, quasdam oraciones ipsius que vocatur Ars notoria in sero quondam protuli. Et ecce de nocte, quasi in excessu mentis positus, talem vidi visionem. Videbatur michi quod eram in pratello quodam iuxta domum matris mee in villa de Otrouiaco, et erat nox, et luna lucebat, et lumen lune erat in muro predicti pratelli a parte occidentis. Et ego habebam faciem meam uersus partem illam. Et ecce, in muro apparebat vmbra quinque digitorum cuiusdam manus. Et vmbra illorum digitorum erat multum horribilis, quod singularis eorum erat ita magnus et grossus quod uere cum quinque manibus humanis inpugillari non posset; set conuersus erga lunam in firmamento aspexi ut viderem vnde veniret vmbra illorum digitorum. Et ecce, vidi figuram cuiusdam maligni spiritus in firmamento, scilicet dyaboli, ita terribilem, ita diformem, ita turpem, ita quod nec auris audiuit nec in cor hominis ascendit. Et manum suam apertam tenebat ante lunam, et sic vmbra digitorum suorum apparebat in muro pratelli."

11. Ibid.: "Capud vero ipsius erat recte supra zenith capitis nostri, et exteriora sua uersus orientem, set erat figura illa ita magna quod a zenith capitis vsque ad orizontem meum durabat corpus suum usque ad coxas–coxas uero, et cetera ipsius exteriora uidere non poteram, quod erant ultra meum orizantem."

12. Ibid.: "Et cum ipsam figuram aspicerem pre nimia turpitudine ipsius eam diu non potui aspicere, set ut ipsam non uiderem pronus in terram cecidi dicens, 'Vere, vere, inexpli-

cabilis est figura demoniorum.' Et cum hec dixissem surrexi et domum meam que erat iuxta pratellum intraui, et dixi hijs qui erant intus, 'Venite et videte mirabilia in celo.' Et ascendens in quodam solarium et quidam mecum ut predicta eis ostenderem, et ecce, prospicientes per fenestram solarij, ostendi eis predictam figuram, terribilem sicut priusquam, cum parum aspicerem. Et ecce, subito illa descendit in pratellum vnde ueneram in specie sancti, et erat ibi valde simplex indutus ueste nigra, et dyadema nigrum gerebat circa capud. Quem cum uidissem penitebam aliquantulum ipsam dixisse malignum spiritum, et continuo excitatus."

13. *Liber florum* I.i.7: "Opere vero illius libri incepto, cum iam in ipso laborassem vsque ad lunam vicesimam nonam, in quo die ipsa luna conplet cursum suum, et in nocte post crepusculum, post prolationem cuiusdam orationis illius libri que uocatur 'Signum gracie,' statim intraui cubiculum candela extincta, quod cum fuissem iacens cecidi in extasim. Et ecce, subito camera illa in qua iacebam repleta est claritate magna, et apparuerunt michi duo homines quos vidi set similitudines eorum recipere non potui, et inter illos aderat tercius, set non potui illum nec audire nec videre set sensi. Vnus illorum quos videbam stetit ad capud cubiculi mei et alius ad pedes, et dixit michi ille ad capud, superbe loquendo, crudeliter, et arroganter, 'Si me per lxxx[ta] dies et amplius deprecatus fuisses, forte ad hoc quod queris attingere potuisses.' Et respondens alter stans ad pedes, 'Audi, Iohannes, que dixit pater.' Et statim credens quod Pater fuisset qui primo loquebatur, et Filius qui locutus fuerat secundo, et Spiritus Sanctus quod non videbam set senciebam, dixi, surgens et flens, manibus iunctis, ad Filium, 'Memento, domine, quia fuisti Deus et homo simul, es, et eris.' Qui continuo respondit, 'Et ego dico tibi quod in octo diebus habebis visionem.' Et cum dixisset continuo excitatus."

14. The prayer *Signum gracie*, involving unknown names, is said to be efficacious for theology. It is found in Véronèse AN, §43; see *Liber florum*, Sources at I.i.7.

15. At that time we did not have the benefit of the glossed versions of the B text, edited by Julien Véronèse, which do contain ritual prescriptions for solicited dreams. See the summary by Véronèse, "Magic, Theurgy, and Spirituality," 37–78, as well as, by the same author, "Le rêve sollicité: Un thème de la magie rituelle médiévale," *Sociétés & Représentations* 23, no. 1 (2007): 83–103. We have since tracked many specifics of the *ars notoria* use in John's visions in the source notes to the *Liber florum*.

16. At *Liber florum* I.i.11.a: "Accidit michi quedam maxima tribulacio, et in ista tribulacione persistens visiones multas horribiles ego singulari die videbam. Et quadam die volui scire quid significabant, et ad hoc sciendum protuli quandam oracionem de prefato libro Artis notorie que ad memoriam dicitur."

17. John's sense that Bridget might be too old to learn to read easily shows a medieval induction about the deterioration of learning abilities that is consistent with current ideas about changes in brain architecture produced by the acquisition of reading skills. There is still believed to be an optimal window early in life for these changes to occur, though the brain is now believed to be more plastic than was once thought, and the window does not shut instantly. See Helen Abadzi, *Improving Adult Literacy Outcomes: Lessons from Cognitive Research for Developing Countries* (Washington, D.C.: World Bank Publications, 2003), 17. Nevertheless, for many reasons, teaching literacy to older students does require different pedagogical techniques, as John recognizes.

18. *Liber florum* I.iii.1: "Consideraui quod per Artem notoriam breui tempore ad cognicionem literarum, non obstante etate sua ita magna, sine dura, posset peruenire. Et ideo tunc primo ad Artem notoriam ipsam posui ut mos est pueros qui nichil didicerunt adiscere, et postea literas ei ostendi, et in tantum didicit ipsa que numquam vidit literas infra computacionem dimidij anni quod legebat et ubique scribebat; et quod plus est, in ecclesia coram omni populo sine defectu vnum Alleluia sola sine adiutorio graciosissime tamquam angelus decantabat."

19. Especially for girls. See Nicholas Orme, *Medieval Children* (New Haven: Yale University Press, 2003), especially chap. 7, "Learning to Read," 237ff. The word "primer" becomes applied to books intended for learning letters through its original use for prayer books.

20. Speeding up short-term memory is vital to the acquisition of literacy in adulthood. Abadzi, *Improving Adult Literacy Outcomes,* describes a study of a method of teaching literacy to adult learners called Neuroalfa, in which "learners practiced reciting digits backwards and forwards, serial recall of unrelated strings of words, story recall, and the repetition of artificial words" (21). Some of these same forms of practice would obviously be encouraged by the *ars notoria* too. For another kind of insight into the training that may be involved here, see Frank Klaassen, "The Subjective Experience of Medieval Ritual Magic," *Magic, Ritual, and Witchcraft* 7, no. 1 (2012): 19–51.

21. *Liber florum* I.iii.2a: "Inter quas vnam sepius uidebat sequentem. Videbat, eciam senciebat, dormiendo in extasi venire quemdam spiritum malignum et iuxta latus suum in lecto suo stabat, et tunc ille malignus spiritus illam puellam ita per latera et dorsum stringebat fortiter ita quod nec loqui nec clamare poterat. Dicebatque semper ad ipsam, minando quod ipsam interficeret et molestaret nec eam in pace dimitteret. . . . et in tantum perterrita fuit ab eo, et tantum timorem incurrit, quod amplius iam non audebat sola de nocte iacere."

22. Nameless in the story, and perhaps invented for the sake of propriety? This girl is not mentioned again. The location of this episode is not given, but the most likely place is the house of John's mother in Autruy, where John could have dropped in on Bridget whenever he traveled between Morigny and Orléans, where his own experiences with the *ars notoria* took place. The year may be 1304, before the delivery of the Thirty Prayers.

23. *Liber florum* I.iii.2: "Et timore percussa clamauit ad me et dixit, 'Frater mi, adest spiritus ille, sencio illum, pro Deo fugetis eum si potestis!' Cui respondi 'Soror mea, quid habes tu? Commendes te Deo, et signes te, et dicas Pater noster, Credo in Deum, Aue Maria, et nullum malum tibi faciet.' Que cum dixisset et ecce spiritus ille magis apropinquabat ei, et eam incepit molestare et flagellare ita quod ipsa quasi amens in altum clamabat, et dixit flendo lacrimabiliter, 'Ha, frater mi, ecce iam tenet me!' Et cum dixisset tacite maximum incurri dolorem et timorem, cogitans quod hec pateretur propter opus Artis notorie. Tunc dixi ei, 'Soror cara, renunccia Arti notorie et pompis eius et operibus, et cras promitte Deo et beate Marie coram ymagine in ecclesia quod de cetero per ipsam Artem non operaberis si remouerit a te beata virgo Maria timorem illius spiritus.' Quod sic promisit se facturam, et statim recessit ab ea longe aliquantulum ille spiritus. Et ego, surgens de lecto meo, feci lumen accendere in camera, et cum vidissem in lecto suo nichil vidi. Et dixit michi, 'Ecce, adhuc sencio illum penes me, set aliquantulum elongatus est a me.' Et ego nichil videbam, set ipsam confortabam melius quam potui, loquens ei de fiducia Dei et amore ipsius, et in illa confortacione omnino recessit spiritus et in crastino fecit ut sibi dixeram."

24. *Liber florum* I.iii.4.a: "Et cum iam diu operatus fuisset in ea, tandem querens per eam ut mos est de quadam interpretacione nominum uel verborum illius Artis talem vidit visionem." In John's original draft of this narrative, the reason for soliciting the vision was slightly different, suggesting that John of Fontainejean did not see visions as frequently as was customary in the *ars notoria,* and he wanted to know why. See *Liber florum* Variants at I.iii.4.

25. *Liber florum* I.iii.4.a: "Ut ipse narrauit, videbatur enim sibi quod ipse erat in claustro abbacie sue, scilicet Fontis Sancti Iohannis, et quod ipse intrabat locum in quo libri sui de hac arte et alij iacebant. Et inuenit ibi unum monachum tenentem vnum psalterium. Legebat in eo illum psalmum: 'Deus iudicium tuum regi da,' et cetera. Et tunc ille monachus incepit respicere in illo psalterio cum eo qui legebat, et videns ille qui legebat dixit ei—quasi indignanter respiciendo illum—'Quid respicis et quid queris? Hoc quod queris non est hic.' . . . . Et cum illud quod quesierat esset de opere Artis notorie, et dictum fuit sibi illud quod querebat non erat in psalterio; et cum psalterium sit de lege diuina et Deo placibile, apparet manifestissime quod Ars notoria non est de lege diuina nec Deo placabilis."

26. On the year 1311, see *Liber florum* table 14, "Later Additions to Phase 3." See also the "Accusacio Auctoris" at the end of the First Procedure in Bodleian Liturg. 160, transcribed in Variants at II.iii.cap 3.14, which seems to document John's sense of having completed the work. It ends, "Lo, the book on whose composition I spent nearly eleven years!" (Ecce enim liber ad cuius compositionem fere per undecim annos vacaui!).

27. These stories are told in *Liber florum* Introductions A and B.
28. John of Morigny, "Prologue to *Liber Visionum*."

CHAPTER 2

1. In various inflections the word "secret" occurs too many times to count, both in John's text and in the *ars notoria*. In John's text a high percentage of these uses is liturgical, referencing the "secret" of the mass. In the *ars notoria*, a high percentage is adverbial (*secrete*), occurring in directives to the operator to do things "secretly."
2. "On comptabilise ainsi 43 occurrences: sacramenta 17, sacramentum 8, sacramentalis 4, sacramenti 4, sacramentorum 3, sacramentis 3, sacramentale 3, sacramentalibus 1. Ce nombre explose si l'on prend en compte la glose." See Julien Véronèse, "L'*Ars notoria* au Moyen Âge et à l'époque moderne: Étude d'une tradition de magie théurgique (XIIe–XVIIe siècle)," 2 vols. (diss., Université Paris X–Nanterre, 2004), vol. 1 online at http://www.univ-orleans.fr/node/653 (as of January 1, 2014). See in particular vol. 1, part II, chap. 2, p. 468. I counted twenty-nine additional instances on a quick search of the gloss.
3. See the extensive discussion in ibid. at 449–88.
4. For differences in usage between "mysterium" and "sacramentum," in contrast to the instances cited here, see Henri de Lubac's excursus, "Mystery," at the end of *Corpus Mysticum: The Eucharist and the Church*, trans. Gemma Simmonds (Notre Dame: University of Notre Dame Press, 2007).
5. *Etymologiarum libri XX*, VI, XIX, 38.
6. For example, Rabanus Maurus, *De rerum naturis* bk. 5, chap. 11; Gratian, *Decretum* II Causa 1. Q. 1 chap. 84; Peter Lombard, *Sentences*, bk. IV, Dist. 1.2.
7. *Liber florum*, I.i.12: "Delatus fuit michi quidam liber a quodam clerico in quo multa nephanda nigromancie artis continebantur. Et de illo quantum potui habui copiam et postea clerico reddidi. Et perscrutatus a dyabolo et temptatus, et temptacione preualente cecatus, cepi cogitare qualiter ad perfeccionem illius sciencie nepharie attingere potuissem. Et a quodam Lambardo nomine Iacobo de Bononia, medico experto, de hoc consilium quesiui. Qui cum ipsum consulerem dixit michi, 'Petas licenciam studia frequentandi, et cum obtinueris quere quemdam librum qui Ars notoria nuncupatur. Et illo non solum de hac sciencia de qua queris set de omnibus invenies veritatem.'"
8. For claims of effective learning through the *ars notoria*, see OC I.iv.8; commenting that he had not used his own book of prayers to obtain the liberal arts, he adds that it was because he had already acquired the liberal, mechanical, and exceptive (or magical) arts through the *ars notoria* ("quia antequam hanc artem incepissem licencia virginis gloriose ad componendum, artes predictas iam comprehenderem ad sufficienciam particulariter per Artem notoriam"). In the Book of Visions he makes specific mention of learning exceptive arts at *Liber florum* I.i.10.a.
9. Alan of Lille [Alanus de Insulis], *De planctu naturae*, metrum 5; see *Liber florum*, Sources at I.i.3.
10. For this passage in full, see *Liber florum* I.i.3.
11. *Liber florum* III.iii.22a: "Cum sedere sit iudicantis and stare pugnantis, et quamdiu sumus in hoc mundo semper bellare nos oportet contra temptaciones et contra aereas potestates, temptacionis bella et huiusmodi per nos vincere non possumus sine adiutorio Virginis gloriose.... Et sic patet quod in celo et in terra stat pro nobis et pugnat."
12. *Liber florum* III.iii.22d: "Ymmo ewangelium legitur in aquilone, id est septemtrione, ad confusionem dyaboli et deiectionem suam a sede sua, quam dixit in lateribus aquilonis se ponendam super altitudinem nubium in monte testamenti ad similitudinem altissimi. Ita visiones huius sciencie et beata Virgo habentur et apparuit in aquilone ad confusionem dyaboli et deieccionem scienciarum suarum nephariarum, in quibus ipse sedem suam docendo posuit et sedit, ostendens eas per fallacias suas esse sanctas et bonas et similes scienciarum altissimi."

13. Guillaume Durand, *Rationale divinorum officiorum* IV.xxiv.21, ed. A. Davril and T. M. Thibodeau, CCCM 140 (Turnhout: Brepols, 1995): "Lecturus autem euangelium transit ad partem sinistram . . . et opponit faciem suam aquiloni . . . ut ostendat nos doctrina euangelii debere armari, et predicationem Christi contra illum specialiter dirigi, qui ait: *Ponam sedem meam ab aquilone et similis ero Altissimo;* nam et secundum Prophetam: *Ab Aquilone pandetur omne malum.* . . . Rursus versus aquilonem Evangelium legitur, juxta illud quod legitur in Canticis iiii: *Aquilo surgat,* idest diabolus fugiat."

14. *Liber florum,* III.iii.22: "Has enim sciencias et artes vniuersas dyaboli destruit beata Virgo per reuelacionem istius sciencie et confundit. Cum non licuit nec liceat dyabolo et angelis eius quin liceat Deo et sanctis eius. Set licet et licuit dyabolo—per invocaciones nepharias, ut in nigromancia, et per oraciones sacrilegas, ut in Arte notoria, custodientibus sua mandata et ceremonias—apparere diuersis malis et figuris. Benigne. ergo, licet Deo similiter et sanctis eius per oraciones deuotas et sanctas suis custodientibus mandata sua apparere benigne."

15. I take Thomas Aquinas as being concerned with a philosophical view when he lists three types of sacrilege concentrating on things rather than words (though the constitution of sacred things can never be wholly be divorced from questions of meaning and signification). Thomas's three types of sacrilege are (1) violations of sacred space (the church and its yard); (2) mistreatment of holy persons (the clergy); and (3) misappropriation or misuse of sacred things (chiefly liturgical instruments and the matter of the sacraments). Verbal ideas enter the picture in the sense that sins committed by clergy were sacrilege by default (II^a II^{ae}, Q. 98 A. 3), but Thomas does not elaborate much on this idea and Daniel 5 does not come up.

16. A group of French and English didactic treatises typically includes Daniel 5 as a story illustrating sacrilege. The earliest may be the *Somme le Roi* of Laurent d'Orléans, dating from the last quarter of the thirteenth century, whose popularity was increasing rapidly in the period of John's composition of the *Liber florum.* Daniel 5 also illustrates the sin of sacrilege in an obviously related work, the Anglo-Norman *Manuel de Pechiez* by Robert of Lincoln and its Middle English translation by Robert of Brunne, "Handlyng Synne," from which the exemplum of Belshazzar's feast is drawn and elaborated as the culmination of the Middle English poem *Cleanness.*

17. Jerome comments on Daniel 5:4, translation by Gleason Archer, *Jerome's Commentary on Daniel* (Grand Rapids, Mich.: Baker Books, 1958), 56. For a critical Latin text, see F. Glorie, ed., *Hieronymus: Commentariorum in Danielem libri III,* CCSL 75A (Turnhout: Brepols, 1964). Selections from this passage (likening the vessels to different types of knowledge) occur in *Glossa ordinaria,* vol. 3, glossing Daniel 5:4, p. 332, right-hand column.

18. John's own explanation of the problem with the *ars notoria* is that demonic names have been subtly inserted among the angel names of the macaronic prayers. See *Liber florum* I.i.9: "bis michi reuelatum fuit ab omnibus spiritibus angelicis quod in oracionibus extranee lingwe illius libri erat invocacio malignorum spirituum interclusa, ita subtiliter et ingeniose quod nullus de mundo quantumcumque esset subtilissimus eam percipere potuisset."

19. In *Genealogies of Religion: Discipline and Reasons of Power in Christianity and Islam* (Baltimore: Johns Hopkins University Press, 1993), chaps. 3 and 4, Asad writes on medieval Christian monasticism; his arguments figure more extensively in my next chapter.

20. Denys Turner, *The Darkness of God* (Cambridge: Cambridge University Press, 1995), 20; the referent for "its" is ambiguous in Turner, too.

21. For methodological overviews, see Bernard McGinn, "Theoretical Foundations: The Modern Study of Mysticism," appendix to his *Foundations of Mysticism* (New York: Crossroad, 1991), and Denys Turner's discussion (in part a critique of McGinn) in chap. 11 of *The Darkness of God,* "From Mystical Theology to Mysticism," 252ff. Both McGinn and Turner are uncomfortable around the term "experiential" as a rubric for the sorts of texts called "mystical" in the middle ages, though they offer different methodological solutions. For a discussion of different but cognate development in Jewish and Christian understandings of "mysticism," see my introduction to *Invoking Angels: Theurgic Ideas and Practices, Thirteenth to Sixteenth*

Centuries, ed. Claire Fanger (University Park: Pennsylvania State University Press, 2012), 23–27.

22. Claire Fanger, "Christian Ritual Magic in the Middle Ages," *History Compass* 11, no. 8 (2013): 610–18.

23. Quoted from the first paragraph of the entry on "Mysticism" in the *Catholic Encyclopedia*, which also has a terse but useful final paragraph on Catholic critique of this idea, describing the theological requirements that made direct and immediate divine union on earth an impossibility: see http://www.newadvent.org/cathen/10663b.htm.

24. Extracts from his defense, as well as the papal bull "In agro dominico" that formally condemned them, are available in translation in the Classics of Western Spirituality volume *Meister Eckhart: The Essential Sermons, Commentaries, Treatises, and Defense*, ed. E. Colledge and B. McGinn (Mahwah, N.J.: Paulist Press, 1981). The introduction to this book lays out the controversy over facets of the condemned propositions. As with John's work among the Benedictines, Eckhart's writings remained popular in his own order after the condemnation.

25. Marguerite's theology does not imply that all souls may be free of sacramental remediation, but does speak of the soul at an advanced stage of spiritual development who does not need to seek God through penitence or other sacraments of the Church; see, for example, chap. 85 of Margaret Porette [Marguerite Porete], *The Mirror of Simple Souls*, ed. Edmund Colledge, J. C. Marler, and Judith Grant (Notre Dame: University of Notre Dame Press, 1999). For recent treatments including discussion of some of the more daring aspects of Marguerite Porete's theology, see Robert Lerner, "New Light on *The Mirror of Simple Souls*," *Speculum* 85, no. 1 (2010): 91–116, and Sean Field, *The Beguine, the Angel, and the Inquisitor: The Trials of Marguerite Porete and Guiard of Cressonessart* (Notre Dame: University of Notre Dame Press, 2012). Useful for the way it lays out the stakes of the dispute in both Marguerite and Eckhart is chap. 6 of Turner's *Darkness*, 137ff.

26. Here, Nicholas Watson's discussion of the filiations between mysticism and Protestant understandings is relevant; see his introduction to *The Cambridge Companion to Medieval English Mysticism*, ed. Samuel Fanous and Vincent Gillespie (Cambridge: Cambridge University Press, 2011), 1–28. Watson does not query the "experiential" category, which is essential to thinking about the link between mysticism and Protestantism.

27. See *Liber florum* II.iii.cap 3.14-15, two chapters discussing how John's art should be taught to boys of less intelligence, uneducated young people, and the elderly afflicted with blindness.

28. For an overview of this topic, see Susan Boynton, "*Libelli Precum* in the Central Middle Ages," in *A History of Prayer: The First to the Fifteenth Century*, ed. Roy Hammerling (Leiden: Brill, 2008), 255–318. Boynton also discusses connections and differences between monastic prayer and the *libelli precum* in her monograph about the monks of Farfa, *Shaping a Monastic Identity: Liturgy and History at the Imperial Abbey of Farfa, 1000–1125* (Ithaca: Cornell University Press, 2006), 88ff. See also Adelaide Bennett's study of a French book that straddles this same divide, "A French Cleric's Prayer Book-Hours of the Early Thirteenth Century," in *Tributes to Nigel Morgan: Contexts of Medieval Art; Images, Objects, and Ideas*, ed. Julian Luxford and M. A. Michael (Turnhout: Harvey Miller, 2010), 23–30. I am grateful to Luis de las Cuevas for this last reference.

29. For these and other precedents for John's experience, see my article "Sacred and Secular Knowledge Systems in the *Ars Notoria* and the *Flowers of Heavenly Teaching* of John of Morigny," in *Die Enzyklopädik der Esoterik: Allwissenheitsmythen und universalwissenschaftliche Modelle in der Esoterik der Neuzeit*, ed. Andreas B. Kilcher and Philipp Theisohn (Paderborn: Wilhelm Fink Verlag, 2010), 157–75.

30. Edited in Claude Lafleur, *Quatre introductions à la philosophie au XIIIe siècle* (Montreal: Institut d'études médiévales and Paris: J. Vrin, 1988), 257: "Philosophica disciplina tribus de causis ab intellectu utentibus est appetenda. Vna est intellectus humani in tantum obumbratione corporis obnubilati informatio; que quidem informatio consistit in habitu scientiarum quantum ad partem speculatiuam et habitu uirtutum quantum ad actiuam uel practicam.

Secunda causa est cognitio magnitudinis Creatoris, potentie, bonitatis et sapientie. Per cognitionem enim philosophicam uel disciplinam prouehimur ad cognitionem uniuersi esse; cuius occulta ui et operatione, quam ei Conditor tribuit, tam mirabili cognita, incitamur ad amorem, et timorem, et reuerentiam tanti Cretoris in tantis creaturis, Eius infinitam potentiam, bonitatem et sapientiam admirantes. Tertia est decentia circumstantiarum quas exigit philosophica disciplina, que sunt tres: *mobilis affluentie contemptus, future felicitatis appetitus, mentis illustratio.*" Translation mine. Essentially the same introductory paragraph also occurs in the first text edited in this volume, *Accessus philosophorum*. Both are thirteenth century.

31. Lafleur, *Quatre introductions*, 301–3: "Nam sicut aer tenebrosus positus inter oculum et colorem tollit uisionem, sic corpus interpositum prohibet erectionem intellectus in Primum. Sicut enim dicit Philosophus primo *Methaphisice noue*, sic se habet intellectus humanus ad illud quod est manifestissimum in natura, sicut oculus uespertilioneis ad lucem Solis. Predictum etiam uidetur confirmare Boetius in libro De consolatione, n quodam metro insinuans statum anime in corpore sub hiis uerbis:

> Nam cum mentem cerneret altam
> (scilicet anima)
> Pariter summa singulaque norat,
> Nunc membrorum condita nube
> Non per totum oblita sui
> Summa retinuit singula perdens,

id est cognitionem confusam et in uniuersali retinuit, discretam et in particulari amisit, corporis mole oppressa.

"Theologica uero causa ponitur lapsus hominis in peccatum. Nam, sicut dicit Eustratius, Adam, primo plamatus ad ymaginem et similitudinem Conditoris siue Creatoris, uiirtutibus et scientiis perfectus, quia legem nature sibi inditam est transgressus, eius oculus intellectualis uersus est in tenebram et errorem, et factus est excecatus, nec non et uirtutibus et scientiis spoliatus." Translation mine.

32. *The "Didascalicon" of Hugh of St. Victor*, trans. Jerome Taylor (New York: Columbia University Press, 1961), III.13, p. 97. The Latin text is edited by Henry Buttimer in *Didascalicon: De studio legendi* (Washington, D.C.: Catholic University Press, 1939).

33. In a usage that seems to begin with Peter Lombard in the second half of the twelfth century and is increasingly common thereafter (though not officially made doctrine until the council of Trent in 1545), the seven sacraments are baptism, confirmation, reconciliation or penance, communion, marriage, ordination, and extreme unction. The number seven is defended by Thomas Aquinas, who refines the definition by distinguishing between "sacraments" and "sacramentals"; *Summa Theologiae* III Q. 65 A.1. In article 3 and 4 of the same question he addresses the order of sacraments, the signal importance of the Eucharist, and the sacraments necessary for salvation.

34. Hugh of St. Victor, *On the Sacraments of the Christian Faith*, trans. Roy Deferrari (Cambridge, Mass.: Medieval Academy, 1951), 3. Latin is available in *De sacramentis christiane fidei*, ed. Rainer Berndt (Münster: Aschendorff, 2008).

35. Unnumbered opening paragraph on p. 3 of Deferrari text.

36. Ibid., I.6.V, 97–98.

37. Boyd Coolman, *The Theology of Hugh of St. Victor: An Interpretation* (Cambridge: Cambridge University Press, 2010), 141; the internal quote is from Hugh's *Archa Noe*, 4.1.

38. *Scriptum super Sententiis*, prooemium, in *Opera omnia: Ad fidem optimarum editionum accurate recognita*, vol. 6 (Parma: P. Fiaccadori, 1856), http://www.corpusthomisticum.org/iopera.html (accessed June 22, 2014): "Per sapientiam enim Dei manifestantur divinorum abscondita, producuntur creaturarum opera, nec tantum producuntur, sed etiam restaurantur et perficiuntur: illa, dico, perfectione qua unumquodque perfectum dicitur, prout proprium finem attingit. Quod autem manifestatio divinorum pertineat ad Dei sapientiam, patet

ex eo quod ipse Deus per suam sapientiam seipsum plene et perfecte cognoscit. Unde si quid de ipso cognoscimus oportet quod ex eo derivetur, quia omne imperfectum a perfecto trahit originem: unde dicitur Sapient. 9, 17: *sensum tuum quis sciet, nisi tu dederis sapientiam?* Haec autem manifestatio specialiter per filium facta invenitur: ipse enim est verbum patris, secundum quod dicitur Joan. 1. . . . Recte ergo dicitur ex persona filii: *ego sapientia effudi flumina.*" Translation mine.

39. On the Sacraments, trans. Roy Deferrari, I.ix, 156.

40. Asad, "Discipline and Humility in Christian Monasticism," chap. 4 in *Genealogies of Religion*, 157–58.

41. For more discussion of the magicality of the *ars notoria*, see chapter 5 below.

CHAPTER 3

1. Miri Rubin, *Corpus Christi: The Eucharist in Late Medieval Culture* (Cambridge: Cambridge University Press, 1991), 84–85.

2. Joseph Goering, "The Internal Forum and the Literature of Penance and Confession," *Traditio* 59 (2004): 176.

3. Ibid.

4. *Liber florum* I Gen Prol.f: "Supponuntur omnia quecumque in hoc libro scripta sunt penitencie sacramento, scilicet ut septem sacramentis spiritualibus principalibus mistice supponantur."

5. *Liber florum* I.i.13: "Cum autem vidisset Deus Creator omnium quod timor eius me a malo non reuocaret, per seueritatem ecclesiastice discipline cohercendo me voluit reuocare. Vnde quadam nocte in extaseo sopore dormiens, vidi hominem in quodam solario vbi eram uenientem indutum toga rubea, vel epythogium, cum quibusdam alijs similiter habitu indutis. Et sedit ibi in kathedra tamquam magister. Et ego, videns Spiritus Sancti reuelacione in corde meo, agnoui ipsum esse dominum Ihesum. Et ego, veniens ante eum prostratus, ueniam pecij, sicut mos est religionis et in capitulo coram magistris ordinis. Et tunc dominus Ihesus, magister meus, precepit cuidam de societate sua ut me acriter verberaret. Et surgens quidam ipsorum et incepit me cum pungno acriter verberare, dicens, 'Tene, quia fecisti et facis que sunt contraria Creatori tuo.' Et multum verberauit me, et in tantum quod pre nimia pena et dolore quas paciebar excitatus fui. Et admirans multum, dolens scapulas, alia loca, in quo uapulatus fueram, et dolui per vnam horam fere. Et sic castigans castigauit me Dominus, et morti non tradidit me."

6. See *Benedictine Rule,* chapters 3, 23, and 28.

7. Unless otherwise noted, English translations of the Bible here and following are Douay-Rheims.

8. Translation mine.

9. Talal Asad, *Genealogies of Religion: Discipline and Reasons of Power in Christianity and Islam* (Baltimore: Johns Hopkins University Press), chap. 3, "Pain and Truth," 110.

10. Ibid., 112.

11. Ibid.

12. The Thirty Prayers, targeting knowledge of the liberal arts, come later, and are generally less autobiographical than the Seven Prayers, though they do return to John's experience at points, notably in prayer 30 and the extracurricular prayer 28B.2. The Thirty Prayers are not requested until after John quits the *ars notoria*, and at this point he is obviously still involved with it. For an overview of the ordering of the *Liber florum*, see the Structure and Referencing System at the front of this book. For more on John's biography, readers are invited to consult the discussion by Watson in *Liber florum* Introduction A.

13. *Liber florum* I.i.10.a: "Quadam nocte videbatur michi quod in camera mea venit vnus ex angelis Cherubin, indutus tunica nigra, et iussit me de camera descendere."

14. *Liber florum* I.i.9: "bis michi reuelatum fuit ab omnibus spiritibus angelicis quod in oracionibus extranee lingwe illius libri erat invocacio malignorum spirituum interclusa, ita

subtiliter et ingeniose quod nullus de mundo quantumcumque esset subtilissimus eam percipere potuisset. Et hiis auditis adhuc de illa sciencia magis dubitaui."

15. *Liber florum* I.i.10.a: "Et tunc cogitaui in corde meo quod si potuissem confessorem inuenire, ego confiterer et peniterem me peccasse et talia fecisse, et quod de cetero non facerem nec peccarem. Et statim ut hoc cogitaui, et ecce, ille inimicus dimisit me et aliquantulum elongauit se a me."

16. *Liber florum* I.i.10.b: "Et dum a predicto confessore recederem, quandam ecclesiam subintraui a parte meridiei. Et ecce, iuxta quoddam altare quod in parte septemtrionis erat, et stabat super gradus altaris predicte ecclesie dulcissima et intemerata Dei genitrix virgo Maria, vestibus candidissimis adornata, cuius pulchritudo erat talis et tanta quod ad eius visionem et declaracionem non potest humana lingwa sufficere. Et admiratus fui nec inmerito cum sol et luna mirantur in societate vero ipsius. Iuxta eam stabat beatus Iohannes ewangelista, indutus habitu Iacobito, mire pulchritudinis vltra modum, quibus visis, omnibus cogitacionibus remotis, tanta leticia exultauit cor meum quod nunquam senseram similem."

17. "Intraui chorum ecclesie": the unnamed church is clearly of substantial size.

18. "Infra accionem misse": the canon of the mass (that is, the part that comes after the offertory and before communion).

19. *Liber florum* I.i.10.b: "intraui chorum ecclesie, et ecce in choro erat altare et quidam in eo celebrabat. Et erat infra accionem misse; et in circuitu altaris ipsius quatuor erant ewangeliste indutis albis. Et ecce, vnus ipsorum capud aquileum habens et corpus et alia membra eius erant hominis venit ad me et amplexatus sum eum. Et ipsum tenendo in gremio meo sedi ibi, et sedendo mecum loquebatur, et in tanta requie positus statim euigilaui."

20. I mean to imply both the medieval sense, an event requiring exegesis, as well as the modern sense, an event of sensual and emotional import experienced as divine news.

21. Gelasian sacramentary, *PL* 74, 1252: "Supplices te rogamus, omnipotens deus, iube haec perferri per manus angeli tui in sublime altare tuum in conspectu diuine maiestatis tuae, ut quotquot ex hac altaris participatione sacrosanctum filii tui corpus et sanguinem sumpserimus, omni benedictione caelesti et gratia repleamur."

22. Stories in which confession loosens the devil's grip are abundant in medieval exempla; see, for example, the third *distinctio* in Caesarius of Heisterbach's *Dialogue on Miracles* (concerning confession).

23. *Liber florum* I.i.10.a: "Et tunc cogitaui in corde meo quod si potuissem confessorem inuenire, ego confiterer et peniterem me peccasse et talia fecisse, et quod de cetero non facerem nec peccarem. Et statim ut hoc cogitaui, et ecce, ille inimicus dimisit me et aliquantulum elongauit se a me, et continuo audiui angelos ita dulciter et melodiose cantantes quod in tota vita mea tam dulce canticum non audiui; set eos videre non poteram."

24. The episode is related in the Book of Visions, *Liber florum* I.iii.2.b, cited and discussed in chapter 1.

25. *Liber florum* I.iii.2.c: "quociens sibi postea apparebat fortis erat contra eum, et contra eum insurgebat et flagellabat et sub pedibus suis conculcabat eum."

26. *Liber florum* I.i.10.b: "Et tunc uere sciui quod Ars predicta notoria penitus erat mala, et aliquantulum ipsam dimisi set non in toto."

27. Ibid.: "Et admirans nec inmerito, gracias Deo reddidi, qui tanta secreta sua michi dignatus est ostendere; et inperpetuam memoriam istius visionis conposui et feci oracionem illam que sic incipit, 'Aue, salue,' et cetera." The link between vision and prayer is explicit in the rubric to the prayer as well, where John notes that he composed the prayer "postquam prima vice apparuit michi beata virgo Maria, in memoriam illius visionis specialiter." See *Liber florum* prayer *4.1 rubric.

28. The prayers preceded by asterisks are the Seven Prayers; see the Structure and Referencing System for the *Liber florum* at the front of this book.

29. The following are the meditation rubrics to prayer *4, each beginning "Cogita hic quod": *4.1 "tu intres aliquam ecclesiam a parte meridie"; *4.2.a "tu videas in eadem ecclesia Virginem gloriosam, cum beato Iohane in humana specie, vestimentis candidis adornatos";

*4.2.b "tibi videatur amplecti a Virgine gloriosa; te aspiciat virgo sancta Maria"; *4.2.c "tibi arrideat sancta virgo Maria"; *4.3.a "tu videas beatum Iohannem stantem in eadem ecclesia iuxta latus virginis Marie, te amplectantem et eum tecum loquentem"; *4.4 "tu videas in eadem ecclesia Virginem gloriosam tecum loquentem."

30. The use of visualizations as visionary prompts is certainly known elsewhere, though it is unusual to have the kind of personal documentation John offers here for the link between vision and visualization. For more on scripted visions, see Barbara Newman, "What Did It Mean to Say 'I Saw'? The Clash Between Theory and Practice in Medieval Visionary Culture," *Speculum* 80, no. 1 (2005): 1–43.

31. Prayer *3 rubric: "I said this prayer when the blessed virgin Mary first appeared to me in dream. And whenever I want her to appear to me I say it, for this, along with its accompanying prayers, is the 'experiment for having a vision'" (Hanc enim oracionem dixi quando primum beata virgo Maria apparuit michi in sompnis. Et quociens desidero ut michi appareat ipsam dico, ipsa enim est experimentum visionis habende, cum suis similibus).

32. *Liber florum* prayer *4.4.a: "O domina dominarum, O regina reginarum, virgo Maria, amica mea et mater, spes mee salutis et venie, mater misericordie, cuius amor omne bonum, cuius pulchritudo splendor paterne glorie. Que amore pulchritudinis tue et concupiscencia decoris tui inflammatum atque succensum me, .N., peccatorem miserum, ad te traxisti. Que per aspectum tuum quasi ab obliquo proiectum super me—et super huius libri compositorem, Iohannem—ex oculis tuis dulcissimis ferientibus et fruendis furibus cor amantis tamquam ex duobus telis acutissimis graciosis, cor meum et animam meam vehementissime perforasti."

33. *Liber florum* I.i.11: "Postquam autem nonam visionem vidi: accidit michi quedam maxima tribulacio, et in ista tribulacione persistens visiones multas horribiles ego singulari die videbam. Et quadam die volui scire quid significabant, et ad hoc sciendum protuli quandam oracionem de prefato libro Artis notorie que ad memoriam dicitur, sicut mos est. Et ecce, in nocte sequente talem vidi visionem. Videbatur michi quod in cubiculo meo erat iacens circa latus meum quidam malignus spiritus. Quo viso, surgens cito ibi ipsum arrepto gladio fugaui violenter, et percussi et recessit. Quo fugato, et ecce, quidam homo adveniens in camera mea, statura satis magna, longam habens faciem et longum nasum in medio altum, indutus vestimento non recte albo set quasi incinerato—i.e. vestis sua colorem cineris habebat—et vocauit me et dixit michi, 'Interpreta michi visionem.' Et tunc ad memoriam reducens pro quo oracionem predixeram, et dixi, 'Ha, Domine, set tu michi interpretaris.' Qui respondit, 'Nichil est. Et amplius non intromittas te de talibus, quia tibi non pertinent—quod si amplius feceris te obmutescere faciemus.'

"Et hoc dicto, iterum dixit michi, 'Veni huc, quia tecum uolo confiteri.' Et accipiens me per manus et duxit me vsque ad scampnum quod erat iuxta cubiculum meum, et ambo prostrauimus nos super scampnum illud ut modus est confitencium. Et incepit confiteri dicens, 'Ego sum vnus homo magnus et fortis et potens, et ego feci misericordiam vbi debuissem facere iudicium, et de hoc volo ut absoluas me.' Cui dixi, 'Domine, videtur michi quod non sit peccatum.' Qui dixit, 'Consciencia mea me reprehendit. Absolue me cito.' Et ego dixi, 'Et ex quo consciencia vestra uos de hoc accusat, ego absoluam vos.' Et cum voluissem ipsum absoluere verbis absolucionis communis, et dixit michi 'Non dicas hec, set aperi os tuum et implebo illud.' Et cum apperuissem os hec verba protuli ad ipsum absoluendum ac si in libro vidissem: 'Rex regum, princeps principum et dominus dominancium, homo Deus filius Marie natus ex virgine.' Et cum hoc vltimum vocabulum dixissem, exclamauit ille uoce magna et dixit, 'O maledicti Iudei,' dicente me sic et illum absoluendo: 'Ipse uos absoluat ab hijs que michi nunc confessus fuistis, ex quo de hijs consciencia uestra uos accusat.' Et hoc dicto a me recessit, et continuo excitatus. Et tunc cognoui, et sine dubio sciui, et expertus fui, quod ille liber Artis notorie omnino erat malignus, et quod Creatori meo non placebat quod amplius per ipsum operari, et in eo quod feceram sibi displicebat. Et propter hoc opus illius libri seu Artis predicte nepharie de hinc omnino dimisi et de hoc quod feceram confessus fui et penitui."

34. *Liber florum* prayer *1.1.a, incipit: "O Rex regum, qui es fortissimus princeps principum, excellentissimus et dominus dominancium, potentissimus homo, Deus iustus et uerus,

iudex faciens iusticiam et iudicium; tu es pius, mansuetus, et gloriosus, faciens misericordiam et graciam." The words "O rex regum, dominus dominantium" also occur in the *ars notoria*. Both texts amplify Revelation 19:16: "Rex regum et dominus dominancium" (king of kings and lord of lords), written on the cloak and thigh of Christ as he appears in the vision of heaven opened.

35. These words are not present in John's early draft of the prayer represented in the manuscript of the Old Compilation text in Oxford, Bodleian Liturg. 160. The fact that they are present only in New Compilation manuscripts of the text suggests that their inclusion resulted from a careful deliberation that took some time.

36. *Liber florum* prayer *1.1.a: "Sine principio principium, sine fine finis, beatus omnium Dux, sapientissimus et incomprehensibilis et eternus qui omnia ex nichilo procreasti; tu es sapiencia Dei Patris ineffabilis et speculum sine macula Dei maiestatis et ymago bonitatis illius, ab eterno sine tempore procreata. Domine Ihesu Christe, Filius clementissimus Dei Patris omnipotentis, tu es saluator meus et redemptor meus, vnus homo magnus, fortis et potens, qui fecisti et facis misericordiam et graciam vbi iudicium et iusticiam facere debuisses. Qui ab arce suprema, de sinu Patris, *ave* ob salutem nostram in vtero beatissime et intemerate gloriosissime Marie virginis descendens, de Spiritu Sancto conceptus, ibi carnem dignatus es assumere preciosam."

37. *Liber florum* prayer *1.1.d: "*Cogita hic quod tu videas passionem domini nostri Ihesu Christi:* O quam medicinalis, curabilis, et sanabilis, pijs et iustis, memoriabilis et compassibilis, tanti hominis mors et passio preciosa; set inpijs Iudeis et alijs infidelibus ipsam non credentibus terribilis et dampnosa."

38. *Liber florum* I.i.11.b: "Et tunc cognoui, et sine dubio sciui, et expertus fui, quod ille liber Artis notorie omnino erat malignus, et quod Creatori meo non placebat quod amplius per ipsum operari, et in eo quod feceram sibi displicebat."

39. Claire Fanger, introduction to *Invoking Angels: Theurgic Ideas and Practices, Thirteenth to Sixteenth Centuries,* ed. Claire Fanger (University Park: Pennsylvania State University Press, 2012), 1–33.

40. Moshe Idel, *Kabbalah: New Perspectives* (New Haven: Yale University Press, 1988), 156. Idel's understanding of "theurgy" is cited and summarized on pages 23–25 of Fanger, *Invoking Angels.*

41. Fanger, *Invoking Angels,* 23, quoting Idel, *Kabbalah,* 158.

42. Fanger, *Invoking Angels,* 24–25.

43. *Liber florum* prayer 30.1 rubric: "que est finis oracionum et conplementum ipsarum et est ad omnes sciencias."

44. Hebrew words given by God in the Bible when Moses asked for his name; commonly translated into English as "I am that I am."

45. *Liber florum* prayer 30.1.a: "Verbum in principio et Verbum apud Deum et Deus Verbum, humanis sensibus et ingenijs inexplicabile misterium et ineffabile sacramentum, Pater, Verbum, et Spiritus Sancte, testimonium celeste, altitudo incomprehensibilis, Trinitas indiuisibilis, essencia inpermutabilis, eyehye heser eyheye, ante mundi principium nullo indigens, set ipse tibi ines sufficiens et in teipso semper permanens et congaudens: deytas eterna, Alpha omnium creaturum, qui in Verbo tuo omnia a principio de nichilo creasti, O in quo omnia terminum et finem corrupcionis mortalis accipient, ut te principium inmortale et incorruptibile in hereditate et stabilitate perpetua reassumant."

46. *Liber florum* prayer 30.1.a–b: "ego . . . qui in peccato conceptus, in peccato natus, et in peccato nutritus, et semper cottidie non cesso peccare. Idcirco volo mundari et desidero. . . . Laua ergo me, Domine, ab vniuersa iniquitate mea, et a cunctis contagijs meis me mundare digneris. . . . digneris hodie in visceribus mentis mee clementer infundere suauissimam dulcedinem amenissimi amoris tui et inconparabilis diuicias multiplicis sapiencie et multiformis gracie tue; ut in sciencia, philosophia, theorica, ethica, et loyca sim perfecte intelligens."

47. John draws on a late medieval tradition of Christian reappropriation of the divine name that begins in the twelfth century with the converted Jew Petrus Alfonsi; see his *Dialo-*

gus contra iudaeos, ed. Klaus-Peter Mieth, trans. into Spanish by Esperanza Ducay (Huesca: Instituto de Estudios Altoaragoneses, 1996), 110–12. Joachim of Fiore follows him in the *Liber figurarum*, in which the letter pairings *je eu ve* are read as *Pater, Filius, Spiritus sanctus*. See *The "Figurae" of Joachim of Fiore*, ed. Marjorie Reeves and Beatrice Hirsch-Reich (Oxford: Clarendon Press, 1972), 38–41.

48. *Liber florum* prayer 30.1.e: "Exaudi me, domine Ihesu Christe, . . . qui iuste hoc nomine vocaris: ✠ Ioth ✠ He ✠ Vaw ✠ Heth ✠ id est Ie ev ve ✠ id est I E V E. Cuius hodie auxilium super me invocaui et ipsum nominaui in auxilium infirmitatis mee, cuius misterium nos a morte redimendo expleuisti. Da gloriam nomini tuo et non michi, et non secundum peccata mea facias michi neque secundum iniquitates meas retribuas michi, set secundum misericordiam tuam qua plena est terra. Miserere mei, tribue michi, per ineffabilem tui graciam, finale sciencie donum, qui mirabiliter omnium scienciarum Salomoni regi et sanctis apostolis tuis donum largiri dignatus es, per quod in me munus largitatis tue patenter agnoscam, vt ab hoc a uia impia me valeam restringere." For Petrus and Joachim, see *Liber florum*, Sources at prayer 30.1.e.

49. *Liber florum* prayer 30.2.h: "Tu es arbor arduissima, virtutum gemmis omnium honorata, cuius fructus est lapis preciosus, sardis karitatis, topasius sciencie, iaspis iudicij, crisolitus reuerencie, onix dominacionis, berillus potestatis, saphyrus virtutis, carbunculus claritatis et smaragdus virginitatis; cuius radices sunt magnes coniunccionis et adamas firmitatis; cuius truncus marmor soliditatis et rami sapiencie margarita. Tu es gramatice congruus intellectus, dyalettice vera memoria argumenti, rethorice eloquencie ornata, libra geometrie, colleccio arismetice, concordia musice; et consideracio astronomie et philosophie congnicio, theologie contemplacio; arcium mechanicarum sciencie, operacio exceptivarum; adiuracionis, impetracionis, et omnium virtutum retribucio, et sapiencie et sciencie perfectio, finis et consummacio gloriosa."

50. Some of the associations of Mary with learning in general are noticed in Miri Rubin, *Mother of God: A History of the Virgin Mary* (New Haven: Yale University Press, 2009), especially in chap. 10, "Mary and Women, Mary and Men" (which mentions John of Morigny). For more development of Mary's association with the trivium, see especially Georgiana Donavin, *Scribit Mater: Mary and the Language Arts in the Literature of Medieval England* (Washington, D.C: Catholic University of America Press, 2011). Mary's association with Wisdom was developed early through the liturgies for Marian feast days; see Barbara Newman's comments in *God and the Goddesses: Vision, Poetry, and Belief in the Middle Ages* (Philadelphia: University of Pennsylvania Press, 2003), chap. 5, "Sapientia: The Goddess Incarnate," 194ff.

51. *Liber florum* prayer 30.2.i–j: "Cum adiutorio tuo completus est liber tuus a fratre Iohanne monacho, de licencia tua et voluntate compositus et factus, ad honorem filij tui, domini nostri Ihesu Christi, et tuum et tocius curie celestis, et in salutem anime mee et omnium ipso fruencium et vtencium bono modo.

"Et nunc, domina et amica, da honorem tibi et non sibi, et vigila super verbo tuo a te sibi, licet indigno, promisso, ut non permittas oraciones tantas istius libri a me dictas et pronuncciatas anullari, ne dyabolus . . . inde gaudeat, forte estimans me ob hoc apud se querere, quod a te possum et per te, si tibi placeat, misericorditer obtinere. Da ergo virtutem, dulcissima domina et amica mea, virgo Maria, verbis sanctis libri in oracionibus a me dictis et prolatis, incepti in tuo nomine et finiti."

CHAPTER 4

1. I discuss the information that points to the shape of the individual installments and possible times of circulation in *Liber florum* Introduction B; it is digested further in *Liber florum* table 14.

2. "Plundering the Egyptian Treasure: John the Monk's *Book of Visions* and Its Relation to the Ars Notoria of Solomon," in *Conjuring Spirits: Texts and Traditions of Medieval Ritual*

Magic, ed. Claire Fanger (University Park: Pennsylvania State University Press, 1998), 231. The reader will note square brackets around the word "book," replacing *"Liber visionum."* We now recognize *Liber visionum* as John's title for the first part of the work only.

3. "Plundering the Egyptian Treasure," 233.

4. *Liber florum* III.iii.35–37.

5. The First Procedure is about 6,000 words; the Book of Figures, about 16,000. The portion of these materials preserved in Clm 276 is only about 1,500 words. The Book of Visions, also missing from Clm 276, is about 9,000 words. These materials together make up roughly half of the New Compilation text represented in our edition.

6. *Liber florum* III.i.2.a.

7. *Liber florum* NC III.iii.2.e: "In 2a parte fiat ymago, et cetera ut prius totaliter, set hec debet tenere rosarium vnum. In 3a parte ut prius set debet tenere vitem cum racemis. In 4a ut prius, set debet tenere olyuam. In 5ta ut prius, set debet tenere palmam. In 6ta parte ut prius, set debet tenere malogranatum. Item, super olyuam debet esse columba; super palmam fenix. In septima figura ut prius, set debet tenere cipressum cum pellicano. Super malagranatum debet esse aquila." All of these iconic elements are well-attested Christian symbols.

8. For comparison of features of images in the two known manuscripts, see *Liber florum,* Variants at NC III.iii.9; 13; 15; 17; 19.a; 21.a; 24. The most complete set of images is contained in Salzburg University Library MI 24. Color images of the apocalyptic Christ and two figures of Mary from this manuscript are reproduced in *Liber florum* plates 6 and 7; a figure of the Virgin with pelican is reproduced in this book at the end of chapter 6. There are also images executed in Bologna, Biblioteca Comunale dell' Archiginnasio, A. 165 (16. b. III. 5), but the set is not complete, since two have been cut out from the book. A few images occur in third compilation manuscripts as well, but these differ from those of the primary tradition; see *Liber florum* Introduction B, IV.2, for discussion and plate 10 for an example in color.

9. The trope is ancient, but item 56 in the *Somniale Danielis* gives a good example and may have been on John's mind, since the book concerns dreamers: "canes latrantes viderit vel eis infestari: inimici tui te superare querunt significat" (someone who sees barking dogs or that he is attacked by them: it means that your enemies seek to conquer you). See *Somniale Danielis: An Edition of a Medieval Latin Dream Interpretation Handbook,* ed. Lawrence Martin (Frankfurt: Peter Lang, 1981), 110. Other users of this figure certainly known to John include Alanus de Insulis, *De planctu naturae,* 14.9, which suggests that you should "te a grege latrantium canum excipias" (withdraw yourself from the crowd of barking dogs) as a remedy for envy. See *De planctu naturae* in *Literary Works: Alain of Lille,* ed. Winthrop Wetherbee (Cambridge, Mass.: Harvard University Press, 2013), 168.

10. *Liber florum* NC III.i.c–d: "Postquam vero licenciam (beata Maria virgine gloriosa procurante et ut eam acciperem in sompnis figuraliter me monente, et quod ipsam obtinerem absque dubio libere michi firmiter promittente) apud Aurelianos obtinui in decretis, audiens et considerans quosdam seminis non Iude set Chaanaam murmurantes morsu rabido more canum latrancium; invidentes contra figuras huius sciencie a me compositas consilio Virginis gloriose et postea ab ipsa confirmatas prout in libro ipsarum antiquo apparet et plenius continetur; detrahentes quidem eidem sciencie et figuris sanctis gracieque Spiritus Sancti lingwa ipsas carpentes toxicata; recedentes a Deo et dicentes eidem, 'Recede a nobis, scienciam viarum tuarum nolumus,' videntes bona et discere contempnentes.

"Tunc, propter hoc quia dicebant ipsas figuras more figurarum nigromancie esse compositas, propter cruces et circulos in eisdem existentes; tunc, propter hoc quia consideraciones planetarum et dierum circulorum in ipsis figuris et oracionibus proferendis constituebantur . . . sic quodammodo secundum istam scienciam scandalum nascebatur. . . . Et ideo, consilio meo cum mandato Virginis gloriose, consideraui—non solum ad predictum scandalum iam ortum euitandum, quia a canibus non a fidelibus fuit ortum, ymmo magis propter dificultatem pronuncciandi ipsas oraciones cum figuris, quia vix posset ab aliquo adimpleri—dictas figuras que prius erant in cruce et circulis ymagines ipsius Virginis gloriose tantummodo transmutare. . . .

"Quod iam, procurante dyabolo in filios diffidencie, tantum inualuerat quod me videntes illudendo capita mouebant; aduersum me loquebantur dicentes, 'Ecce, Sompniator,' credentes quod ego non agnoscerem corda eorum."

11. *Liber florum* I.i.1.b: "[P]repositus nostre camere factus fui infra octauam diem post predicta, quod officium est ualde laboriosum et mobile." See also Sources at I.i.1.b.

12. John's awareness of the possibility and consequences of condemnation is visible in his comments on the *prosa* of Philip Chancellor. John resorts to visionary means to remove doubt that he should make liturgical use of this little poem; see *Liber florum* I.ii.3 and Sources. Other noteworthy early fourteenth-century theological condemnations originated with the archbishop of Sens, Philip of Marigny, including condemnation of Marguerite Porete, burnt as a heretic in 1310 after she refused to withdraw her book from circulation (itself burnt in 1308). See discussion by Watson in *Liber florum* Introduction A, §88.

13. The book of prayers was mostly written at Orléans, and since it was transmitted from an early period, it clearly did circulate outside of Morigny. For analysis of evidence pertinent to early circulation, see *Liber florum* Introduction B, esp. III.2–5. The prayers would probably not have appeared objectionable without the figures.

14. Most directly, "Ecce, sompniator" echoes the aspersion cast at Joseph of the coat of many colors in Genesis 37:19–20: "And said one to another: Behold the dreamer cometh [Ecce, sompniator venit]. Come, let us kill him, and cast him into some old pit." Thus it may be a trope that John used to attract sympathy for his own position by linking himself to a biblical dreamer who likewise suffered insult from his own family. On the other hand, it may really have happened. The Vulgate gives other precedents for uses of the word that parallels it to diviners and sorcerers—for example, Jeremiah 27:9: "Therefore hearken not to your prophets, and diviners, and dreamers [somniatores], and soothsayers, and sorcerers," and in this usage the term appears in the title of a work on spiritual discernment by John's contemporary Augustine of Ancona, *Tractatus contra divinatores et sompniatores*, published in 1310. Thus it is possible that this insult really was cast at John in 1315.

15. And incidentally supports the notion that proliferation of the figures could not have been especially rapid.

16. Richard Hunt and Falconer Madan, *A Summary Catalogue of Western Manuscripts in the Bodleian Library at Oxford Which Have Not Hitherto Been Catalogued in the Quarto Series* (Oxford: Clarendon Press, 1895–1953), 850.

17. The ending with "heth" instead of "he" was widely transmitted among Christian Latin writers.

18. The prayer appears in slightly different forms at *Liber florum* II.Rit Prol.d., and in a slightly simpler version at the end of the book, NC III.iii.37.d, here quoted: "Ioth: Deus intellectus et intelligencie / (*Ihesu Christe vite principium*) / He: Deus perfecte reminiscencie et memorie / (*Qui per crucis patibulum*) / Vaw: Deus racionis et eloquencie; / (*Qui per passionis obitum*) / Heth: Deus stabilitatis perfeccionis et perseuerancie, fons tocius sapiencie sciencie et prudencie / (*Vita factus es omnium*): / Incipe nunc, pone, perfice, fac, comple in me qui es ut predixi, per signaculum annuli et figurarum. Amen."

19. *Liber florum* NC III.iii.36.b: "Ipsa enim oracio in Antiqua Compilacione habet figuram propriam, set in ista non.... Vnde ipsam dicendo, ymaginetur in mente annuli forma." In the Salzburg manuscript, University Library M I 24, fol. 1r, following this directive, the scribe wrote a careful gloss near the instruction "here there should be a figure": "let the figure of a ring be inscribed mentally."

20. For examples of necromantic figures, see the plates in Richard Kieckhefer, *Forbidden Rites: A Necromancer's Manual of the Fifteenth Century* (University Park: Pennsylvania State University Press, 1997); for examples of *Ars notoria* figures, see the plates in Véronèse AN.

21. Oxford, Bodleian Liturg. 160, fol. 1: "Cogita hic hiis dictis quod <tu sis ad por>tam paradisi et quod tibi ab angelo aperiatur." See *Liber florum* Variants at II. Rit Prol for more on manuscript representations in this section.

22. *Liber florum* OC III.1.rubric: "Hic incipit Liber Figurarum beate et intemerate Dei genitricis Marie. Qualiter debet operari per omnes oraciones, figuras, et ymaginaciones ipsius artis beate Marie ad omnes artes sciendas et optinendas per preces eiusdem Virginis."

23. "Mater misericordie" is an epithet of Mary, part of the address to Mary in the opening line of "Salve Regina," a very familiar Marian hymn traditionally said or sung after night prayer from the end of Eastertide until the beginning of Advent.

24. For examples of the pentangle in necromancy, see, for example, Kieckhefer, *Forbidden Rites*, 364–65.

25. The description of Gawain's shield comes at lines 619–65; see the edition by Tolkien and Gordon, *Sir Gawain and the Green Knight* (Oxford: Oxford University Press, 1967).

26. *Liber florum* OC III.19.l: "Maria: mater misericordie Ihesu Christi, aula altissimi Ihesu Christi, regina reginarum Ihesu Christi, iusticia iustorum Ihesu Christi, altitudo angelorum Ihesu Christi. Amica: auxilium mei, Galfridi, illuminacio, consilium adiuuamen: miserere mei, audi me, respice me, instrue me, adiuua me." Galfridus (Geoffrey) is the name of the operator, the person who either copied or commissioned the manuscript now called Oxford, Bodleian Liturg. 160.

27. *Liber florum* OC III.19: "Capitulum de literis et scriptis figurarum."

28. *Liber florum* OC III.19.rubric: "In figuris beate Marie et 7tem planetarum, duodecim signorum et domorum, in eodem libro post ipsas manifeste scribitur quid in eis continetur."

29. For a complete list, see *Liber florum* table 17, "The Figures of *Liber florum*."

30. To be further discussed in the next chapter.

31. There is too little information to know what these might have looked like. They might have involved anthropomorphized representational images, as the planetary figures do; or, on the other hand, they could have been more diagrammatic, or involved arrangements of dots such as geomantic figures have.

32. *Liber florum* OC I.iv.6: "Litere uero figurarum litere sunt nominis operantis mixte cum literis nominis beate Marie et cum literis nominum proprietatis figurarum et situate in figuris ad modum crucis sic: vna litera accipitur de nomine beate Marie, scilicet prima, uel alterius nominis secundum proprietatem figure, et altera de nomine opificis; et coniunguntur et vna post aliam sic ad modum crucis in figuris situantur. Et ita faciendum est de aliis literis nominis beate Marie et nominum proprietatis figurarum et nominis opificis semper repetendo literas nominis opificis tociens quot erunt litere in nomine beate Marie et in nominibus proprietatis figurarum. Et hoc intelligendum est de figuris que sunt a principio usque ad figuras 12 domorum. In aliis uero figuris que inde sequuntur sufficiunt due litere nominis opificis cum nomine beate Marie et cum nominibus proprietatis figurarum." The kind of letter play John prescribes here has devotional precedents elsewhere in the tradition of *carmina figurata*. See chapter 4, "Acrostics, *carmina figurata*, and Other Poetic Devices," in Dag Norberg, *An Introduction to the Study of Medieval Latin Versification*, trans. Grant Roti and Jacqueline de Chapelle Skubly (Washington: Catholic University of America Press, 2004). For an example see Raban Maur's *De laudibus sanctae Crucis* in the lovely manuscript viewable online at http://gallica.bnf.fr/ark:/12148/btv1b8490076p/f9.image (as of November 1, 2014).

33. *Liber florum* OC III.3: "Postquam enim oraciones prescriptas, cum practica quadam ipsarum particulari seu eciam preambulanti vel preparatiua, composui, ut dictum est, de licencia et voluntate Virginis gloriose ad figuras componendas operam dedi. Et de hac composicione licenciam a domina mea et amica Virgine gloriosa petij, deuotissime exorando et deprecando corde perfecto et mundo. Et ego, Iohannes, in exstasi positus. Ipsa apparuit michi in ecclesia nostra Sancte Trinitatis de Moriginaco super altare. Dixique ei:, 'Domina mea et amica, potero numquid facere perfecte librum quem incepi?' Que ridendo dulcissime respondit, 'Non.' Et pedem suum tetendit ad me vt deosculer. Et deosculatus sum eum et continuo excitaui.

"Et admirans et timens dixi in corde meo, 'Forte ipse michi negauit primo, non ut librum non incipiam, set ut ardencius ipsum componendo ipsam rogem de eo. Et hoc michi signum quia ridebat quando negauit, et propter hoc librum hunc incipiam melius quam potero semper ipsam rogando pro eo.' Et sic feci. Verumptamen in responsione predicta duo sunt intellectus, quorum vnum dixi, alter uero sequitur, set statim non intellexi donec post maximum tempus. Et iste est: verum dixit michi Virgo beata quando dixit michi quod librum meum 'perficere' non poteram, scilicet quantum ad effectum omnium operacionum eius et non quantum ad scripturam composicionis—quia de hoc non intelligebat nisi quod ardencius quererem. Quia in perfeccione effectuali huius artis, oportet quod opifex per omnes operaciones eius ad omnes artes et sciencias operetur, et ego ad hec omnia per librum hunc non fui operatus racione illa que scribitur superius ante oraciones in capitulo ultimo de Visionibus, et sic dixit michi verum in vtroque intellectu."

34. For the book of thirty prayers, John requested "license to compose a book of only thirty simple prayers" through which he might come to "knowledge of all scripture, arts, and sciences" (licenciam peterem conponendi vnum librum tantummodo de triginta orationibus simplicibus librum componam de triginta orationibus simplicibus tantummodo, per quem possim ad cognicionem omnium scripturarum, arcium, scienciarum pervenire). This vision is described at *Liber florum* I.ii.5; similar words are used at II.Prol.d.

35. The reference to "the last chapter of the Visions" seems to refer to OC.I.iv.8: "But everyone should know that I worked through this art only for the arts of virtue and for having visions of the blessed and undefiled mother of God, Mary, and not for the liberal, mechanical, and exceptive arts, because I grasped enough of those arts already in their particulars through the Notory Art" (Set cognoscant omnes quod ego per artem istam operatus sum solummodo ad artes virtutum et ad habendas visiones beate et intemerate Dei genitricis Marie et non ad artes liberales mechanicas et exceptiuas, quia antequam hanc artem incepissem licencia virginis gloriose ad componendum, artes predictas iam comprehenderem ad sufficienciam particulariter per Artem notoriam).

36. Quoted from *The Rule of St. Benedict in Latin and English*, ed. Timothy Fry (Collegeville, Minn.: Liturgical Press, 1980).

37. *Liber florum* OC I.iv.10.e: "Item, aliquando quesita uel petita petenti primo negat, non ut ea non optineat, set ut postea illa ardencius querat; et postea concedit ea cum sollicite querantur."

38. *Liber florum* OC III.5: "Apparuit michi virgo Maria in quodam pilario depicta et subito in specie et forma pulcherime mulieris transmutata. Rogaui eam ut daret michi licenciam componendi Librum Figurarum suarum quem iam inceperam componere. Et dixit michi, 'Et ego dico tibi quod licenciam non dabo tibi. Set quando ipsum librum feceris libenter ipsum videbo.' Et videbatur michi quod soror mea Burgeta erat iuxta me quando virgo Maria dixit michi verba predicta. Et dixit michi soror mea, 'Sufficiant vobis que dixit virgo Maria; faciatis librum vestrum, et quando erit factus ipsa videbit si bene erit factus vel non, et secundum hoc vobis respondebit.' Et regraciaui Virginem gloriosam et excitaui, et librum hunc usque ad finem composicionis ipsius auxilio eius suffragante perduxi."

39. *Liber florum* OC III.7–8: "Satis bene factus" and "peroptime factus."

40. *Liber florum* I.iv.2.c: "Tunc dixit, 'Et ego dico tibi quod nolo oraciones neque figuras neque ymaginaciones nisi cor.'"

41. *Liber florum* OC III.6: "Virgo Maria iterum apparuit michi propter predicacionem meam sic. Ego enim, Iohannes, fui sepius post visiones predictas a sociis meis rogatus; immo eciam ab abbate nostro fuit michi preceptum et iniunctum quod in capitulo nostro pupplice predicarem, de quo multociens me excusaui. Set ipsi perseuerantes semper rogabant me, et abbas similiter precipiens michi. Ego tanquam bonus obediens voluntati et precepto rogatiuo acquieui ipsorum; set sine licencia Virginis gloriose—tamen parum sciebam de his, quantum ad hoc quod predicare pupplice debuissem uel potuissem—non ausus fui hoc tantum officium subintrare. . . . Tandem apparuit michi in sompnis, in pilario eiusdem ecclesie depicta, et dixi ei, 'Domina mea, rogo vos quod vobis placeat ut predicacionem subintrem.' Que respondit, 'Placet michi; predica.' Et excitatus sum, et predicacionem sui gracia subintraui adiuuante, deinde secure."

42. For other references to John's gift of prophecy in the Old and New Books of Figures, see *Liber florum* OC III.21.c, OC III.25.a–d, OC III.28.c, and NC III.i.14.b.

43. *Liber florum* OC III.25.a–b: "In extaseo sopore positus, post donum spiritus prophecie, vidi diabolum in claustro nostro in similitudine bouis, et pugnaui contra ipsum et vici. Iterum, ego vidi quod ego dedi sertum rosarum beate Marie et ipsa posuit in capite suo illud dicens, 'Amicus meus dulcis dedit michi illud, dulcis et mitis.' Iterum, ego vidi me iacentem et obdormientem supra pectus virginis Marie, et posuit mammam eius in ore meo et lactaui et dormiui. . . . Item, ego vidi me ludentem cum Christo puero ad pelotam. Item, ego vidi quod dominus noster Ihesu Christus me deosculatus fuit in ore, et in crastino officium predicationis subintraui. Iterum, ego vidi quod crucifixus erat super calicem meam, et gutte sanguinis pedum eius descendebant in calicem meam. Iterum, ego vidi quod ego ascendebam in cruce vbi crucifixus erat, et sanguis pedum crucifixi defluebat super capud meum."

44. The reference to the "book of prophecies" is proleptic. In *Liber florum* OC III.21.c it is clear that he has not yet written this book; he proposes to do so if death does not interfere. Such a book is not extant, so far as is known.

45. *Liber florum* OC III.25.d: "Prophecias omnium istarum visionum in *Libro propheciarum beate Marie* quere. Hic aliter non scripsimus eas ratione breuitatis et quia non sunt de corpore huius artis visibilis, licet sint de inuisibili operacione ipsius. Vnde si quis interogauerit quomodo ista sciui et vbi accepi que scripsi, et scripturus sum, cogitatis et inspectis visionibus meis, sic ei respondebo: ex sacro osculo spirituali pedum beatorum virginis Marie gloriose, quod est reconsiliacionis. Et manuum eius sanctarum quod est remuneracionis. Et oris eius, benedicti odore inbalsamati mellito, et eiusdem filii domini nostri Ihesu Christi, quod est contemplacionis. Et adhuc ex eo quod plus est, scilicet ex sacro fonte pectoris eiusdem Virginis, in quo spiritualiter recubui et dormiui, atque ex emanancione lactis spiritualis gracie et misericordie sancte eius mamille, cum quo nutritus est Christus, et ego spiritualiter lactatus et confortatus. In cuius cibi spiritualis fortitudine, perrexi vsque ad montem Dei, Oreb. Et inde que scripsi et scripturus sum, sacra huius libri verba fluenta potaui."

46. I have analyzed the elements of this passage more extensively elsewhere; see Claire Fanger, "Complications of Eros: The Song of Songs in John of Morigny's *Liber Florum celestis doctrine*," in *Hidden Intercourse: Eros and Sexuality in the History of Western Esotericism*, ed. Wouter Hanegraaff and Jeffrey Kripal (Leiden: Brill, 2010), 153–73, esp. 165–67.

CHAPTER 5

1. The necromantic episodes are the tenth and eleventh visions of the Book of Visions, at *Liber florum* I.i.12–13.

2. *Liber florum* I.i.12. The *Four Rings of Solomon* is mentioned in *Speculum astronomiae* as among the "detestable" (though not "abominable") works of image magic, which include inscribed characters and other dubious components; see *Liber florum*, Sources at I.i.12 for further information on the *Four Rings*.

3. These are the visions grouped in the second part of the Book of Visions, *Liber florum* I.ii.

4. *Liber florum* I.ii.1: "Videbatur enim michi quod eram in ecclesia magna Carnocensi beate Marie ante magnum altare ipsius ecclesie, et rogabam ibi Virginem gloriosam. Et cum aliquantulum rogassem eam, ecce, ymago argentea, in ipsa Virgine carnaliter et corporaliter transmutata, desuper descendit de altari et venit ad me, accipiens me per manus et duxit me per medium gradus ante altare, et dixit michi, 'Hic sta, et Deum adora, et redde ei gratias.' Et cum voluissem orare orationibus communibus, beata Virgo dixit, 'Non, set sic: "Gracias ago tibi."'" Et cum fuissem ibi, genibus flexis, manibus conplosis, omnis chorus cantabat 'Te Deum laudamus' propter miraculum quod in persona mea fecerat beata virgo Maria et in conspectu omnium. Et dum cantabant, ego cogitaui in corde meo, et dicebam, 'Maria, si libri istius artis nephandissime nigromancie apud me inuenientur, dicetur quod hoc non est miraculum set per artem illam feci ymaginem ita descendere et transmutare? Et quid faciam libris istius

sciencie? De societate mea remouebo et abscondam?' Et dum hec cogitarem euigilaui, et in memoriam illius visionis orationem illam composui 'Gloriose flos celorum' et aliam que sequitur, 'Gratias tibi ago.'"

5. *Liber florum* I.i.12.

6. Ibid.: "non solum de hac sciencia de qua querisset de omnibus invenies ueritatem."

7. John says that nothing can be done in necromancy without it. See *Liber florum* I.i.3: "sine ipso de nigromancia aliquid exerceri non potest."

8. *Liber florum* I.i.10.a: "nigromanciam sciui in vtraque specie."

9. Burnett, "Talismans: Magic as Science? Necromancy Among the Seven Liberal Arts," in *Magic and Divination in the Middle Ages: Texts and Techniques in the Islamic and Christian Worlds* (Aldershot: Variorum, 1996).

10. Ibid., 3.

11. A translation of this work, known as *Ghāyat al-ḥakīm* in Arabic, was commissioned by Alfonso X in the twelfth century. Chapter 2, concerning "what necromancy is and its proper nature," is a good example of a neutral usage of the word "necromancy," one that is not principally focused on demonic involvement. Here it states that necromancy is a term for a subtle art that worked in such a way that the causes and operations are hidden, not readily visible to men; mostly this implies that the astrological forces at work are invisible, though it can be an art of illusion too. See the Latin edition by David Pingree, *Picatrix: The Latin Version of the "Ghāyat al-ḥakīm"* (London: Warburg Institute, 1986), I.ii.

12. See the extended treatment by Nicolas Weill-Parot, *Les "images astrologiques" au Moyen Âge* (Paris: Honoré Champion, 2002). Chapter 1, concerning the *Speculum astronomie*, is especially important in delimiting the terms of art now in use; Weill-Parot offers a shorter treatment in English, "Astral Magic and Intellectual Changes (Twelfth–Fifteenth Centuries): 'Astrological Images' and the Concept of 'Addressative' Magic," in *The Metamorphosis of Magic from Late Antiquity to the Early Modern Period*, ed. Jan Bremmer and Jan Veenstra (Leuven: Peeters, 2002), 167–84. For the *Speculum*, see Paola Zambelli et al., *The Speculum astronomiae and Its Enigma: Astrology, Theology, and Science in Albertus Magnus and His Contemporaries* (Dordrecht: Kluwer, 1992), though the attribution to Albertus Magnus has been disputed; see discussion in Weill-Parot, "*Images astrologiques,*" 27–32.

13. While it might be objected that standard prayers and liturgies are also "addressative," Weill-Parot attempts to clarify the ground of his terminology when he writes, "from a theological point of view, any 'addressativity' occurring outside the divine order and framework of the Church was condemned as demoniac: the Christian Church had a monopoly on 'addressativity'" ("Astral Magic," 169).

14. Ibid., 175.

15. See *De doctrina christiana* II.xxiii.36, ed. William Green, CSEL 80 (Vienna: Hoelder-Pichler-Tempsky, 1963), 59: "Omnes igitur artifices huius modi vel nugatoriae vel noxiae superstitionis, ex quadam pestifera societate hominum et daemonum, quasi pacta infidelis et dolosae amicitiae constituta, penitus sunt repudianda et fugienda Christiano."

16. For a capsule history of the transmission of the primary Augustinian passages on magic, see Claire Fanger, "Magic," in *The Oxford Guide to the Historical Reception of Augustine*, ed. Karla Pollmann and Willemien Otten (Oxford: Oxford University Press, 2013), 860–65.

17. Weill-Parot comments on the Thomistic passages I am about to quote here in "Astral Magic," 175. He notes it as one of the parameters he uses to date the work of the Magister Speculi, since it involves an early use of the term "astrological image." However, he does not comment on how Thomas here is reacting to a problem with the Augustinian terminology.

18. For another discussion of Thomas's influence on the later traditions of condemnation of the Notory art, see Julien Véronèse, "L'*Ars notoria* au Moyen Âge et à l'époque moderne: Étude d'une tradition de magie théurgique (XIIe–XVIIe siècle)," 2 vols. (diss., Université Paris X–Nanterre, 2004). Volume 1 is online at http://www.univ-orleans.fr/node/653 (as of June 1, 2014); see in particular volume 1, part II, chap. 6, "Condemnations doctrinales de l'Ars notoria."

19. Thomas's use of these terms "augury" and "lots" is distinctive. He is not following Isidore, as he appears to be elsewhere in this article, but rather subsumes a number of nontraditional subcategories in these two types. In the category of "augury," Thomas indicates that he means to include divinations in which someone reads the future in the disposition or movement of natural things (stars in astrology, birds in augury, and so on); in "lots" or "sortes" he means to include divinations in which someone performs an action to find out something hidden (this would include practices such as casting dice, drawing lots, geomancy, and other allied actions, including trial by ordeal). *Summa theologiae*, II^a II^{ae}, Q. 95 A. 3.

20. Ibid., Q. 96 A. 2: "Cuius signum est quod necesse est eis inscribi quosdam characteres, qui naturaliter ad nihil operantur, non enim est figura actionis naturalis principium. Sed in hoc distant astronomicae imagines a nigromanticis, quod in nigromanticis fiunt expressae invocationes et praestigia quaedam, unde pertinent ad *expressa pacta cum Daemonibus* inita, sed in aliis imaginibus sunt quaedam *tacita pacta* per quaedam figurarum seu characterum signa." Quoted from the Leonine edition, online at http://www.corpusthomisticum.org.

21. *Liber florum* III.i.1, quoted in chapter 4.

22. "Under dem namen ist auch ein kunst, haisst Notarey, das ainer durch ettlich wort, vigur und caracter alle kunst lernen macht. Die kunst ist nit mangel der verpintnuss der bösen tüffel, wann die verporgen wort, die machen gesellschaft und gemain zwischen dem tüffel und dem menschen. Wie wol die kunst zugåt mit vasten båten und rainem, keüschen leben, yedoch ist sy verpoten und sünd, wann in disem gůten schein verpergen die bösen tewfel ir verlaitten und verfüren der armen menschait. Darumb, durchleüchtiger fürst, fliůch die kunst, wann sy von der hailigen kirchen verdambt ist." My translation is based on the modern German translation from chap. 29 of the edition of Hartlieb, *Das Buch aller verbotenen Künste*, ed. Falk Eisermann and Eckhard Graf (Ahlerstedt: Hugendubel Heinrich, 1989), 42–43.

23. *Liber florum* I.i.3: "Quia sine ipso de nigromancia aliquid exerceri non potest."

24. *Liber florum* I.i.6: "Omnibus alijs studijs dimissis, cepi in ipsa frequencius studere, et in tantum studui quod qualiter operari deberem sciui."

25. Láng, *Unlocked Books: Manuscripts of Learned Magic in the Medieval Libraries of Central Europe* (University Park: Pennsylvania State University Press, 2010), 165.

26. *Liber florum* III.ii.5 in the reference system of our edition.

27. See appendices translated by Jerome Taylor in *The "Didascalicon" of Hugh of St. Victor* (New York: Columbia University Press, 1961), 152–56. I have suggested that this type of "exception" of magic from the order of knowledge may be behind the term "exceptive"; see my article "Sacred and Secular Knowledge Systems in the *Ars Notoria* and the *Flowers of Heavenly Teaching* of John of Morigny," in *Die Enzyklopädik der Esoterik*, ed. Andreas B. Kilcher and Philipp Theisohn (Paderborn: Wilhelm Fink Verlag, 2010), 157–75. Later fifteenth-century uses of the term "exceptive arts" in texts circulating in central Europe are documented by Benedek Láng, *Unlocked Books*, in regard to Egidius of Corintia (33ff.) and Conrad Kyeser (76ff.).

28. It is not possible to determine whether Hartlieb knew the *Liber florum* itself. On the one hand, copies of John of Morigny's work were certainly circulating in fifteenth-century Germany, and Hartlieb was widely read in literature of that kind. If he was familiar with the work, however, it is odd that it goes unmentioned here. Frank Fürbeth traces Hartlieb's sources from Thomas Aquinas through the *Tractatus de superstitionibus* of Nicolaus Magni de Jawor, neither of which really explains Hartlieb's curricular structure, though it is evident that Nicolaus may have had a special concern about works in the notory art tradition. See Fürbeth, *Johannes Hartlieb: Untersuchungen zu Leben un Werk* (Tübingen: Max Niemeyer, 1992), 88–108. For more on magical curricula, including Hartlieb's, see also Andreas Kilcher, "*Ars memorativa* und *ars cabalistica*: Die Kabbala in der Mnemonik der Frühen Neuzeit," in *Seelenmaschinen: Gattungstraditionen, Funktionen und Leistungsgrenzen der Mnemotechniken vom späten Mittelalter bis zum Beginn der Moderne*, ed. Jörg J. Berns and Wolfgang Neuber (Wien: Böhlau Verlag, 2000).

29. Orthography is highly variable, as noted above.

30. In the wording of the A text, "sub astrologia" might apply to either *neonegia* or *geonogia*, though editorial punctuation attaches it to *neonegia*: "mechanice autem septem sunt iste: ydromantia, pyromantia, nigromantia, cyromantia, geomantia, geonogia, sub astrologia neonegia" (Véronèse AN §71).

31. Benedek Láng documents a couple of fifteenth-century uses of the term "exceptive arts" in central Europe in *Unlocked Books*; see note 27 above. Neither Egidius of Corintia nor Conrad Kyeser evidently owes a debt to John of Morigny in his conception of the *artes exceptivae*, though John's work was certainly known in central Europe in this period; see the discussion by Láng in chap. 6, 162ff.

32. Véronèse AN §71: "Sequitur: est enim nigromantia quasi sacrificium animalium mortuorum, quo sine peccato quedam antiqui magistri misteria comprehendere consueverunt. Unde Salomon precepit ut .v. libros artis ejus justus aliquis sine peccato legeret, duos vero quasi sacrilegium reptaret, duo enim libri ijus arrtis sine peccato legi non possunt."

33. Véronèse AN §71 Glose: "Istarum vero mechanicarum artium est quedam que vocatur nigromantia, de qua non est licitum operari per istam artem propter peccatum quod operatur in ea, sacrificando malignis spiritibus. Sed tamen dicit Salomon quod in nigromantia sunt septem libri, quorum quinque cum minori peccato possunt legi et per eos in scientia nigromantie operari. Duo vero illorum penitus prohibentur operari, de quibus siquis operatus fuerit sacrilegium facit offerendo sacrificium spiritibus malignis, quia sine sacrificio oblato et presentato ipsis spiritibus de illis duobus libris nemo potest operari, et quicumque offert sacrificium demonibus de sanguine humano vel aliis rebus corporalibus offendit Deum et negat eum et secum irascitur mortaliter et animam suam penitus amittit nisi per penitentiam peractam eam evadat. Qua de causa prohibiti sunt illi duo libri specialiter, et quamvis peccatum sit operari de illis in quibus non est necesse sacrificari, tamen minus peccatum est quam de illis, quales vero sunt illi quinque libri de quibus non est peccatum magnum operari sine illi duo de quibus maximum peccatum est nunc omitto, quia de illa scientia non est bonum facere mentionem alicui et specialiter in libro isto in quo sunt pura et sacramenta Dei et sanctorum angelorum."

34. Burnett, "Magic as Science," 4–5; the quote comes from Petrus Alfonsi, *Dialogue Against the Jews*. There is a translation of the work by Irven M. Resnick (Washington, D.C.: Catholic University of America Press, 2006); this passage may be found on p. 221 of the translation.

35. Burnett, "Magic as Science," 4 n. 13.

36. *Liber florum* prayer 28.6.

37. Ibid.: "*Ab illo loco,* Cherubin lanifici, *posset nomina dimitti usque ad* Cherubin paciencie."

38. The presence of this name shows that the book was intended to be consecrated and used, as John's instructions require a personalized copy to be made by any potential operator.

39. This is from the Old Compilation Liber Figurarum, *Liber florum* OC III.19.i.i: "Litera figure gramatice et artium sub ea contentarum: [Y] e v e Deus Maria spiritus intellectus Galfridi. Et gramatice Saturni Galfridi. Et lanificii Saturni Galfridi. Et nigromencie Saturni Galfridi. Et patiencie Saturni Galfridi."

40. *Liber florum* OC III.18.a–b: "hec verba (que sequuntur secundum suas proprietates) non lingua exprimi set in corde ymaginari vel premeditari. . . . In die quando operatur de gramatica, dum figure mentaliter ymaginantur: debet opifex in corde suo et non ore hec verba cogitando exprimere."

41. *Liber florum* OC III.3.18.h.i: "Hec ymaginabis ad astronomiam: Vellem intelligere *Tractatum de spera materiali,* et scire Alfraganum, Arthabicium, tabulas Toletanas, astrolabium, indicia, cursus et loca et naturas planetarum, duodecim signorum et duodecim domorum." References are to astronomical treatises current as textbooks in John's day. The *Treatise on the Sphere* by thirteenth-century mathematician Johannes de Sacrobosco was a textbook based on Arabic commentaries on Ptolemy. Alfraganus (al-Farghani) was a ninth-century Arab

astronomer who wrote a summary of Ptolemy and two treatises on astrolabes. Arthabicius or Alcabitius (al-Qabisi) was a tenth-century Arab astronomer whose *Introduction to Astrology* was popular in Latin. The Toledan Tables were a set of astronomical tables formulated by eleventh-century Arab astronomers in Toledo.

42. *Liber florum* OC III.18.c.ii: "Hec ymaginabis ad artem theatricam: Vellem scire et intelligere omnem artem theatricam: choreare, ludere omnimodo, et debellare, saltare, tympanizare, balare, et omne tedium et malencoliam remouere per ludos in theatralibus et alibi."

43. *Liber florum* OC III.18.b.iii: "Ad artem nigromencie hec cogitantur in corde: Vellem scire et intelligere, set non facere, omnes artes nigromancie: sacrificatiuam, suffumagatiuam, et auscultatiuam." I do not know exactly what he meant by "auscultative" knowledge, though the word relates to listening.

44. In a seemingly analogous case, an episcopal visitation of 1500 at Sulby monastery turned up a monk who had consulted "books of experiments" but "for speculation merely and never for operation." See *Collectanea Anglo-Premonstratensia*, ed. Francis A. Gasquet, Royal Historical Society, Camden Third Series, 12, vol. 3 (1906), 117–18. I thank Richard Kieckhefer for this reference.

45. *Liber florum* OC III.18.h.iii: "*Hec ymaginabis ad geonegiam artem:* Vellem scire et intelligere omnes artes geonegie (set non operari): libros *De ymaginibus* Tholomei Regis, *Librum prestigiorum Abel, Librum de septem senatoribus, Librum de duodecim firmamentis,* et *Librum Semhemforas.*"

46. A Ptolemaic work, *On Images,* is one of two texts admitted as licit in the catalogue of the Magister Speculi, the other being a work that traveled under the same name by Thabit ibn Qurra. Several manuscripts of Ptolemaic image magic are given by Lynn Thorndike in his "Traditional Medieval Tracts Concerning Engraved Astrological Images," in *Mélanges Auguste Pelzer* (Louvain: Bibliothèque de l'Université, 1947), 259. Francis Carmody discusses a Ptolemaic book of images in *The Astronomical Works of Thabit B. Qurra* (Berkeley: University of California Press, 1960), 170–72. Trithemius mentions two different works of image magic by Ptolemy, both of which he considers dubious, one called *De imaginibus* and another *De componendis imaginibus*; see the chapter of *Antipalus maleficorum* annotated by Jean-Patrice Boudet as app. I to *Entre science et nigromance: Astrologie, divination et magie dans l'Occident médiéval (XIIe–XVe siècle)* (Paris: Sorbonne, 2006), items 58 and 65. See also Charles Burnett, "The Arabic Hermes in the Works of Adelard of Bath," in *Hermetism from Late Antiquity to Humanism,* ed. Paolo Lucentini, Ilaria Parri, and Vittoria Perrone Compagni (Turnhout: Brepols, 2003), 369–84.

47. On this text, see Burnett, "Arabic Hermes," 370, and Vittoria Perrone Compagni, "'Studiosus incantationibus': Adelardo di Bath, Ermete e Thabit," *Giornale critico della filosofia italiana* 80 (2001): 36–61 (cited in Burnett, "Arabic Hermes," 370). On the *Liber planetarum ex scientia Abel,* see also Nicolas Weill-Parot, "*Images astrologiques,*" 493 and 792.

48. One was the *Almandel* (edited by Julien Véronèse, *L' "Almandal" et l' "Almadel" latins au Moyen Âge* [Florence: Sismel, 2012]). According to Véronèse, "an altitude is a heavenly location bound to a sign of the zodiac and to a month of the year determined by the sun's course ... it is populated with angels governed by princes whose names are given in the text" (43). Véronèse goes on to note (44–45) that twelve altitudes are also mentioned in one of the books constituting the Latin *Liber Razielis,* the *Liber Samayn,* potentially though not certainly a source for the altitudes in *Almandel.* Another work, edited as *Liber de essentia spirituum* by Sophie Page, also alludes to twelve orders of separated substances, though these are not tied to the zodiac but related to the four elements and eight spheres—that is, seven spheres of the planets and the outermost sphere of Urania. (The known manuscript has a text that is incomplete, breaking off after only eight orders are mentioned, but twelve orders are discussed by William of Auvergne, who evidently had access to a complete copy; see *De universo* II.2.29 and II.3.6.) For an edition of the text, see Sophie Page, "Image-Magic Texts and a Platonic Cosmology at St Augustine's, Canterbury, in the Late Middle Ages," in *Magic and the Classical Tradition,* ed. Charles Burnett and W. F. Ryan (London: Warburg Institute, 2006), 69–98.

The text is further discussed and translated by Page in *Magic in the Cloister: Pious Motives, Illicit Interests, and Occult Approaches to the Medieval Universe* (University Park: Pennsylvania State University Press, 2013; see chap. 5 and app. 2).

49. Occurring in numerous variant spellings in Latin works, *Semyforas, Semaphoras, Seminafora*, and so on, all meant as approximations of the Hebrew *Shem ha-Meforash*, preeminent name of God, which would normally refer to the Tetragrammaton. In the *Liber Semhemforas*, the term is evidently adopted to refer to names of God more broadly.

50. See discussion of the *Liber Semiphoras* in Jan Veenstra, "Honorius and the Sigil of God: The *Liber iuratus* in Berengario Ganell's *Summa sacre magice*," in *Invoking Angels: Theurgic Ideas and Practices, Thirteenth to Sixteenth Centuries*, ed. Claire Fanger (University Park: Pennsylvania State University Press, 2012), 169–72.

51. See *Magic in the Cloister*, chap. 4.

52. *De imaginibus*, edited in Carmody, *Astronomical Works*, 193, first column: "Et scito quod hee imagines discurrunt in uniuersis quibus filii Ade disponuntur de aptatione scilicet et destructione et salute atque infirmitate et amore et odio ... si fuerit auctor eorum prouidus ac peritus in opere ac complemento planetarum. Serua ergo hec quia sunt ex secretis planetarum et ex occultis sapiencie philosophie; et hec est sapientia magna quam uoluit Deus altissimus patefacere suis seruis ad aptationem terrarumque suarum. Et Deus dirigat qui est fortitudo incomprehensibilis magnus et altissimus."

53. *Liber florum* OC III. 26.b–c: "Ymaginaciones planetarum. In prima, fiat capud Cherubin cum alis. In secunda, fiat capud femineum, coronatum diademate aureo. In tercia, fiat capud Christi ad modum magistri tonsorati cum capucio remoto. In quarta, fiant capita Virginis gloriose duo, vnum antiquum et alterum iuuene, simul iuncta tergum contra tergum. In quinta, fiat capud Dei ad modum hominis senioris cum barba prolixa. In sexta, fiat caput Christi ad modum regis aurea corona coronatum. In septima, fiat capud Christi ad modum vnius militis armati et aureo diademate coronati.

"Ymaginaciones omnium aliarum figurarum quales debent esse inferius manifestatur. Et est notandum quod in solis figuris duodecim signorum sunt mixta nomina sillabarum. In omnibus aliis literatim. Et nota quod in spacia in qua fieri debent ista capita, si fuerint tam ampla quod in eis tota ymago fieri possit, fiat."

54. A nice example of a manuscript with varied but still recognizable images of planetary gods is the treatise by Albumazar in a fourteenth-century manuscript in London, British Library, Sloane 3983. Some images may be seen at http://www.bl.uk/catalogues/illuminated manuscripts/record.asp?MSID=7959&CollID=9&NStart=3983.

55. *Picatrix*, II.vii.capitulum tercium: "Forma Mercurii secundum opinionem sapientis Beylus est forma iuvenis barbati et in manu dardum tenentis. Et hec est eius forma. Forma Mercurii secundum opinionem sapientis Mercurii est forma hominis in eius capite gallum habentis, et supra cathedram erecti; et eius pedes similes pedibus aquile; et in palma sinistre manus ignem habentis. et sub pedibus signa que inferius dicentur. Et hec est eius forma. Forma Mercurii secundum opinionem Picatricis est forma hominis erecti et in dextro eius latere alas extensas habentis, et in sinistro gallum parvum tenentis, et in manu dextra dardum, in sinistra vero concham rotundam tenentis. et in capite medio cristam galli. Et hec est eius forma. Forma Mercurii secundum opinionem aliorum sapientum est forma baronis coronati. equitantis supra pavonem, in eius dextra calamum. in sinistra vero cartam habentis; et eius vestes sunt omnium colorum mixte. Et hec est eius forma."

56. There is only one known manuscript of *Picatrix* with illustrations, in a fifteenth-century manuscript in Kraków, Biblioteka Jagiellońska 793, which is useful in resolving some of the ambiguities of the descriptions: it shows the small chicken preferred to the shell in the example above, and also depicts the "wings" extending from the right side of the figure as a kind of elaborate sleeve. All of the images of the planets are reproduced in *Picatrix*, ed. Pingree, plates 3–9. The images of Mercury are on plate 8.

57. See *Liber florum* OC III.19.k for the original instruction and Hebrew letters; for the repeal of this instruction, see John's comments at NC III.i.2.c and gloss, and the dream of God

the Father at NC III.iii.1. A discussion may be found in Claire Fanger, "Covenant and the Divine Name," in Fanger, *Invoking Angels*.

58. *Liber florum* NC III.iii.36.b: "Ipsa enim oracio in Antiqua Compilacione habet figuram propriam, set in ista non, quia omnes figure restringuntur ad 7tem et annulum. Vnde ipsam dicendo, ymaginetur in mente annuli forma."

59. The elegant manuscript of this text, Kassel Universitätsbibliothek 4 MS astron. 3, formerly owned by John Dee, may be viewed online at http://orka.bibliothek.uni-kassel.de/viewer/image/1343812736802/1 /. For figures with Hebrew in them, see especially the *tabula shemamphoras* with its four alphabets centered on the crowned name of God, fol. 38r (image 83), and the revolutions of the divine name depicted on fols. 61v-62r (images 130-31). The *Summa sacre magice* was first noticed by Carlos Gilly, "Between Paracelsus, Pelagius, and Ganellus: Hermetism in John Dee," in *Magic, Alchemy, and Science, 15th-18th Centuries*, edited by Carlos Gilly and Cis van Heertum (Florence: Centro Di, 2002), 1:286. For more information on smaller texts incorporated into the work, see Veenstra, "Honorius and the Sigil of God," 151, and Damaris Gehr, "'Spiritus et angeli sunt a Deo submissi sapienti et puro': Il frammento del Magisterium eumantice artis sive scientiae magicalis. Edizione e attribuzione a Berengario Ganello," *Aries* 11, no. 2 (2011): 189-217. (Gehr has an edition of the whole work in progress.)

60. Rome, Vatican Library, Reg. lat. 1300, fol.137r, p. 269. There is no printed edition of the Latin *Liber Razielis*, though greatly abbreviated English versions of the text, drawn from early modern manuscripts, are available on the Internet. Joseph Peterson transcribes an early modern English *Raziel* in British Library, Sloane 3846, http://www.esotericarchives.com/raziel/raziel.htm#book7. The *Liber Samayn* in Sloane 3846 is no more than a précis of the part of that work in the Latin text concerning the seven heavens (omitting the armies and altitudes, all the prayers, and almost all the angel names). To me, the English version looks almost like a set of notes on a Latin text that the scribe must have had in hand, with translations of some parts, linked by Latin lemmata. For more information on the Latin *Raziel*, with bibliography, and a chapter synopsis drawing on Reg. lat. 1300, see Sophie Page, "Uplifting Souls: The *Liber de essentia spirituum* and the *Liber Razielis*," in Fanger, *Invoking Angels*, 79-112.

61. *Liber florum* OC III.19.c.

62. For the sigil of God, Joseph Peterson gathers a number of interesting examples, all bearing these names, online at Esoteric Archives, http://www.esotericarchives.com/esoteric.htm (see under "Sigillum Dei Aemeth"). See also Kieckhefer, *Forbidden Rites: A Necromancer's Manual of the Fifteenth Century* (University Park: Pennsylvania State University Press, 1998), 181-82, where these angels are listed corresponding to the days of the week. In the *Liber Razielis*, Vatican manuscript Reg. lat. 1300, fol. 135r, p. 265, the names of these seven angels occur clustered at the beginning of a much longer list. Multiple instances of this cluster of seven angels may also be found in *The Key of Solomon*, ed. S. L. MacGregor Mathers, rev. Joseph H. Peterson, online at Esoteric Archives, http://www.esotericarchives.com/solomon/ksol.htm. This list is not exhaustive.

CHAPTER 6

1. Though pragmatic exceptions to this principle are quite imaginable for medieval readers. Caesarius of Heisterbach has a story about a bishop dealing with two men he deems heretics who have gained a following in Besançon. The bishop goes to a (reformed) expert at *nigromancia* and successfully pleads with him to return to his art to discover why the heretics are able to work miracles and so convert followers. The devil discovers where the false holy men are concealing their amulets, and the story ends happily for bishop and necromancer (not so much for the heretics). See *Dialogus miraculorum*, Dist. V, Cap. XVIII; in the edition by Joseph Strange (Cologne: H. Lempertz, 1851), 1:296ff.

2. Inasmuch as they evidently did not suggest that the *Liber florum* as a whole actually constituted or could be reduced to "nigromancia" but only that the figures were made in a similar way: "ipsas figuras more figurarum nigromancie esse compositas" (NC III.i.1.c).

3. *Liber florum* OC III.1.a: "Moyses enim dicit esse quedam non solum sancta, set eciam sancta sanctorum, et alia non solum sabbata set eciam sabbata sabbatorum. Sic nos dicimus esse quedam non solum sciencia, set eciam sciencia scienciarum. Et sicut ille beatus est qui ingreditur sancta, et beacior ille qui ingreditur sancta sanctorum; et beatus qui sabbatum sabbatizat, et beacior qui sabbata sabbatorum; ita beatus qui scienciam ingreditur et sapienciam, set multum beacior qui ingreditur scienciam scienciarum et sapienciam sapienciarum, quia omnia bona pariter veniunt cum sciencia et sapiencia, et innumerabilis honestas per manus illarum. Meliores enim sunt super negociacione auri et argenti, et diuicias nichil esse dixi in comparacione illarum; per ipsas enim reges regnant et legum conditores iusta discernunt; ipse enim diligentes se diligunt, et qui mane vigilauerint ad ipsas inuenient eas, et qui eas inuenient inuenient vitam et haurient salutem a Domino. Beatus ergo vir qui scienciam et sapienciam ingreditur, et cuius cor in ipsis vigilat. Quia sciencia est cognicio vniuersi cuius descriptio est in anima, que in presenti est summa nobilitas et in futuro causa felicitatis eterne. Sapiencia est vapor virtutis Dei et emanacio quedam claritatis omnipotentis Dei sincera, et ideo nichil iniquitatum incurrit. Candor enim lucis eterne et speculum sine macula maiestatis Dei et ymago bonitatis illius."

4. *Homiliae in Canticum canticorum,* in *Origenes Werke,* ed. W. A. Baehrens, vol. 8 of Griechische Christliche Schriftsteller 33 (Leipzig: J. C. Hinrichs, 1925), p. 27, lines 7–15: "Quomodo didicimus per Moysen esse quaedam esse non solum sancta, sed et 'sancta sanctorum'; et alia non tantum sabbata, sed et 'sabbata sabbatorum'; sic nunc docemur scribente Solomone esse quaedam non solum cantica, sed et 'cantica canticorum.' Beatus quidem et is, qui ingreditur in sancta, sed multo ille beatior, qui ingreditur in 'sancta sanctorum.' Beatus, qui sabbata sabbatizat, sed beatior, qui sabbatizat sabbatorum sabbata. Beatus similiter et is, qui intelligit cantica ... sed multo beatior qui canit 'cantica canticorum.'"

5. *Glossa ordinaria,* vol. 2, p. 707: "Dicitur autem canticum canticorum eo quod omnibus canticis preferatur sicut in lege quedam dicuntur sancta quibus maiora sunt sancta sanctorum." Comments on the song as "Holy of Holies," like other parts of Origen's preface, go back to Jewish tradition. See also *The Glossa Ordinaria on the Song of Songs,* trans. Mary Dove (Kalamazoo: Medieval Institute Publications, Western Michigan University, 2004), preface, paragraph 7, p. 4.

6. For *sciencia,* some versions read *philosophia*; see *Liber florum,* Sources at OC III.1.a

7. *Liber florum* OC III.11.a–b: "Set dicat aliquis quod hic sit nouus modus orandi, et quod ab eclesia non s<anc>itur; quia falsum esset dicere talia. Quia ecclesia tripliciter orat in missa: primo oracionibus quas nos vocamus 'collectas' et in principio siue introitus misse; secundo orat in oracionibus et figuris et hoc in secretis et in principio canonis (quod sine figura crucis fieri non potest); et tercio orat in ymaginacionibus mentis, oracionibus, et figuris, et hoc in memento primum et vltimum (quod fit sola mentis ymaginacione, et aliis signis crucis que exinde sequntur, et oracionibus tam in illis que in canone sunt quam in illis que sunt de graciarum accionibus). Et tamen non sunt tres misse set vna missa. Ita et hic.

"Et nota quod in quacumque figura in hac arte, vltra signa crucis quicquid fuerit illud (siue rotunditas siue quadratura vel triangulatura uel plus uel minus uel quicquid aliud), hoc pro circumstancia figure habetur, et non pro ipsa figura. Solum signum crucis (vnum vel plura) pro figura habentur.... Et si aliquam figuram inueneris in qua expressum non fuerit signum crucis ... tamen semper mistice subintelligitur.... Occultatur enim in illis propter hoc: ut ostendatur quod in ips<is> efficacie proprietatis—ipsarum figurarum illud signum crucis—finiri sensu et intellectu humano non potest spiritualiter."

8. Véronèse AN §Var 1 glose, p. 142: "Item sciendum est quod in ista arte mirabili tria inspiciuntur, scilicet nota, figura et oratio. Nota autem quid sit ipsa arte describitur. Figura vero est quedam sacramentalis et ineffabilis oratio que nequid per sensum humane rationis

exponi. Oratio autem est piamentis deprecatio in vocem deprecantis non temptando, sed legendo suauiter prorumpens: in hiis ergo tribus tota ista ars consistit."

9. Isidore, *Etymologiarum sive originum libri XX*, ed. W. M. Lindsay (Oxford: Clarendon Press, 1911), 7.1.15: "Nonum Tetragrammaton, hoc est quattuor litterarum, quod proprie apud Hebraeos in Deo ponitur . . . dicitur autem ineffabilis, non quia dici non potest, *sed quia finiri sensu et intellectu humano nullatenus potest;* et ideo, quia de eo nihil digne dici potest, ineffabilis est" (my emphasis).

10. *Glossa ordinaria*, vol. 1, p. 183, left-hand column, near bottom of page: "Bene autem in fronte pontificis quattuor litteris significans totidem partes dominicae crucis quam in fronte portamus."

11. Ibid., on Exodus 28:36–38, immediately following previous passage: "Ineffabile nomen domini quattuor litterarum constans, he scilicet quod interpretatur iste, ioth, quod est principium, heth, quod est passionis, vau hoc est vite. Quod totum sonat iste principium passionis vitae, quia Christus principium vitae in adam amisse quam reparauit sua passione."

12. In his discussion of these chapters, Nicholas Watson includes, as part of the packet on the work's defense, an additional chapter following NCIII.iii.5 on apocrypha. It is true that this chapter shares the apologetic goals of the first three; however, it is also clear from the surrounding context that the three chapters under discussion below share a single writing occasion, and so I speak of a triptych. See *Liber florum*, Watson's Introduction A, §94.

13. *Liber florum* NC III.i.5.a: "Contra morsus latrancium et adversas lingwas toxicatas ista sancta sciencia et mirabilis defendit et resistit." The "barking" evokes the parties who condemned the figures, but it is a common figure in medieval Latin for raging or blustering; the "poisonous tongue" is a common trope for backbiting.

14. These arguments are found in *Liber florum* NC III.i.5 and NC III.iii.3 (the two chapters are presented out of order, for reasons I will touch on shortly).

15. *Liber florum* NC III.iii.3.f: "Set totum beneficium istius sciencie consistit in sompnis: ergo est permissiua, et veritatis discipuli sunt ipsam sectantes, vt patet sacrorum canonum auctoritate."

16. *Liber florum* NC III.iii.5: "Sacris canonibus obpungnatur ista sciencia que habentur xxvj^a, questione 3^a et 4ta in capitulo 'Sciendum,' circa medium, et cetera."

17. Augustine, *De divinatione daemonvm* V.9.

18. *Liber florum* NC III.iii 5.a: "Sacris canonibus obpungnatur ista sciencia que habentur xxvj^a, questione 3^a et 4ta in capitulo 'Sciendum,' circa medium, et cetera. Ex quo quod colligitur quod demones quedam futura aut presencia facienda vel advenienda hominibus prenuncciant et predicunt, et hec 'swadunt invisibilibus modis per illam subtilitatem quam habent, qua corpora hominum non senciencium penetrant, et se cogitacionibus eorum inmiscunt per quedam ymaginaria visa, siue vigilando siue dormiendo.' Set ista sciencia docet et est de quibusdam futuris aut presentibus faciendis vel adveniendis miris et invisibilibus modis, per quedam ymaginaria, et cetera, sicut patet per totum istum librum. Ergo videtur quod ista sciencia sugestione demonum sit facta."

19. Augustine, *De doctrina christiana*, II.20.

20. *Liber florum* NC III.iii.5.b: "Item, in eodem causa dicitur, in qua illud quod est in 2^a questione: 'Quod quidquid institutum est ab hominibus ad colendum creaturam sicut Deum, illud est supersticiosum et vanum; vel ad consultacionem et pacta quedam significacionum cum demonibus placita atque federata, qualia sunt volumina magicarum artium, que quidem commemorare pocius quam docere solent poete.' Set videtur quod institutum sit in ista sciencia magis adorare 'creaturam,' scilicet virginem Mariam, quam Deum vel tamquam Deum; et quod volumen illud quedam 'pacta et placita atque federata significationum' ad consultacionem contineat, et vanum."

21. As discussed in chapter 5.

22. *Liber florum* NC III.iii.5.c: "Item, colligitur ex lxviij^a Distinccione, de capitulo 'Pres<ci>teri,' quod dubia in deteriorem partem interpretantur in hijs in quibus ver<titur> periculum anime; et quamuis in deteriorem partem tamen tuciorem, ut 'De consecracione,'

Di<stinctio> 4ª, capitulo 'Paruulos.' Set dyabolus potest se transformari vsque in angelum lucis, et sic in similitudine Virginis gloriose. Ergo dubium est si sit ipsa Virgo vel dyabolus. Et quia in istis potest cadere periculum anime, quia ipsa dubia sunt, in deteriorem partem debemus interpretari quia tucior est. In hoc casu, ergo, visiones istius sciencie debemus dicere prouenire ex dyabolo, et non ex virgine Maria." Gratian, *Decretum* D. 68 c. 2, compares the procedures to be used in cases of doubtful consecration with those used in baptisms: "sicut de quo dubium est, an sit baptizatus an non, debet baptizari ... nec pertinet hoc ad reiteracionem baptismi, sed ad cautelam salutis." *De consecracione*, D. 4 c. 110, lays out the procedures used in cases of doubtful baptism. "Quamuis in deteriorem partem tamen tuciorem" again apparently draws not on the text, but on a principle of Roman law: see, for example, Justinian, *Digest* 50.17.87.

23. *Liber florum* NC III.iii.5.d: "Item, ex dictis Virginis gloriose, que dixit michi in quadam visione viijº ydus Septembris, petenti ab ipsa quid sibi videbatur de me. Que respondens ait, 'Tu es Spiritus Sancti receptaculum.' Et statim, sine interuallo, cum indignacione mouens capud omne, naribus et oculis subsannando subiunxit, 'Et tu es fantasma omnium aliorum.' Ac si voluisset dicere, 'Quia tu es Christianus monachus et sacerdos, in hoc es aptus natus ad Spiritus Sancti receptaculum. Set quia scribis et doces alios fantasmata sompniorum istius sciencie, in hoc es effectus fantasma omnium aliorum.' Ergo ista sciencia fantastica est. Ex quibus auctoritatibus et similitudinibus ista sciencia inpungnatur."

24. *Liber florum* NC III.iii.5.i–j: "Ad 4ᵐ sic respondetur: interpretacio verborum visionis ibidem facta stare non potest, quia modus illius visionis talis fuit sicut omnium aliorum. Et sic sequitur totalis visio esset fantastica, sicut et omnes alie. Et sic non esset credendum verbis ipsius, nec standum, sicud nec alijs, quod non est tenendum. Et ideo non stare potest interpretacio predicta, et sic non obstat.

"Ymmo totaliter debet interpretari: 'Quia tu composuisti istam scienciam et multas gracias reuelacionum habuisti, et ideo patebit et patet cunctis factum de contemplatoribus et vere Deum diligentibus, quia tu es Spiritus Sancti receptaculum. Set et omnium aliorum Deum vere non diligencium nec vere contemplatorum in quorum manibus aliquociens est ventura' (ut patet per verba visionis subtiliter intuenti) 'effectus es fantasma, quia tales hanc scienciam non reputabunt veram set fantasticam. Et ideo dicit "aliorum" quod ipsi erunt alieni a gratia Spiritus Sancti.'"

25. *Liber florum* NC III.iii.5.f: "Secundo argumento sic respondetur: quod ibi capitulum allegatum intelligitur de hoc quod instituitur ab hominibus ad faciendum ydola et colenda et ea contingencia, quia illud supersticiosum et vanum est solummodo. Set hic loquitur de institucionibus ad colendum Deum, et Virginem gloriosam, et contingenciam, et cetera. 'Quia nulla est conparacio Christi ad Belial.' Nec obstant 'pacta,' quia permittuntur in Genesi, vbi sic dicitur: 'Recordabor federis mei quod pepegi tecum,' qua autoritate ostenditur 'pacta federata' esse inter Deum et hominem. Ergo, et cetera. Non quod Deus ualeat constringi per talia federa set homo."

26. *Liber florum*, Watson's Introduction A, §§94–96.

27. *Liber florum* NC III.iii.5.g: "3º respondetur: quamuis dyabolus se possit transformari in angelum lucis et sic apparere loco Virginis gloriose, hoc intelligendum est semel, vel bis, vel ter, aut alias pluries, non tamen semper—nisi in illis peruersis de quibus dictum est in primo responso. Quia iam sequeretur vnum valde inconueniens et erroneum: scilicet, quod omnia illa que per gratiam spiritus sancti sompniorum nostris predecessoribus fuerunt ostensa, et visa, et facta essent sugestione dyaboli reuelata. Quod non solum esset absurdum credere, ymmo erroneum. Nec est credendum quod Deus esset ita iniustus quod illos perfecte cogitantes ad se, in summa contemplacione existentes, non curantes terrena, ymmo despicientes, et celestia toto corde et anima cupientes, spe et fide excellentes et caritate feruentes—qui tales sunt circa hanc scienciam intendentes—semper dimittat nepharie decipi, quamuis aliquociens bis, vel ter, vel pluries hoc permittat, non vt ipsos interimat set ut fidem suorum approbet."

28. These assumptions about the monastic lineage of prophecy are not peculiar to John. It has been pointed out generally that prophecy is associated with monasticism from an early period and is a routine charism attributed to founders of religious orders. See, for example,

Hvidt, *Christian Prophecy: The Post-Biblical Tradition*, (Oxford: Oxford University Press, 2007), 91-105, and Lubac, *Medieval Exegesis*, trans. Edward M. Macierowski, vol. 2 (Grand Rapids, Mich.: William B. Eerdmans, 2000), 148-49.

29. "Diligentibus Deum omnia cooperantur in bonum his qui secundum propositum vocati sunt sancti." John references Romans 8:28 in *Liber florum*, I.i.5.

30. The figures are described in the chapter just above.

31. *Liber florum* NC III.i.3.f, gloss and text: "*Figuras vero, et cetera*. Hic in isto paragrapho primo fuerunt figure huius libri hic posite, set ex causa vsque ad 3^{am} partem translate—et incipit hic error noster floridus.

"Figuras vero consequenter hic primo posuimus secundum quod superius sunt diuise. Set postea ex causa inferius, ipsas posuimus et transtulimus."

32. The descriptions of the forms of the figures in chapter 2 (NC III.i.2) contain some directives that are cancelled by later visions related in NC III.iii.

33. *Liber florum* NC III.i.4.a-b: "*Que fuit causa translacionis figurarum de isto loco ad alium*. Quesiui enim a Uirgine gloriosa in visione positus <si> placeret sibi quod instituciones et figuras huius libri antiquas propter morsus quorumdam latrancium et propter profectum multorum successorum meorum de nouo compilarem. Que, per archangelum Michael michi respondens, dixit: 'Non remoues nec mutes adhuc; benedicemus tibi quando tempus erit.' Et me ab huiusmodi visione excitato, nec exspectaui tempus promissum, set instituciones huius sciencie et figuras de nouo incepi compilare, et figuras di<u>isi faciendas prout superius diuiduntur, volens postea omnia ea credens a gloriosa Virgine confirmari, sicut prius feceram in Antiqua Compilacione....

"Set tempus non exspectaueram; et quia non exspectaui tempus, in errorem cecidi—tantummodo quantum ad formas figurarum, sicut inferius apparet, non autem quemadmodum institucionum. Et ideo errorem meum volens corrigere tali modo quod sit in exemplum omnium aliorum successorum meorum, ad hoc quod facere pertimescant quod in hac sciencia fuerit inhibitum et facere secundum quod fuerit preceptum, et dictum modum formandi figuras nobis superius ante tempus dictum inperpetuum volumus et decreuimus remanere et in loco vbi ipsas instituimus fieri et poni.

"*Capitulum sequens quod est de defensione huius sciencie quod debuisset situari in tercia parte huius libri, ut ibidem videbitur, in signum punicionis erroris mei in manu propria scripsi.*"

34. *Decretum* D. 6, c. 1: rubric: "De multiplici genere illusionis."

35. *Liber florum* NC III.i.5.c: "in loco vbi prius error continebatur, locus veritatis succedat."

36. Ibid.: "Et iste error noster sine causa a Deo et Virgine gloriosa non fuit permissus, ut magis claresceret veritas profutura, quia secundum quod dicitur super primum psalmum: 'Non potest melius excellencia vniuscuiusque rei ostendi quam si sui contrarij vilitas ostendatur.' Et ita concluditur quod error noster florem veritatis excellencie fecit et peperit. Et ab illo loco predicto vbi incipit vsque ad presentem locum in signum veritatis, qui voluerit floribus et frondibus ymagines foliorum huius libri faciat depingi."

37. The sole exception is the Klosterneuberg manuscript, Augustiner-Chorherrenstift Cod 950, which is an exemplar copy.

38. *Liber florum* NC III.iii.3.h: "deberet scribi et situari post ista, capitulum quod est de <def>ensione istius sciencie, set illud posuimus floribus et frondibus circumdatum in prima parte huius libri, et ex causa ibidem expressa, scilicet in signum correctionis erroris nostri et excellencie veritatis."

39. Our edition attempts to sort out text from gloss. See *Liber florum* NC III.i.2-9 and Variants.

40. In OC III.3, John reports that the Virgin appeared to him and he said to her, "'my Lady and my beloved, will I be able to finish the book that I began?' Smiling sweetly, she answered 'no.'" (Ipsa apparuit michi in ecclesia nostra Sancte Trinitatis de Moriginaco super altare. Dixique ei:, "Domina mea et amica, potero numquid facere perfecte librum quem incepi?" Que ridendo dulcissime respondit, "Non.")

41. *Liber florum* NC III.iii.35.g–i: "Quereret aliquis quare Compilatio Figurarum facta et edita a nobis in principio non valuit vel non potuit confirmari sicut Antiqua. Respondeo quod Antiqua erat confirmata et ista erat reuelanda; et sic esset superfluum si alia interponeretur que similiter esset reuocanda; et cessaret misterium significatum per Antiquam ex qua ergo reuelanda erat ista. Quare permisit Deus nos ipsam componere cum sciret ipsam nullius momenti et aliam reuelandam? Respondeo: hoc ideo fuit vt magis veritas istius claresceret.... Item, nota quod ista Noua Compilacio fuit presignata quod futura erant a principio Antique Compilacionis argumento cuiusdam visionis, set non intelleximus donec ipsa Noua Compilacio fuit completa. In qua visione petebamus si librum ad finem ut componeremus, et, ridendo, respondit beata virgo Maria quod 'Non.'" Et verum dixit et hystoriace, quamuis alio modo interpretati sumus dictam visionem in Antiqua Compilacione, et tamen bene. Quia patet quod nos non finimus istum librum, set ipse Deus et beata virgo Maria." I discussed some passages from this chapter in my chapter "Plundering the Egyptian Treasure: John the Monk's *Book of Visions* and Its Relation to the Ars Notoria of Solomon," in *Conjuring Spirits: Texts and Traditions of Medieval Ritual Magic*, ed. Claire Fanger (University Park: Pennsylvania State University Press, 1998).

42. *Liber florum* NC III.ii.1.

43. *Liber florum* NC III.iii.3: "Item, nota quod Vetus Testamentum figura fuit Noui Testamenti. Ita Compilacio Antiqua est et fuit figura istius Noue Compilacionis."

44. The vision in which John is directed to replace the Hebrew letters with nails is recounted in NC III.iii.1. The theme of supersession is discussed more extensively in Fanger, "Covenant and the Divine Name," in *Invoking Angels: Theurgic Ideas and Practices, Thirteenth to Sixteenth Centuries*, ed. Claire Fanger (University Park: Pennsylvania State University Press, 2012), 198–201.

45. *Liber florum* NC III.iii.35.j–k: "Vnde lac nobis in principio istius sciencie beata Virgo dedit in potum, ut satis significatur per mamillam suam sanctam quam posuit in ore meo lacte gracie spiritualis, me lactando, ostendens me adhuc iuuenem esse. Et ideo permisit me cingere in ista sciencia et ambulare per ipsam quocumque vellem, ludendo cum puero domino nostro Ihesv Christo cum p<ilo>ta voluntat<e>, constituendo et inveniendo figuras qualescumque volebam et institucciones ipsarum dicendarum. Et omnia michi tamquam puero, ne flerem fletu dimissionis vel renuncciationis huius sciencie sancte, ab ipso domino Ihesv Christo et ab ipsa beata Virgine fuerunt confirmata, vt hec omnia ex Antiqua Compilacione colliguntur.

"Set quia creui iam et senui in sciencia, iam amplius non lac set escam dedit michi ipsa Virgo in cibum, ita quod amplius non possum me cingere set oportet brachia virtutis extendere et alius cinget me, scilicet, ipsa Virgo, ducendo me quo non volo (tamen placet); tradendo michi et reuelando istas figuras et earum aptaciones quoniam non ad voluntatem meam set Dei et ipsius Virginis, oportuit fieri et eciam confirmari. Ex hiis ergo omnibus patet hanc scienciam fuisse propheticis visionibus designatam, quasi miraculis prenuncciatam et figuris et enigmatibus presignatam."

46. *Liber florum* OC III.25; Latin passage cited in chapter 4, note 43.

47. Ibid.

48. *Liber florum* NC III.iii.35.j–k; complete passage in Latin at note 45, above.

49. *Glossa ordinaria*, on 1 Corinthians 3:1–2, vol. 4, p. 310, right-hand column, middle: "Sicut enim crux Christi alijs stultitia est alijs scandalum vocatis autem est virtus dei, ita idem alijs est lac alijs cibus est secundum quod capacitas eorum plus vel minus capit. Vt hi qui dicunt ego sum illius vel illius, aliter acceperunt de Christo crucifixo quam qui dicit *Mihi absit gloriari nisi in cruce domini*. Eadem simul audiunt, spirituales et carnales, et quique pro modo suo capiunt nec necesse est vt aliqua secreta taceantur paruulis, dicenda perfectis. Ideo quia dicit apostolus, 'Non potui vobis loqui quasi spiritualibus,' quod est, 'Non potuistis quae dicebam intelligere ut spirituales, sed vt carnales.'"

50. *Glossa ordinaria* on John 21:18, vol. 4, p. 270, starting three lines up from the bottom of the left-hand column: "*extendes manus*. Hoc est, crucifigeris, et quomodo hoc fiet, subdit:

Et alius te cinget et ducet quo non vis, quia ad illam molestiam nolens est ductus, nolens ad eam venit, sed volens eam vicit, et reliquit affectum infirmitatis, quo nemo vult mori, que adeo est naturalis, vt eum nec senectus abstulerit petro. Unde & dominus: Transeat a me calix iste. Sed quantumcumque sit molestiam mortis, vincat eam vis amoris, si nulla esset vel parua molestia mortis, non esset tam magna gloria martirum."

51. *Liber florum* OC III.11.b; Latin passage cited in note 7 above.

52. The other images of Mary follow this general pattern, with shifts in the plants and birds. For more images from this manuscript, see *Liber florum*, plates 6 and 7. See also close-up images online at the Salzburg University Library catalogue page, http://www.ubs.sbg.ac.at/sosa/handschriften/mI24.htm.

CONCLUSION

1. *Liber florum* NC III.iii.1.e: "Hoc idem intelligendum est de forma annuli, qui similiter in metallo cordis debet sculpi, et in digito consciencie portari, sicut et liber iste describi debet in pergameno cordis et legi litera consciencie—quamuis causa exempli manu debeat scribi—ut patet in penultimo capitulo istius libri."

2. *Liber florum* NC III.iii.37.d; the Latin is cited above at chapter 4, note 18.

3. A pseudo-Jerome commentary on Lamentations (*PL* 25:787–92) offers a gloss on each letter of the Hebrew alphabet that is clearly connected to these instances: *jod* is "principium," *he* is "ista," *vau* is "et," and *heth* is "vita." A variant of the gloss on the Tetragrammaton in Rupert of Deutz's *De Trinitate et operibus ejus* runs "For Joth is interpreted 'beginning,' He is 'that,' Vau 'and,' He 'that.' And it is the continuous sense of the letters, 'that beginning, and that,' which I say rightly delights us, because 'that beginning' is the Father, and 'that beginning' is the Son." (Interpretatur enim Joth principium, He, iste, Vau et He iste. Estque continuus litterarum sensus, principium iste, et iste, hoc, inquam, jure nos delectet, quia principium iste Pater, et principium iste Filius est; *PL* 167:725B.) This reading, while more faithful than some others to the Hebrew orthography, does not include any words for "life" or "passion." The word "passionis" cannot be fit into this schema at all (the pseudo-Jerome commentary does not include a letter meaning "passion"), but there are witnesses for it outside John, including in the *Glossa ordinaria* passage on Exodus 28:36-38 quoted in chapter 6 (p. 136), which takes "passionis" the reading for "heth." Durand has a version which reads "heth," as "vita" and takes "vau" as "passionis"; see *Liber florum*, Sources at II Rit Prol.d.

4. *Philosophical Investigations* #31, trans. G. E. M. Anscombe, P. M. S. Hacker, and Joachim Schulte, 4th ed., rev. Hacker and Schulte (Malden, Mass.: Wiley-Blackwell, 2000).

5. A common translation of Wittgenstein's "übersichtlichen," in Anscombe's translation rendered by the more accurate but also less handy "surveyable."

6. First published in 1995, reprinted in Smith, *Relating Religion: Essays in the Study of Religion* (Chicago: University of Chicago Press, 2004) p. 218.

7. For example, Birgit Meyer and Peter Pels, eds., *Magic and Modernity: Interfaces of Revelation and Concealment* (Stanford: Stanford University Press, 2003); for the term "haunting," see 30, 79, 127, 203, and 216. See also Randall Styers, *Making Magic: Religion, Magic, and Science in the Modern World* (Oxford: Oxford University Press, 2004), 8.

8. "Remarks on Frazer's *Golden Bough*," in Ludwig Wittgenstein, *Philosophical Occasions, 1912–1951*, ed. James Klagge and Alfred Nordmann (Indianapolis: Hackett, 1993). The two quotations here are found on pp. 127 and 133. They bracket a discussion of the need for "perspicuous" representations.

9. Douglas, *How Institutions Think* (Syracuse: Syracuse University Press, 1986). This book looks at how institutional knowledge form, and how it is sustained, and why.

10. Kuhn, *The Structure of Scientific Revolutions*, 50th anniv. ed. (Chicago: University of Chicago Press, 2012), 116.

11. David Bloor, *Wittgenstein, Rules and Institutions* (London: Routledge, 1997), 136.

12. See Klaassen, *The Transformations of Magic: Illicit Learned Magic in the Later Middle Ages and Renaissance* (University Park: Pennsylvania State University Press, 2012), especially chap. 7, as well as his "Medieval Ritual Magic in the Renaissance" *Aries* 3, no. 2 (2003): 166–99.

13. It is worth remarking that the *ars notoria* does not show a strong life as a practice in the early modern period, even though the text is preserved and transmitted as a part of the Solomonic tradition, where, according to Frank Klaassen, "it sits (almost like a museum piece) but does not seem to influence.... Catholic piety at that time simply did not have the expansiveness of the later middle ages and was very much intent upon reasserting simple, fundamental, and obviously conventional aspects of Roman piety." Personal communication, February 17, 2014.

14. Patricia Meyer Spacks, *On Rereading* (Cambridge, Mass.: Harvard University Press, 2011), 275.

SELECTED BIBLIOGRAPHY

This bibliography includes all primary texts cited, works relevant to methodology, and secondary texts with historical or literary substance relevant to John's *Liber florum* and its medieval context. It omits incidental works mentioned in notes that do not directly touch on the historical and medieval situation of John of Morigny (such entries in modern dictionaries, books on the neurology of adult literacy, works of John Keats, and so on).

MANUSCRIPTS

Albumazar
    London, British Library, Sloane 3983
John of Morigny
    Bologna, Biblioteca Comunale dell' Archiginnasio MS A. 165 (16. b. III. 5)
    Klagenfurt, Universitätsbibliothek, Cart. 1
    Klosterneuberg, Augustiner-Chorherrenstift Cod. 950
    Oxford, Bodleian Library, MS Liturg. 160.
    Salzburg, Studienbibliothek Salzburg Cod. M I 24
    Seitenstetten, Benediktinerstift Cod. 273
    Vienna, Schottenkloster, MS 140 (61).
Liber Razielis
    Città del Vaticano, Vat. Reg. lat. 1300
    London, British Library, Sloane 3846
Summa sacre magice
    Kassel Universitätsbibliothek 4 MS astron. 3

PRIMARY

Alanus de Insulis. *De planctu naturae*. In *Literary Works: Alain of Lille*, edited by Winthrop Wetherbee, 22–217. Cambridge, Mass.: Harvard University Press, 2013.
L' *"Almandal" et l' "Almadel" latins au Moyen Âge*. Edited by Julien Véronèse. Florence: Sismel, 2012.
Arnoul de Provence. *Divisio scientiarum*. In *Quatre introductions à la philosophie au XIIIe siècle*, edited by Claude Lafleur, 295–355. Montreal: Institut d'études médiévales; Paris: J. Vrin, 1988.
Augustine. *De doctrina christiana*. Edited by William Green. CSEL 80. Vienna: Hoelder-Pichler-Tempsky, 1963.
Benedict of Nursia. *The Rule of St. Benedict in Latin and English*. Edited and translated by Timothy Fry. Collegeville, Minn.: Liturgical Press, 1980.
Caesarius of Heisterbach. *Dialogus miraculorum*. Edited by Joseph Strange. 2 vols. Cologne: H. Lempertz, 1851.

Chronique latine de Guillaume de Nangis de 1113 à 1300: Avec les continuations de cette chronique de 1300 à 1368. Edited by H. Géraud. Vol. 2. Paris: Jules Renouard, 1843.
Collectanea Anglo-Premonstratensia. Edited by Francis Aidan Gasquet. Vol. 3. Camden Third Series 12. London: Royal Historical Society, 1906.
Corrozet, Gilles. *Les Antiquitez, croniques et singularitez de Paris.* Paris: Nicolas Bonfons, 1581.
Durand, Guillaume. *Rationale diuinorum officiorum I–IV.* Edited by A. Davril and T. M. Thibodeau. CCCM 140. Turnhout: Brepols, 1995.
———. *William Durand on the Clergy and Their Vestments: A New Translation of Books 2–3 of the "Rationale divinorum officiorum."* Translated by Timothy M. Thibodeau. Scranton: University of Scranton Press, 2010.
Eckhart. *The Essential Sermons, Commentaries, Treatises, and Defense.* Edited by E. Colledge and B. McGinn. Mahwah, N.J.: Paulist Press, 1981.
The Glossa Ordinaria on the Song of Songs. Translated by Mary Dove. Kalamazoo, Mich.: Medieval Institute Publications, Western Michigan University, 2004.
Grandes Chroniques de France. Edited by Jules Viard. Vol. 9. Paris: Librairie ancienne Honoré Champion, 1937.
Hugh of Saint Victor. *De sacramentis christiane fidei.* Edited by Rainer Berndt. Münster: Aschendorff, 2008.
———. *Didascalicon: De studio legendi.* Edited by Henry Buttimer. Washington, D.C.: Catholic University Press, 1939.
———. *The "Didascalicon" of Hugh of St. Victor.* Translated by Jerome Taylor. New York: Columbia University Press, 1961.
———. *On the Sacraments of the Christian Faith.* Translated by Roy Deferrari. Cambridge, Mass.: Medieval Academy, 1951.
Isidore of Seville. *Etymologiarum sive originum libri XX.* Ed. W. M. Lindsay. Oxford: Clarendon Press, 1911.
Jacobus Magnus. *Sophologium.* Lyon: de Vingle, 1495.
Jerome. *Hieronymus: Commentariorum in Danielem libri III.* Edited by F. Glorie. CCSL 75A. Turnhout: Brepols, 1964.
———. *Jerome's Commentary on Daniel.* Translated by Gleason Archer. Grand Rapids, Mich.: Baker Books, 1958.
Joachim of Fiore. *The "Figurae" of Joachim of Fiore.* Edited by Marjorie Reeves and Beatrice Hirsch-Reich. Oxford: Clarendon Press, 1972.
Johann Hartlieb. *Das Buch aller verbotenen Künste.* Edited by Falk Eisermann and Eckhard Graf. Ahlerstedt: Hugendubel Heinrich, 1989.
John of Morigny. "Prologue to *Liber Visionum.*" Edited by Claire Fanger and Nicholas Watson. *Esoterica* 3 (2001): 108–217. Online at http://www.esoteric.msu.edu/VolumeIII/Morigny.html. Accessed June 22, 2014.
The Key of Solomon. Edited by S. L. MacGregor Mathers. Revised by Joseph H. Peterson. Esoteric Archives. http://www.esotericarchives.com/solomon/ksol.htm.
Margaret Porette [Marguerite Porete]. *The Mirror of Simple Souls.* Edited by Edmund Colledge, J. C. Marler, and Judith Grant. Notre Dame: University of Notre Dame Press, 1999.
Origen. *Homiliae in Canticum Canticorum.* In *Origenes Werke,* edited by W. A. Baehrens. Vol. 8 of Griechische Christliche Schriftsteller 33. Leipzig: J. C. Hinrichs, 1925.
Petrus Alfonsi. *Dialogue Against the Jews.* Translated by Irven M. Resnick. Washington, D.C.: Catholic University of America Press, 2006.
———. *Dialogus contra iudaeos.* Edited by Klaus-Peter Mieth. Translated into Spanish by Esperanza Ducay. Huesca: Instituto de Estudios Altoaragoneses, 1996.
Philosophica Disciplina. In *Quatre introductions à la philosophie au XIIIe siècle,* edited by Claude Lafleur. Montreal: Institut d'études médiévales; Paris: J. Vrin, 1988.
Picatrix: The Latin Version of the "Ghāyat Al-ḥakīm." Edited by David Pingree. London: Warburg Institute, 1986.

Raziel (Cephar Raziel/Liber Salomonis). Transcribed by Joseph Peterson from British Library, Sloane 3846. Esoteric Archives. Online at http://www.esotericarchives.com/raziel/raziel.htm#book7. Accessed June 22, 2014.
Sir Gawain and the Green Knight. Edited by E. V. Gordon and J. R. R. Tolkien. Oxford: Oxford University Press, 1967.
Somniale Danielis: An Edition of a Medieval Latin Dream Interpretation Handbook. Edited by Lawrence Martin. Frankfurt: Peter Lang, 1981.
The "Speculum astronomiae" and Its Enigma: Astrology, Theology, and Science in Albertus Magnus and His Contemporaries. Edited by Paola Zambelli et al. Dordrecht: Kluwer, 1992.
Thābit ibn Qurra al-Ḥarrānī. "De imaginibus." In *The Astronomical Works of Thabit B. Qurra*, edited by Francis Carmody, 167–97. Berkeley: University of California Press, 1960.
Thomas Aquinas. *Scriptum super Sententiis*. In *Opera omnia: Ad fidem optimarum editionum accurate recognita*. Vols. 6–7. Parma: P. Fiaccadori, 1856–58. Online at http://www.corpusthomisticum.org/iopera.html. Accessed June 22, 2014.
———. *Summa Theologiae. Opera omnia iussu edita Leonis XIII P.M.* [Leonine edition]. Vols. 4–12. Rome: Ex Typographia Polyglotta S.C. de Propaganda Fide, 1888–1906. Online at http://www.corpusthomisticum.org/iopera.html. Accessed June 22, 2014.
Modlitewnik Wladyslawa Warnenczyka w zbiorach Bibljoteki Bodlejanskiej [Wladislas Warnenczyk's Prayer Book]. Edited by Ludwik Bernacki and Ryszard Ganszyniec. Kraków: Anczyc i Spólka, 1928.

SECONDARY

Asad, Talal. *Genealogies of Religion: Discipline and Reasons of Power in Christianity and Islam*. Baltimore: Johns Hopkins University Press, 1993.
Barnay, Sylvie. *Le ciel sur la terre: Les apparitions de la Vierge au Moyen Âge*. Paris: Cerf, 1999.
———. "Désir de voir et interdits visionnaires ou la 'mariophanie' selon Jean de Morigny (XIVe siècle)." In *Homo Religiosus: Autour de Jean Delumeau*, 519–26. Paris: Fayard, 1997.
———. "La mariophanie au regard de Jean de Morigny: Magie ou miracle de la vision mariale?" In *Miracles, prodiges et merveilles au Moyen Age*, by Société des Historiens Médiévistes de l'Enseignement Supérieur Public, 173–90. Paris: Publications de la Sorbonne, 1995.
———. "La mariophanie de Jean de Morigny ou les manipulations de la vision mariale au début du XIVe siècle." *Rivista di storia e letteratura religiosa* 33 (1997): 483–50.
———. "Un moment vécu d'éternité: Histoire médiévale des apparitions mariales (IVe–XVe siècle): Lire et traduire le langage visionnaire." Diss., Université de Paris X–Nanterre, 1997.
Bennett, Adelaide. "A French Cleric's Prayer Book-Hours of the Early Thirteenth Century." In *Tributes to Nigel Morgan: Contexts of Medieval Art; Images, Objects, and Ideas*, edited by Julian Luxford and M. A. Michael. Turnhout: Harvey Miller, 2010.
Boudet, Jean-Patrice. *Entre science et nigromance: Astrologie, divination et magie dans l'Occident médiéval (XIIe–XVe siècle)*. Paris: Sorbonne, 2006.
Bourdieu, Pierre. "History and Truth." In *Science of Science and Reflexivity*, 71–84. Cambridge: Polity, 2004.
Boynton, Susan. "*Libelli Precum* in the Central Middle Ages." In *A History of Prayer: The First to the Fifteenth Century*, edited by Roy Hammerling, 255–318. Leiden: Brill, 2008.
———. *Shaping a Monastic Identity: Liturgy and History at the Imperial Abbey of Farfa, 1000–1125*. Ithaca: Cornell University Press, 2006.
Burnett, Charles. "The Arabic Hermes in the Works of Adelard of Bath." In *Hermetism from Late Antiquity to Humanism*, edited by Paolo Lucentini, Ilaria Parri, and Vittoria Perrone Compagni. Turnhout: Brepols, 2003.

———. "Talismans: Magic as Science? Necromancy Among the Seven Liberal Arts." In *Magic and Divination in the Middle Ages: Texts and Techniques in the Islamic and Christian Worlds*. Aldershot: Variorum, 1996.
Compagni, Vittoria Perrone. "'Studiosus incantationibus': Adelardo di Bath, Ermete e Thabit." *Giornale critico della filosofia italiana* 80 (2001): 36–61.
Coolman, Boyd Taylor. *The Theology of Hugh of St. Victor: An Interpretation*. Cambridge: Cambridge University Press, 2010.
Donavin, Georgiana. *Scribit Mater: Mary and the Language Arts in the Literature of Medieval England*. Washington, D.C.: Catholic University of America Press, 2011.
Dupèbe, Jean. "L'ars notoria et la polémique sur la divination et la magie." In *Divination et controverse religieuse en France au XVIe siècle*, ed. Jean Céard, 123–34. Cahiers V.-L. Saulnier 4. Paris: L'É.N.S. de Jeunes Filles, 1987.
Fanger, Claire. "Christian Ritual Magic in the Middle Ages." *History Compass* 11, no. 8 (2013): 610–18.
———. "Complications of Eros: The Song of Songs in John of Morigny's *Liber florum celestis doctrine*." In *Hidden Intercourse: Eros and Sexuality in the History of Western Esotericism*, edited by Wouter J. Hanegraaff and Jeffrey J. Kripal, 153–74. Leiden: Brill, 2010.
———, ed. *Conjuring Spirits: Texts and Traditions of Medieval Ritual Magic*. University Park: Pennsylvania State University Press, 1998.
———. "Covenant and the Divine Name." In Fanger, *Invoking Angels*, 192–217.
———, ed. *Invoking Angels: Theurgic Ideas and Practices, Thirteenth to Sixteenth Centuries*. University Park: Pennsylvania State University Press, 2012.
———. "Magic." In *The Oxford Guide to the Historical Reception of Augustine*, edited by Karla Pollmann and Willemien Otten, 3:860–65. Oxford: Oxford University Press, 2013.
———. "Plundering the Egyptian Treasure: John the Monk's *Book of Visions* and Its Relation to the Ars Notoria of Solomon." In Fanger, *Conjuring Spirits*, 216–49.
———. "Sacred and Secular Knowledge Systems in the *Ars Notoria* and the *Flowers of Heavenly Teaching* of John of Morigny." In *Die Enzyklopädik der Esoterik: Allwissenheitsmythen und universalwissenschaftliche Modelle in der Esoterik der Neuzeit*, edited by Andreas B. Kilcher and Philipp Theisohn, 157–75. Paderborn: Wilhelm Fink Verlag, 2010.
Faubion, James D. *An Anthropology of Ethics*. Cambridge: Cambridge University Press, 2011.
———, ed. *Rethinking the Subject: An Anthology of Contemporary European Social Thought*. Boulder, Colo.: Westview Press, 1995.
Field, Sean. *The Beguine, the Angel, and the Inquisitor: The Trials of Marguerite Porete and Guiard of Cressonessart*. Notre Dame: University of Notre Dame Press, 2012.
Fürbeth, Frank. *Johannes Hartlieb: Untersuchungen zu Leben und Werk*. Tübingen: Max Niemeyer, 1992.
Gehr, Damaris. "'Spiritus et angeli sunt a Deo submissi sapienti et puro': Il frammento del Magisterium eumantice artis sive scientiae magicalis. Edizione e attribuzione a Berengario Ganello." *Aries* 11, no. 2 (2011): 189–217.
Gilly, Carlos and Cis van Heertum, eds. *Magic, Alchemy, and Science, 15th–18th Centuries*. 2 vols. Florence: Centro Di, 2002.
Goering, Joseph. "The Internal Forum and the Literature of Penance and Confession." *Traditio* 59 (2004): 175–227.
Hunt, Richard, and Falconer Madan. *A Summary Catalogue of Western Manuscripts in the Bodleian Library at Oxford Which Have Not Hitherto Been Catalogued in the Quarto Series*. Oxford: Clarendon Press, 1895–1953.
Hvidt, Niels Christian. *Christian Prophecy: The Post-Biblical Tradition*. Oxford: Oxford University Press, 2007.
Idel, Moshe. *Kabbalah: New Perspectives*. New Haven: Yale University Press, 1988.
Kieckhefer, Richard. *Forbidden Rites: A Necromancer's Manual of the Fifteenth Century*. University Park: Pennsylvania State University Press, 1998.

Kilcher, Andreas B. "*Ars memorativa* und *ars cabalistica:* Die Kabbala in der Mnemonik der Frühen Neuzeit." In *Seelenmaschinen: Gattungstraditionen, Funktionen und Leistungsgrenzen der Mnemotechniken vom späten Mittelalter bis zum Beginn der Moderne,* edited by Jörg J. Berns and Wolfgang Neuber, 199–248. Wien: Böhlau Verlag, 2000.

Klaassen, Frank. "Medieval Ritual Magic in the Renaissance." *Aries* 3, no. 2 (2003): 166–99.

———. "The Subjective Experience of Medieval Ritual Magic." *Magic, Ritual, and Witchcraft* 7, no. 1 (2012): 19–51.

———. *The Transformations of Magic: Illicit Learned Magic in the Later Middle Ages and Renaissance.* University Park: Pennsylvania State University Press, 2012.

Láng, Benedek. *Unlocked Books: Manuscripts of Learned Magic in the Medieval Libraries of Central Europe.* University Park: Pennsylvania State University Press, 2010.

Lea, Henry Charles. *A History of the Inquisition of the Middle Ages.* Vol. 3. New York: Macmillan, 1887.

Lerner, Robert. "New Light on *The Mirror of Simple Souls.*" *Speculum* 85, no. 1 (2010): 91–116.

Lubac, Henri de. *Corpus Mysticum: The Eucharist and the Church in the Middle Ages.* Translated by Gemma Simmonds. Notre Dame: University of Notre Dame Press, 2007.

———. *Medieval Exegesis: The Four Senses of Scripture.* Translated by Edward M. Macierowski. Vol. 2. Grand Rapids, Mich.: William B. Eerdmans, 2000.

McGinn, Bernard. *The Foundations of Mysticism.* New York: Crossroad, 1991.

Nainfa, John Abel. *Costume of Prelates of the Catholic Church, According to Roman Etiquette.* Rev. ed. Baltimore: John Murphy, 1926.

Newman, Barbara. *God and the Goddesses: Vision, Poetry, and Belief in the Middle Ages.* Philadelphia: University of Pennsylvania Press, 2003.

Norberg, Dag. *An Introduction to the Study of Medieval Latin Versification.* Translated by Grant Roti and Jacqueline de Chapelle Skubly. Washington, D.C.: Catholic University of America Press, 2004.

Orme, Nicholas. *Medieval Children.* New Haven: Yale University Press, 2003.

Page, Sophie. "Image-Magic Texts and a Platonic Cosmology at St Augustine's, Canterbury, in the Late Middle Ages." In *Magic and the Classical Tradition,* edited by Charles Burnett and W. F. Ryan, 69–98. London: Warburg Institute, 2006.

———. *Magic in the Cloister: Pious Motives, Illicit Interests, and Occult Approaches to the Medieval Universe.* University Park: Pennsylvania State University Press, 2013.

———. "Uplifting Souls: The *Liber de essentia spirituum* and the *Liber Razielis.*" In Fanger, *Invoking Angels,* 79–112.

Pennycook, Alastair. "'Press 1 for English': Practice as the 'Generic Social Thing.'" In *Language as a Local Practice,* 17–33. Abingdon: Routledge, 2010.

Rubin, Miri. *Corpus Christi: The Eucharist in Late Medieval Culture.* Cambridge: Cambridge University Press, 1991.

———. *Mother of God: A History of the Virgin Mary.* New Haven: Yale University Press, 2009.

Thorndike, Lynn. *A History of Magic and Experimental Science.* 8 vols. New York: Columbia University Press, 1923.

———. "Traditional Medieval Tracts Concerning Engraved Astrological Images." In *Mélanges Auguste Pelzer,* 212–73. Louvain: Bibliothèque de l'Université, 1947.

Turner, Denys. *The Darkness of God: Negativity in Christian Mysticism.* Cambridge: Cambridge University Press, 1995.

Veenstra, Jan. "Honorius and the Sigil of God: The *Liber iuratus* in Berengario Ganell's *Summa sacre magice.*" In Fanger, *Invoking Angels,* 169–72.

Véronèse, Julien. "Les anges dans l'*Ars notoria:* Révélation, processus visionnaire, et angélologie." In "Les Anges et la magie au Moyen Âge: Actes de la table ronde, Nanterre, 8–9 décembre 2000," edited by Henri Bresc and Benoît Grévin, special issue, *Mélanges de l'École Française de Rome, Moyen Âge* 114, no. 2 (2002): 813–49.

Watson, Nicholas. "Introduction." In *The Cambridge Companion to Medieval English Mysticism*, edited by Samuel Fanous and Vincent Gillespie, 1–28. Cambridge: Cambridge University Press, 2011.

———. "John the Monk's *Book of Visions of the Blessed and Undefiled Virgin Mary, Mother of God*: Two Versions of a Newly Discovered Ritual Magic Text." In Fanger, *Conjuring Spirits*, 163–215.

Weill-Parot, Nicolas. "Astral Magic and Intellectual Changes (Twelfth–Fifteenth Centuries): 'Astrological Images' and the Concept of 'Addressative' Magic." In *The Metamorphosis of Magic from Late Antiquity to the Early Modern Period*, edited by Jan Bremmer and Jan Veenstra, 167–84. Leuven: Peeters, 2003.

———. *Les "images astrologiques" au Moyen Âge et à la Renaissance: Spéculations intellectuelles et pratiques magiques (XIIe–XVe siècle)*. Paris: Honoré Champion, 2002.

Wittgenstein, Ludwig. *Philosophical Investigations*. Translated by G. E. M. Anscombe, P. M. S. Hacker, and Joachim Schulte. 4th ed. Revised by Hacker and Schulte. Malden, Mass.: Wiley-Blackwell, 2000.

———. "Remarks on Frazer's *Golden Bough*." In *Philosophical Occasions, 1912–1951*, edited by James Klagge and Alfred Nordmann, 115–55. Indianapolis: Hackett, 1993.

INDEX

Adam of Saint Victor, 47
addressative texts and magic, 113, 115, 116, 117, 189n13
Agrippa von Nettesheim, Heinrich Cornelius, 161
Alan of Lille, 38, 47, 67
Alfonso X, King of Castile and Leon, 189n11
Alfraganus (al-Farghani), 123, 192n41
Anthropology of Ethics, An (Faubion), 171nn19, 21
Antiquitez, croniques et singularitez de Paris, 3
Arnoul de Provence, 49
ars notoria
    abuse of beauty and, 43
    access to knowledge via, 38, 175n8
    Bridget's use of, 65–66
    characteristics of, 37, 56–57
    condemnation of, 3
    discovery of knowledge and, 111–12
    evil nature of, 43, 66
    figures (*notae*) in, 94
    influence of, 87
    John of Morigny's use of, 2, 28–29, 32, 34, 68, 109, 128
    language of, 35, 39
    vs. *Liber florum*, 38, 43–44, 90–91
    magic and, 56, 117
    as metascience, 118
    necromancy and, 41, 116, 117–18, 121
    notae of, 99
    perception and criticism of, xiii, 37–38, 56
    preservation and dissemination of, 201n13
    printed editions of, 22, 23, 172n6
    scholarly works on, 3, 20, 22, 23, 172n6
    sources of, 160
    teaching literacy with, 29
    versions of, 23–24, 25
Arthabicius, 123, 192n41
Asad, Talal, 44, 55, 61
Augustine, Saint, Bishop of Hippo, 2, 113–14, 158. *See also individual books*
Autruy (village), x, 25, 174n22

baptism, 59, 136
Barking Dogs
    condemnation of Book of Figures by, xv, 11, 79, 105, 116, 136, 142, 157, 165
    John's reference to, 88–89
    origin of trope, 184n9
    perception of figures as necromantic, 2, 89–91, 95, 107, 116, 123, 131–32
    provenance of, x
    training in canon law, 89
Barnay, Sylvie, xi, 4, 22, 170n11
Belshazzar's feast, 42, 176n16
Benedictine Rule, 103
Bloor, David, 165
Bodleian Library, 33, 79, 86, 151
body
    Christ's, 52, 64, 146
    human intellect and, 49–50
    as medium, 61
    metaphor of book's, 146, 149
    as obstacle to knowledge, 61
Boethius, 49
Bonaventure, 48, 162
Book of All Forbidden Arts, The (Johan Hartlieb), 117, 119
Book of Figures. *See* New Compilation of Figures; Old Compilation of Figures
Book of Particular Experiments, xv
Book of Prayers, x, xiii–xv, 79, 185n13. *See also* Seven Prayers; Thirty Prayers
Book of Prophecies, references to, 106, 188n44
Book of Seven Senators, 124
Book of Talismans of Abel, 124
Book of the Semhemforas, 124
Book of Thirty Prayers. *See* Thirty Prayers
Book of Twelve Firmaments, 124
Book of Visions
    absence of in Clm 276, 87
    characteristics of, 2, 32, 33–34, 59
    content of, xiii, 2
    description of Bridget's visions in, 29

Book of Visions *(continued)*
    editions of, 170n11
    necromantic episodes in, 109–10, 188n1
books, experience of writing, 9
Bourdieu, Pierre, 8, 10, 154, 171n18
Bridget (sister of John of Morigny)
    demon and, 65
    dreams of, 29–30, 174n22
    learning experience of, 29, 103, 173n17
    name spellings, ix
    testimony against *ars notoria,* xiii, 65
Burchard, Bishop of Worms, 114
Burnett, Charles, 112, 120, 121
burning of *Liber florum,* 4–5, 20, 22, 24, 30, 88, 132, 166
Byatt, A. S., 15

Caesarius of Heisterbach, 194n1
canon law, x, 1, 2, 5, 9, 58, 59, 88–90, 114, 116, 137
carmina figurata, 99–100
cataphatic, 44, 46, 78
Cecco, d'Ascoli, 23
Chartres (France), ix, 91, 110, 114
cherubim, xiv, 19, 63, 121–23
chess, game of, 154, 160–61
Christ. *See* Jesus Christ
confession
    John's book as, 25, 32–33, 39
    sacrament of, 55, 58–59, 64–65, 68–71, 131
Confessions (Augustine), 33, 158
Conjuring Spirits (Fanger), 22, 25, 33, 84, 86, 87, 100
Coolman, Boyd, 53
Copernicus, Nicolaus, 164
cross, figure of, 150

Dante Alighieri, 59
De doctrina christiana (Augustine), 113
De imaginibus (Thābit), 125, 131
demons
    ars notoria and, 3, 65, 117
    forms of, 26
    in medieval narratives, 26–27, 38–39
    necromancy and, 41, 43, 109, 113, 116, 117, 120
    pacts with, 113–15, 138–40
    prayers and, 65
    visions of, 25–31
De occulta philosophia (Agrippa), 161
De Trinitate et operibus ejus (Rupert of Deutz), 200n3
De vanitate (Agrippa), 161
devil
    appropriation of God's throne, 37, 40–41
    appearing as angel of light, 138, 141
    Bridget's engagement with, 66
    John's engagement with, 37, 62–63, 65, 105

    Theophilus' pact with, 110, 111
    visions of, 25–27, 105–6
Divisio scientiarum (Arnoul de Provence), 49
Douglas, Mary, 16, 164, 200n9
Dupèbe, Jean, 3, 23, 170n5
Durand, Guillaume, 40, 43, 135

Eckhart, Meister, 46–47, 177n24
Elijah (prophet), 106, 107, 148
error
    of intellect, 50, 83, 160
    of magic, 34, 56
    as path to truth, 83
    of will, 84, 167
    of words, 42
Esoteric Archives (Twilit Grotto), 194n62
ethical action, 9, 171n19
Eucharist, 58, 59, 64, 148
exceptive arts, 118–20, 122, 123, 124, 191n31. *See also* liberal arts; mechanical arts

Faubion, James, xi, 171nn19, 21
figures. *See also* Oxford Manuscript
    definition of, 135
    of gate of paradise, 94
    letters on, 96–98, 99–100
    meaning and design of, 150–51
    of necromancy, 96
    prayers and, 94–95
    of seven angels, 130–31
First Procedure, xv, 79, 87, 184n5
Forbidden Rites (Kieckhefer), 22, 130
Foucault, Michel, 44, 61–62
Frazer, James, 163
Fulton, Rachel, xi

Ganell, Berengario, 124, 128
Gawain and the Green Knight, 96, 144
Genealogies of Religion (Asad), 55
geonegia, category of, 120, 124, 125, 131, 191n30
Ghazali, Muḥammad al-, 134
gifts of Holy Spirit, 118–19
Glossa ordinaria, 42, 134, 136, 148, 200n3
God
    appearance in dreams and visions, 30–31, 39, 68–69, 71, 105–6
    chastisement of, 61
    devil's appropriation of throne of, 37, 40–41
    interpretations of acts of, 72
    intervention in John's life, 33, 109–10
    Jewish sources on power of, 73
    in prayers, 69–70, 92–93, 158–59
    qualities of, 158
    revelation of, 141–42
    as savior and redeemer, 70–71
    trust in, 141

Goering, Joseph, 58, 59
Golden Bough (Frazer), 163
Golden Flowers (Apollonius), 23
Google, 22, 172n5
Gospel, 40
Grandes Chroniques de France
    on condemnation of *Liber florum,* 3, 4, 5, 22
    description of book burning in, 20, 132
    on images of Virgin Mary, 86
Gratian, 37, 114, 116, 137–40, 143
Graz manuscript, 24, 25, 32, 87, 170n11. *See also* Liber florum
Guillaume de Nangis, 3
Gundissalinus, Dominicus, 112, 121

habitus, idea of, 8
Hartlieb, Johannes, 117, 119, 124, 190n28
Hildegard of Bingen, 47
Hill Monastic Manuscript Library in Minnesota (HMML), 24, 172n9
historical research, 17, 84–86
history, practice of, 167–68
History of Magic and Experimental Science, The (Thorndike), 4, 23
How Institutions Think (Douglas), 164
Hugh of Saint Victor
    on act of writing, 52
    De sacramentis, 11, 51
    Didascalicon, 48, 50, 118
    on learning, 50–51
    on magic arts, 118, 120, 161
    on sacraments, 54–56
    on subject matter of Divine Scriptures, 51
    theology of, 53

Idel, Moshe, 73, 74
idolatry, 132, 138
interest, definition of, 171n2
Isidore of Seville, 37, 41, 135, 190n19
Itinerarium mentis in Deum (Bonaventure), 48, 162
Ivo, Saint (bishop of Chartres), 114

Jacob of Bologna, 38
Jerome, Saint, 42, 43, 134
Jesus Christ. *See also* God
    child of Virgin Mary, 153
    in dreams and visions, 60, 61
    kisses of, 106, 147
    monograms of, 97–98
    prediction of martyrdom of Peter by, 149
Johannes de Carnoto (John of Chartres, early byname of John of Morigny), 91
John the Evangelist, 63, 64, 66, 69, 78
John of Fontainejean, xiii, 31, 39, 132

John of Morigny
    on *ars notoria,* 38, 56, 65–66, 117–18, 160, 175n8, 176n18
    on Barking Dogs, 88–89, 90
    on Bridget's visions, 29–30, 174n22
    charges against, 137–39, 140–41
    condemnation of, 89–90, 161, 165
    confessions of, 32, 33, 64, 65, 68
    on construction of knowledge, 9–11
    conversations with Virgin Mary, 103–5, 110, 138–39, 149, 198n40
    conversation with God, 68–69, 71
    on designs of flowers and leaves, 144
    on desire to be cleansed from sins, 76
    devil and, 27, 63, 65
    dreams of, 26, 27–29, 60, 137
    education of, x, 1, 59, 112
    engagement with magical art, 24
    engagement with necromancy, 2, 11, 37–38, 111, 125, 131
    errors of, 34, 85, 143, 144
    on exceptive arts, 122
    exegesis of, 31, 165
    experience of pain, 61
    on figures, 4, 39–40, 98–99, 118, 142–43, 144
    figures designed by, 88–89, 92, 96, 128, 150–51, 152, 153
    on *geonegia,* 124, 125
    God's intervention in life of, 33, 109–10
    home village of, x
    as inspirational character, xi–xii
    interest in necromancy, 109, 116
    interpretations of visions of, 71–73, 139
    knowledge and intellectual abilities of, 2, 5–6, 90, 146–47, 162, 167–68, 187n35
    language and vocabulary of, 35, 43, 175n1, 185n14
    on liberal arts, 48
    on *Liber florum,* 145
    on link between vision and visualization, 181n30
    as literacy teacher, 29, 103, 173n17
    on magic and heresy, 5, 120
    manuscripts of, x, 16–17, 24
    as medieval scholar, 162
    monastic community and, 90, 105
    mysticism of, 45, 46
    pact with demon, 139–40
    penance of, 61
    perception and use of *ars notoria* by, 28–29, 32, 34, 35, 63, 109
    personality of, 47, 74–75, 105, 168
    on personalization of books, 4, 171n14
    on planetary figures, 126
    prayers of, 66–70, 76–78, 109–10, 134, 158–59, 181n31, 182n35

212 INDEX

John of Morigny *(continued)*
    on praying, 134–35
    on purpose of reading Gospel, 40
    relatives of, ix, 25
    on sacrament of penance, 58, 59, 60–61
    scholars on, 3–4, 6, 7, 10, 170n11
    self-revelation of, 141–42
    on the sign of the cross, 135, 150
    sources of, 40, 44, 47, 86, 111–12, 128, 131
    spiritual journey of, 106–7, 146–48
    on spiritual nourishment, 146–48
    on Tetragrammaton, 76, 136, 146
    theology of, 44
    views of, 48
    visions of, 25–26, 60–64, 66–68, 71–72, 105–6, 109–10, 139, 141–42, 147–48
    works of, ix, 1–2, 4, 86–88, 159–60, 165–66, 187n35
    writing techniques of, 5, 11–12, 32, 102, 157, 158
John XXII, Pope, 46

Kabbalah: New Perspectives (Idel), 73
kabbalistic writings, 73–74
Keats, John, 17
Kieckhefer, Richard, xi, 16, 20, 22, 130
Klaassen, Frank, xi, 20, 24, 166, 201n13
knowledge
    acquisition and discovery of, 5, 7–8, 15–17, 36, 38
    ars notoria and access to, 38, 111–12, 175n8
    body as obstacle to true, 49
    as communal project, 62
    corruption of, 42
    heavenly *vs.* earthly, 161
    human and divine, 50, 53, 54
    institutional, 10, 164, 167
    integration of, 132–33
    loss of, 50, 153
    magic and, 159–60, 162
    medieval and modern systems of, 164–65
    nature of, 168
    necromancy and, 111
    origin of mystical, 16
    personal, 10
    reading and, 15
    representation of different types of, 122–23
    scholarly discourse on, 8–9
    systematization of, 121–22
    transformation of, 8
    as triumph over sin and temptation, 76–77
Kuhn, Thomas, 164

Láng, Benedek, xi, 118, 191n31
language game, 8, 10, 163
Laurent d'Orléans, 176n16
Lea, Henry Charles, 4

Le Grand, Jacques, 4
Lewis, C. S., 1
liberal arts, 19, 48, 50, 118–19, 123, 125. *See also* exceptive arts; mechanical arts
Liber figurarum. See Book of Figures
Liber florum celestis doctrine (Flowers of Heavenly Teaching). *See also individual books and manuscripts*
    vs. *ars notoria*, 38, 43–44, 90–91
    as autobiography of John of Morigny, 32
    characteristic of, 2–3, 5, 8, 44, 48, 59–60, 85
    charges against, 137–39
    circulation of, 183n1, 185n13, 190n28
    communal awareness of, 105
    comparison with Bible, 146
    compilations of, xiii, xv, 103
    condemnation of, 2, 3, 4–5, 132, 137–38, 170nn3, 9
    content of, xiii–xv
    discovery of, 3, 4, 19
    distribution of, 1, 4
    First Procedure, xv, 79, 87, 184n5
    historical value of, 168
    identification of authorship, 22
    Latin edition of, 155–56
    necromancy and, 112, 116, 195n2
    publications of, ix, 1, 7
    scholarly research on, 6, 18–19, 24, 155–57
    Second Procedure, xv, 2, 79
    structure of, 2, 11–12, 79, 169n2
    surviving manuscripts, x, 4, 18–19, 157–58, 171n13
    Thirty Prayers, xiv, 59, 77–78, 121–23, 179n12, 187n34
    titles, ix
Liber iuratus, See Sworn Book
Liber Razielis
    circulation of, 124
    figures and images in, 130, 131, 160
    English versions, 194n60
    as source for John of Morigny, 133
    Vatican manuscript, 128, 129
Liber Samayn, 128, 130, 194n60
Liber Semhemforas, 124, 131, 193n49
literacy, 29, 174n20
Lombard, Peter, 37, 53, 178n33
Luther, Martin, 166

magic
    ars notoria and, 56, 117
    categorization of, 119–20
    historians' view on, 163
    John's experimentation with, 2
    knowledge and, 159–60, 162
    mysticism and, 45
    nature of, 159

as product of intellectual elite, 45
types of, 115–16
magical images, 124–25, 128
Magic in the Middle Ages (Kieckhefer), 20
magic texts, 5, 112–13, 160, 161–62
Magister Speculi, 113, 115, 121, 160, 189n17
martyrdom, metaphor of, 149
Mary at Chartres (church), 110
McMaster manuscript, 19–20, 21–22, 23, 24. *See also* Liber florum
mechanical arts, 118–20, 123. *See also* exceptive arts; liberal arts
medieval manuscripts
  burning of, 171n16
  cataloguing and description of, 21
  circulation of magical, 166
  decoration of, 144
  discovery and study of, 83–84, 85
  nature of, 84
Mercury, 126–27
Metaphysica (al-Ghazali), 134
Mirror of Simple Souls (Porete), 46
model city, metaphor of, 6–7
monastic discipline, 61–62
Morigny (France), 89, 91
Mount Horeb, 107
Munich manuscript (Clm 276), 23, 24, 32, 87
mysticism, 45, 46, 176n21, 177n23

necromancy
  vs. ars notoria, 41, 116, 117–18, 121
  characteristics of, 91, 132
  definition of, 112, 169n3, 189n11
  elements of, 120–21
  figures of, 96
  Hebrew and Arabic texts and, 131
  heresy trials and, 194n1
  John's engagement with, 2, 11, 37–38, 111, 125, 131
  knowledge and, 111
  as liberal art, 120
  Liber florum and, 112, 116, 195n2
  in medieval literature, 38–39, 112–13
  prayer for art of, 123
  vs. sin of sacrilege, 42
  Thomas Aquinas on, 115
neonegia, 120, 191n30
New Compilation of Figures
  comparison with Old Compilation, 93, 145–46
  on decoration of manuscripts, 144
  figures of Virgin Mary and Christ in, 151, 152
  on knowledge, 39
  origin of, 90, 116
  study of, 101, 156
  surviving manuscripts, 87–88
New Metaphysics, 49

New Testament, 52, 146
  Corinthians 3:1–2, 148
  Corinthians 6:9, 60–61
  Ephesians 3:3, 36
  Hebrews 12:6, 61
  John 21:18, 149
  Revelation 3:19, 61
  Revelation 4:6–8, 64
  Revelation 16:16, 69
  Romans 8:28, 44, 141
nigromancia. See necromancy
North, as location of God's throne, 40–41
nourishment, idea of sacred, 106–7

Old Compilation of Figures
  comparison with New Compilation, 93, 145–46
  content summary of, xv
  figures in, 98, 126, 151
  idea and origin of, 101–4
  inscription on figures of, 98
  John's revision of, 101
  manuscript of, 86, 118, 151
  on sign of cross, 150
  personalization of, 122
  reconfiguration of, 107–8
  scandal of, 2, 89–90, 107–8, 136
  sources and analogues of, 133–34
  study of, 33, 100
  visions of Christ in, 147–48
Old Testament, 52, 146
  3 Kings 19:8, 107
  Daniel, 41, 176nn15–16
  Ecclesiasticus 24:17, 151
  Exodus 28:36–38, 200n3
  Exodus 34:27, 140
  Ezekiel 1:4–10, 64
  Genesis 6:18, 140
  Genesis 9:15, 140
  Genesis 37:19–20, 185n14
  Isaiah 14:13–14, 40
  Jeremiah 1:14, 40
  Jeremiah 27:9, 185n14
  Lamentations, 200n3
  Leviticus 26:42, 140
  Psalms 80:11, 69
  Psalms 117:18, 60
  Wisdom 7:25–26, 134
On Images (Ptolemy), 192n46
On Rereading (Spacks), 166
Origen, 134
Orléans (France), x, 89
Oxford manuscript (Bodleian Liturg. 160). *See also* Liber florum
  catalogue record of, 91
  dates of composition, 91

Oxford manuscript *(continued)*
  description of, 86–87, 93
  images and figures in, *92, 93, 95, 96,* 97–98
  invocation of Tetragrammaton in, *92, 93*
  transcription of, 101

Page, Sophie, xi, 124, 192n48
pain, experience of, 61
penance, 58, 59, 72, 97, 106, 109, 142, 144, 151, 159
Pennycook, Alastair, 171n18
Pesikta de-Rav Kahana, 73
Peterson, Joseph, 22, 194n62
Petrus Alfonsi, 112, 120, 121
Philosophica disciplina, 49
Picatrix, 112, 126, 127, 189n11, 193n56
Plaint of Nature (De planctu naturae, Alan of Lille), 67
planetary figures, 126, 127, 186n31, 193n54
Pontifical Institute Library, 23
Porete, Marguerite, 46, 47, 177n25, 185n12
prayers, 29, 66, 94–95, 123, 135
prophecy, 141, 197n28
pseudo-Jerome, 200n3
Ptolemy, 124, 191–92n41

Rationale divinorum officiorum (Durand), 40
reading, act of, 15, 52, 166–67
Reed College, 18
restoration, work of, 51–52
Rewriting Magic (Fanger), xi, 6
Rigg, George, 21
Ritual Prologue, xiii, 93, 94
Rubin, Miri, 58
Rupert of Deutz, 200n3

sacraments, 35–37, 51, 54–56, 58, 175n4, 178n33
sacrilege, 41–43, 176nn15–16
Sacrobosco, Johannes de, 191n41
Salzburg manuscript, 151, *152,* 184n8
Sapientia, 77
self, concept of, 16, 62
self-formation, 62
seraphim, xiv, 19
Sens (France), x
Sentences (Lombard), 53
Seven Prayers, xiv, 11, 62, 67, 75. *See also* Book of Prayers
sins, 50, 76
Smith, Jonathan Z., 162
Somme le Roi (Laurent, d'Orléans), 176n16
Song of Songs, 133, 134
Sophologium (Jacques Le Grand), 4, 170n10
Spacks, Patricia Meyer, 166
Speculum astronomie (Magister Speculi), 113

Summa sacre magice (Berengario Ganell), 124, 128
Summa Theologiae (Thomas Aquinas), 114
Sworn Book (*Liber iuratus*), 22, 130

telos, 8, 9, 125
Tetragrammaton, 92–93, 128, *129,* 135–36, 150, 200n3
Thābit ibn Qurrah, 125
Theophilus (deacon), 110, 111, 114
theurgy, 56, 73, 74, 153
Thirty Prayers, xiv, 59, 77–78, 121–23, 179n12, 187n34. *See also* Book of Prayers; Seven Prayers
Thomas Aquinas
  on creation as divine communication, 53
  on demonic pact, 113, 115, 138
  on divination, 114
  on necromancy, 114, 115
  on sacraments, 178n33
  on terms "augury" and "lots," 190n19
  on types of sacrilege, 176n15
  on work of Wisdom, 54
Thorndike, Lynn, 4, 20
Toledan Tables, 123, 192n41
Treatise on the Sphere (Sacrobosco), 123, 191n41
Turner, Denys, 44
Twilit Grotto (Esoteric Archives), 22

Vatican Library, 128–29
Veenstra, Jan R., 124
Véronèse, Julien, xi, 22, 35, 119, 172n6, 173n16, 192n48
Virgin Mary
  beauty of, 63
  epithet of, 95, 186n23
  images of, 3, 86, 88, 151, *152,* 200n52
  John's conversations with, 103–5, 110, 138–39, 149
  kisses of, 106
  milk of, 146–48
  monograms of, 96–99
  planetary figures and, 98–99
  prayers to, 19, 67, 77–78
  restoration of knowledge and, 77
  spiritual children of, 153
  standing figures of, 39–40
visionary exegesis, 134, 135, 138, 153
Vulgate, 29, 36, 37, 140, 185n14

Watson, Nicholas
  authentication of Oxford manuscript, 101
  on John of Morigny, 141
  on link between mysticism and Protestantism, 177n26

personality of, xii, 18
publications of, 169n1
as researcher, 7, 155–56
scholarly works of, ix, x, 10, 18, 170n11, 171n18
Weill-Parot, Nicolas, 113, 115, 189n13, 189n17
West, Rebecca, 154
whole, concept of, 15–16
William, of Auvergne, Bishop of Paris, 160

wisdom, 49, 52-4, 69-70,72, 75-7, 93-4, 125, 133-4, 151, 160
Wittgenstein, Ludwig
  on language game and chess, 160–61, 200n5
  metaphor of language, 1, 6, 8, 9
  on Frazer's *Golden Bough*, 163
  on path to truth, 83, 84
  perspicuous view, 161, 165

Typeset by
COGHILL COMPOSITION COMPANY

Printed and bound by
SHERIDAN BOOKS

Composed in
MINION PRO

Printed on
NATURES NATURAL

Bound in
ARRESTOX

www.ingramcontent.com/pod-product-compliance
Lightning Source LLC
Chambersburg PA
CBHW021403290426
44108CB00010B/362